THE PLUMB LINE

a journey through agriculture and politics

The Greycoat Press

ISBN 1 899908 03 X

Contents

ACKNOWLEDGEMENT

Without the support of a tolerant wife, Marjorie, who kept the family together and the home fires burning over many years, this story could not have been told.

Without the help and encouragement of Dr Robert Ramsay who worked with me as an expert on European affairs over most of my twenty years in the European Parliament and of Dr Puck Wertwyn who was mastermind of the whole work, it would not have been written. I enjoy working as a team leader and before volunteering to take on the marathon task of producing *The Plumb Line*, I had experienced Puck's qualities in our work together in my Cotswold Constituency.

Many colleagues have willingly contributed to various parts of the book as memories tick back through struggle and progress in Agriculture and our entry into the European Community.

Seeing some of the real problems in developing countries made me appreciate the good fortune we have to live in Europe. It was also my good fortune to have the assistance of Bryan Rose from the European Secretariat who is an expert on African issues.

Readers may ask why I have enjoyed a career of deep ends! Well I did, not because I was ambitious but because I believe that keeping the adrenalin flowing is a stimulant for a good life.

Henry Plumb

September 2001

FOREWORD

The Rt. Hon. Lord Hurd of Westwell, CH., CBE

The arguments about Europe swirl round the media and Parliament in an endless circle. Often they are based on theoretical anxieties rather than fact and experience. Sometimes they concentrate heavily in their criticism of the way Europe is handling its agriculture.

In this book Henry Plumb gives us the chance to test our theories against his own life, which has been remarkable by any standard. A Warwickshire lad, removed from school at the age of 15 to help his father run the farm, Henry rose to the top of the English farming industry. He then moved across to European politics and became not only the head of the Conservatives there, but also President of the European Parliament. This career is itself a refutation of some of the stories about the European Union. No one could be further removed from the sinister Eurocrat of myth and legend. On the way Henry Plumb developed strong views which he sets out here about British agriculture, about the relationship between the British Government and farming, about Britain in Europe, about the place of Europe's institutions in the world, and most recently about how we should handle the problems of international development. There is plenty of sustained argument in these pages, but it is characteristic of Henry Plumb that he often crowns the argument with an anecdote from practical experience.

I have known Henry Plumb for many years, when I was Foreign Secretary and when he was Member of the European Parliament representing the Cotswolds where I live. I have always admired the straightforward and cheerful way in which he has tackled each position he has occupied, and each argument with which he has been confronted. No one who knows Henry Plumb or reads his book can believe that Britain is going to be swallowed up in a European superstate in which our identity as Britons will be smothered. It seems equally impossible, at the other end of the spectrum, that we would ever find it in our interest to leave and thus disrupt a community which, despite its many faults, has notched up the kind of progress recorded in these pages.

No one could be more British than Henry Plumb; no one could be more committed to a sensible Europe.

INTRODUCTION

No man is a statesman who is ignorant of wheat.
(Socrates)

As I lived through the forty years of my public career, I had the impression that day by day I was engaged in what was essentially a frenetic struggle to meet and deal with the many new challenges that presented themselves at national, European and global levels. That seemed the reality – but on reflection, I realise that my own career, as it progressed, reflected like ripples on a pond a pattern of ever-widening and overlapping circles of development at those same three levels.

That career traced its path from my beginnings in local farming, and continued on to national farming, to being concerned in the Common Agricultural Policy, to the European integration process, to the internationalisation of agricultural (and of course other) trade issues within the General Agreement on Tariffs and Trade (GATT) and the World Trade Organisation (WTO), and so finally to involvement in the special problems of the relationship between the developed and the developing parts of the world.

I know that my personal profile may, at first sight, appear to sit somewhat incongruously with that evolution. Certainly, in the generations before mine the 'yeomen of England' would not naturally have followed such a path. But I believe my personal choices and convictions have sprung from drawing pragmatic conclusions from developments in Europe and the world at large. I do not claim prophetically to have foreseen all that would happen, but it is true that I instinctively felt early on in the 1960s that in both agriculture and national/international politics, the trend was likely to be towards a greater coming together, and that independence and isolation was not going to be the way of the future.

At that time 'globalisation' had not yet been coined as a concept. Looking back, though, we can now see that it has been that force, more than any other, that has made so many profound transformations in our world possible, and indeed necessary. The thinking of the European founding fathers predated the serious onset of globalisation and was inspired by other goals – principally the desire for permanent European peace and the building up of a prosperous society. But it is the surge of globalisation that makes the longer-term vision of those founding fathers ever more realisable.

Globalisation is neither a 'policy' nor a philosophy. It is the practical consequence, in the economic, social and political spheres, of rapid scientific advances, particularly in relation to information technology, the application of science-based methods in all fields of production, and the general shrinking of the world through modern transportation and communications. It is neither 'good' nor 'bad' – its effects will ultimately depend on what we make of it. It did not arrive as the fulfilment of some ideological theory. Instead, it was the practical consequence of scientific advance at a moment in history propitious to its widespread adoption and application.

The existence of the EEC/EC/EU has facilitated this advance in Europe. Indeed, you might say that if the process of European integration had not already been well under way, it would have been necessary to start it, in order to derive maximum benefit from globalisation.

In the global village in which we all now live, 'you in your small corner, and I in mine' is no longer a valid approach. Nor, I would add, a desirable one. We in the UK must face up to realities of this shrinking and fast-changing world. For in every sphere it is one of increasing competition. We have to ensure not only that our efficiency – whether as an economic sector such as agriculture, or as a country overall – is being constantly reviewed and improved, but also that we are fitting into the right framework, whether that framework relies on a common policy or an alliance.

Since my earliest days, I have always been a 'participator', not only by nature but out of a conviction that only by joining with others can one influence events and get things done. That applies equally at the level of the Young Farmers, the Conservative Party and the European Union.

At the same time, looking back, I realise that my approach has been a highly individualistic one – I have always applied my own 'Plumb line'. In practical terms this has meant a very pragmatic view of life: looking at any situation realistically, deciding which is the best option for action, seeking like-minded allies to reinforce such action, and, above all, being ready to adapt to changing circumstances.

I gradually came to believe that party politics, while by no means the only valuable forum of action, were, for what I wanted to achieve, a usefully mobile vehicle for my actions. The Conservative Party was clearly the only one for me, since it has at its core that same pragmatic dynamic while emphasising the fundamental values of freedom, fairness and responsibility, both in respect of the individual and towards our fellow men and women. That is what Conservatives mean whenever they say that we are not driven by 'ideology' – we are not attempting to work outwards from a political theory, such as Marxism or Socialism, but from a realistic view of the world, which we strive to improve through the application of pragmatic policies.

The book I have written is therefore not an ideologically committed view of current affairs. It is certainly political in nature, and in some respects even party political. It is political in the widest sense of the word, in that it is about public problems and how they have been tackled by representative bodies, including governments – but it is essentially my own story and the record of my personal views.

This story goes from the life of the son of a Warwickshire farmer to the House of Lords, by the way of the Young Farmers, the National Farmers Union and the European Parliament. It has been a journey full of interest and, occasionally, of drama. The variety has been immense – from grappling with the foot-and-mouth outbreak in 1967, to establishing links, post-Falklands, with Argentina, to visiting rural China, to pioneering a role for the European Parliament at Euro-summits, to helping bring assistance to war-torn Rwanda.

And underlying that variety, I can see a pattern. For in my public career I have been privileged to see at first hand, and to play a leading part in, three profound transformations:

> · the metamorphosis of British agriculture from a 'national' sector into part of an integrated European industry;
> · the accession of the United Kingdom to the European Community and that Community's continuing evolution and expansion; and
> · the development of a co-ordinated European policy towards the countries of Africa, the Caribbean and the Pacific.

As President of the National Farmers Union (1969–1979), President of COPA (the *Comité des Organisations Professionelles Agricoles de la CEE* 1975–1977), member of the European Parliament (1979–1999) and President of that institution (1987–1989), and Co-President of the EP–ACP Joint Parliamentary Assembly (1994–1999), I have been in the thick of it as the multiplicity of changes have taken place.

It has not been my ambition to write a comprehensive historical account of these changes – such factual material exists elsewhere, in abundance. Rather, I have tried to give a personal account of my involvement in the events that took place. Inevitably, such a view is much narrower than that taken by a historian, and no doubt it is coloured by my personal preferences and prejudices. But I trust the book will present the reader with a little slice of 'history with a human face', and perhaps give some new insights into the processes of change I describe.

My intention has been not only to give a personal record of the past but to offer some pointers for the future. Few of the developments I describe has come to finality; indeed, by their nature most are in on-going mutation. On the basis of my personal experience in these three fields I am by no means happy with what I see:

· I have doubts about whether European agriculture will be sufficiently reformed to face up to the challenges of EU enlargement, the requirements of the World Trade Organisation, and the present crisis in farming in Britain and other member states;

· I fear for the UK's future role in the European Union – and in particular, I have to say I think the Conservative Party has in recent years been led up a blind alley in that regard; and

· I believe that the European Union is not facing up energetically enough to the challenges of helping the developing countries to help themselves.

It is my hope that the 'Plumb line' on these subjects will at least stimulate some fresh debate on them. They are all of immense importance to every citizen, especially every taxpayer, in Britain and throughout the European Union.

1

THE EARLY YEARS

While the earth remaineth, seedtime and
harvest . . . shall not cease.
(Genesis 8:22, Authorized Version)

As a young boy, I used to daydream about selling things to an imaginary crowd. I would spend time valuing furniture, livestock or implements – in fact, anything that caught my eye. Although I was born and brought up on a farm, with traditions of at least four generations of farming families, and had farming very much in my blood, I felt more than anything that I wanted to be an auctioneer.

It was an ambition lost to circumstance, for one day in 1940, when I was fifteen, the headmaster of my school – the King Edward VI, in Nuneaton – called me into his study, where my father was standing. He said at once, 'You're leaving school. We need you at home.' The Headmaster added, consolingly, 'Plumb, this war can't last more than six months, so there will still be a place for you.'

My immediate reaction was to throw my satchel in the air and shout 'So long, chaps!' – quite oblivious, at that moment, to the impact these unexpected responsibilities would have on the rest of my life.

This was to be the first of many occasions in my lifetime that I was 'thrown in at the deep end'. I thus began my time of learning at the 'University of Life' by working full-time in farming through the war years. And I was obliged to learn some hard lessons – unlike farmers' sons in peacetime, who typically go to agricultural college for at least a year or two. I was working with one other fifteen-year-old boy. Together we milked all the cows – by hand, of course – and kept 300 acres in order on one of the three farms between Coventry and Birmingham. My father had hardly any other men left.

The working days were very long. Sometimes when our work went on late, it would be illuminated by the glowing light from bomb blazes on the horizon – conflagrations that had been triumphantly predicted in the pro-German propaganda broadcast daily on the radio by 'Lord HawHaw'.

It was during this learning experience that I found a confidence and a belief in my own personal judgement – a judgement, mind you, that was based solely on intuition as the only survival kit available to me then. Looking back at that learning now, I appreciate something that has stood me in good stead through the rest of my life: the importance I attached even at that early age to teamwork, to working towards common objectives on the basis of mutual respect.

In 1942, when we were joined by two skilled farmworkers, both over sixty years of age, I put my teamworking skills into practice. In deference to my role as boss, they called me 'Young Master Henry', and I used to make sure that each morning after milking I discussed with them every single farm-related plan. Although generally agreeing with my ideas, it was *they* who made the decisions on my proposals. Perhaps at first unwittingly, that is the way I have always worked with a team. It may also explain how I have been fortunate enough to work with very many loyal teams throughout the various stages of my career. It was *they* who contributed to my positive thinking during the most trying times.

Further progress in my development came about because some of my time was freed up a little when the 1942 team was augmented by three landgirls. One of the tasks we had to do in those days was riddling potatoes that were stored in 'potato clamps' out in the field. The clamps were no more than heaps of potatoes covered by a deep layer of straw, and then buried under earth on top of that. 'Riddling' meant shovelling them out with a *scuven*, and then sizing and sorting them into one-hundredweight bags. (A hundredweight, for those who don't know, is 112 pounds in imperial weight, or 50.8 kilograms.) Although it was physical work, there was opportunity to work with a swing, and I can still hear Beryl singing Franz Léhar's *Dehlia* – 'I stand here, at the top of a hillock', and so on – while for seemingly endless periods of time we riddled mountains of potatoes from those field clamps.

This extra help meant that I had a little more time for other things. I studied as many farming books as I could lay my hands on, scientific and technical, convinced that farming would be my main aim in life.

My next experience taught me all kinds of other things that have stood me in good stead in my public life. I joined the Young Farmers Club (YFC) of Coleshill, in Warwickshire. The YFC movement provided a background for learning new skills that I was barely aware of. For example, we were all encouraged to take part in many activities, including competitions in such rural disciplines as ploughing, stock-judging and, of all things, public speaking. For the first of these competitions – the one in public speaking – I remember being taught the slogan 'Get up. Speak up. Shut up.' It was a rule I did not manage to adhere to.

The story goes that a good friend of the family once said, 'I'm sure that when Henry was a very young baby, he lay in a little cradle on top of the wireless while the news was on – because he has never stopped talking since.'

In my first speaking contest, I chose the subject 'What I Consider a Good Farm'.

'A good farm', I duly declaimed, 'is a farm that works 300 acres. It has to be sloping the right way, so it will not get the rough winds. Water has to be available for irrigation and feeding the stock.' For in my view, this was the ideal of a good 'mixed farm' (as it was typically described in those days), with so much arable, so much grass – enough to feed the animals, with a milking herd, beef and pig units.

The judge, well known in the district as a farmer who had started from scratch and with practically no education, looked me up and down and asked quizzically, 'You are a very ambitious young man. *Can* a ploughman become a farmer?'

'Oh yes, sir,' I said. 'You are a fine example, sir!'

In my next competition I fancied I would live up to being called 'ambitious', and chose 'Citizenship' as my subject. I came last. 'Speak on a subject you understand,' the judge advised me afterwards. The winner had spoken about ducks!

Fortunately, I was just as interested in the other competitions being held – the ploughing contests and the stock-judging. The ploughing competition involved an unexpectedly large number of people. Everyone in the YFC connected with the event stood to learn from it. It didn't matter whether they were taking part in the ploughing, involved with the stewarding or responsible for organising the whole thing. And ever since, ploughing and ploughing contests have been one of my enduring enthusiasms – specifically because they embody the realisation, amounting to a common bond among ploughmen, that land has to be treated with care and respect.

That I was in due course to become Patron of the British Society of Ploughmen, and in the year 2000 would perform the opening ceremony at the 47th World Ploughing Contest in Lincolnshire, was of course way beyond the scope of my thoughts at the time.

Then there was the stock-judging. We were trained to judge pigs, sheep, beef cattle and dairy cattle. My own particular interest was judging dairy cattle. And it was at that time that I fell in love with Ayrshires. I asked an old Ayrshire breeder, a canny Scotsman, how I could convince my father that we should have Ayrshires, and not Shorthorns or Friesians. 'Choose your breed like you choose your wife,' he told me. 'If you really like 'em, that is the breed you should go for. Just remember you have to look at 'em 365 days of the year!'

In time, we managed to build up quite a good Ayrshire herd – some pedigree, some not. Our milk yield was a good average, and we were concentrating on a high-quality product. And that in itself was not without particular significance. For in my political life in later years, when I stressed the importance of high-quality products backed up with good marketing, I would draw on my experience of selling our own milk at that time. We supplied only the best milk for our milk-round, even for milk supplied via vending-machines. I always believed in giving the customers the best deal – 'delivering the highest added value to the consumer', as the commercial types warble today – by getting our milk to them as immediately as possible. I still believe in that principle, and probably even more so, today.

On our waxed carton, showing an Ayrshire cow's head, I had a slogan printed stating 'Ayrshire milk is easier to digest'. An inspector from the local authority called in one day to say that he had sent one of our cartons to a doctor in the area who had testily asked him, 'How can Plumb claim that this milk is more easily digested than other milk?'

It was evident that the inspector thought he'd caught me out. 'What's your answer to that, eh?' he demanded. I had to think quickly.

'I don't say what it's more easily digested *than*, do I?' I replied after a moment. 'I might mean that Ayrshire milk is more easily digested than . . . than Ayrshire cows.' And he went away laughing.

But in fact, I always believed that Ayrshire milk was easier to digest because the fat globules in it are much smaller than the fat globules in the high-quality Channel Island milk with which Ayrshire milk most often has to compete.

It was in 1943 – still during the war – that I began to feel I could do more for the agricultural industry than just farm for myself and our customers. I was first elected Chairman of Coleshill YFC in that year, and as time moved on, I became Chairman of the North District Young Farmers of Warwickshire. Over the following nine years, two personally traumatic events then took place.

As Chairman of the North District Young Farmers I couldn't help but become well acquainted with the organisation's vivacious secretary. Indeed, it was the greatest of pleasures to become even better acquainted with Marjorie, for she became my wife. We were married in 1947, and our partnership has continued to this day.

Only the first five of those years, however, were in farming partnership with my father. For in 1952 my father died suddenly, at the age of 58 – and my world collapsed. I was 'thrown in at the deep end' once more. He had been a man of great stature and wisdom, and a believer in 'service before self'. I fought my way out of emotional and practical confusion, out of death duties and other matters beyond the scope of my previous experience, and managed to reorganise our farming business – thanks in particular to the assistance of the secretary of the county branch of the National Farmers Union (NFU), of which my father had been Chairman.

The period that followed was more significant to my later life than I could have imagined at the time.

My involvement as a keen, active member and office-holder in the Warwickshire County Federation of Young Farmers, together with my father's dedicated service to the NFU and to various politically-focused local and district organisations, might have made it seem natural for me to follow in his footsteps and get more involved in agricultural politics. But in 1952 I had a young family – three children under five – and a dairy, livestock and arable farm, together with a retail milk business to run. Why on earth should I bother with politics? I was very much a hands-on farmer.

It was loyalty to the memory of my father that persuaded me to follow in his footsteps nonetheless, at least along the lines of his main aim: to live a life practising 'service before self'. That was the motto also of the Rotary Club – which was an incentive to take up his place in the Coleshill Rotary, of which he had been a founder-member. Similarly, I became Churchwarden. But I was by no means so well disposed at that time towards the NFU county branch as my father had been – actually, he'd been Chairman at one stage. To tell the truth, I felt rather anti-NFU because those who seemed to enjoy their never-ending meetings appeared to be so much older than I was.

During the next few years, up to 1959, I gradually gathered further confidence, and probably even better judgement. I certainly increased contact with people outside farming through Rotary and the Church – and this might just explain why, after such a lengthy period, I allowed myself to be coaxed back into the NFU. For in due course I was elected to represent the farmers from my home county, Warwickshire, on the Council of the NFU, an august body that met at Agriculture House in London. There, I was joined by farmer and grower delegates from all corners of England and Wales

The first year in this new role on the Council, I served under the leadership of Lord Netherthorpe, not only a man of great physical stature (24 stone – 336 pounds or 152.4 kilograms – in his heyday) but also a legendary figure who had achieved a reputation as the pillar of the agricultural industry, and who is still remembered as a pioneer of the post-war Agriculture Act of 1947.

It was an educational experience in itself to witness the art of leadership as he demonstrated it. He once said to me that he would back the Council of the NFU – all 150 of them – more than the administrative body of any other organisation to come to a sensible decision on any subject. But he saw to it that he pretty well always got his own way. Farmers today owe him more than they perhaps realise for his ability to influence Ministers and Governments towards providing the current framework for the stability of the farming industry. Many of us who had lived through the wartime days of 'Dig for Victory', ploughing up every bit of pasture available in order to grow food for human consumption, had been convinced that we would soon revert to 'dog and stick' farming, particularly under a post-war Labour Government. But the legislation Netherthorpe helped to frame brought about a very different scheme of things.

The Agriculture Act of 1947 required Ministers each year to conduct a general review of the economic conditions and prospects of agriculture, in the light of which economic guarantees would be provided for a list of commodities. The guarantees were related to 'such part of the nation's food and other agricultural produce as in the national interest it is desirable to produce in the United Kingdom'. It was also stipulated that the financial returns on their commodities should be sufficient to provide proper remuneration and living conditions for farmers and farm-workers, together with an adequate return on capital invested in the industry. As a statement of intent, this was a radical departure from pre-war policies and implied unprecedented opportunities.

An apocryphal story tells how Jim Netherthorpe and Tom Williams, Minister of Agriculture, went to a meeting with the Chancellor of the Exchequer, Stafford Cripps. Cripps asked mildly how much the new policy would cost in its first year. At once, Jim pulled out the cigarette packet that he was well known for also using as his notebook. He glanced down at it briefly, raised his eyes again, and said, 'Around seventy-eight million pounds.'

'Let's call it eighty million, and get started,' said the Chancellor.

The fact that there was nothing at all written on the cigarette packet escaped his notice.

As Price Review succeeded Price Review thereafter in an annual ritual, Ministers and the Presidents of the NFU of England and Wales, together with their counterparts from Scotland and Ulster, met and negotiated, eyeball to eyeball, for at least three weeks in February every year. The NFU steadily consolidated its position. It was more than a pressure-group of loyal farmers – it became the seat of the agricultural establishment, and reflected the moods and needs of all its members.

At this time, in comparison with previous years, fortune favoured the home producer. The country was short of food and willing to pay for it. The NFU was the farmer's friend and protector – its decisions made news, and there was an army of able agricultural correspondents who were thirsting for positive stories of growth. Accordingly, the NFU became the universal provider.

Feeling very much part of this influential and promising body, I was pleased to find myself placed on the Milk and Pigs Committee, and even more delighted to be one of the Committee for Animal Diseases, later to become the Animal Health Committee. By no means everyone's cup of tea, sickness in farm animals was a topic of specific personal interest to me, although I hardly thought at the time that I would one day write a Minority Report to the European Parliament's Temporary Committee of Inquiry on BSE ('mad cow disease') – as I did in February 1997.

New delegates to the NFU were usually made welcome at a formal dinner hosted by the NFU President and the office-holders, so that they might meet all the senior staff together. General Secretary and Administrator at that point was Ken Knowles. A former President, and a formidable man who had dedicated his life to farming and the NFU, Ken was a very effective partner to Jim Netherthorpe during his fifteen years in office.

I sometimes felt humble and inadequate, as a young farmer aged 34 rubbing shoulders with men of great farming experience, many of whom had waited a decade or more for their sons to take responsibility on the farm before committing themselves to greater NFU involvement. In my house we took the opposite view: give it three years, think of it as good experience, and then get home to be there to give the children much-needed fatherly guidance.

But as my experience as a representative on the NFU Council continued, I became more and more impressed with the general standard of debate and the articulate way so many delegates were able to express their views.

It is worth recording one such contribution from a young delegate who said on one occasion:

'If we regard security as our due – as those with long memories may be tempted to do – the Agriculture Act may be thought of as a maintenance ration, designed to keep us alive for as long as the nation can meet the cost. If, on the other hand, we regard security as something to be earned and paid for out of maximum production, the Agriculture Act confers a right – and the dollar crisis dictates a need – to *produce*. Then, as farmers we must take our resources of skill, enterprise and labour, our assets of land, stock and machinery, and work them as never before. We must aim at feeding more of the people to save foreign exchange. We must aim at lowering our costs by increasing our technical, commercial and corporate efficiency in all practical ways. Unless we keep these aims before us, we shall not play our part in this country's struggle for economic revival.'

These were stirring words that expressed the mood of the time. They were amplified by a chorus of exhortation and argument to which the industry responded with a quite remarkable sense of purpose.

Back in this period, the NFU was secure in the sense that as long as there were subsidies, price reviews and farmer protection, the NFU was free to speak for all, affording to both landlords and tenants an appreciable element of support within the farming community.

My first year also gave me an insight into the wider world of farming. One of my duties was to make a monthly report on the decisions of the various Committees back to my county executive. I hadn't intended to be so quickly or so personally involved, but at my first meeting of the Pigs Committee, I made myself most unpopular by pressing for a resolution of no confidence in the Pig Industry Development Authority

(PIDA), a body meant to advise on production and marketing for producers, and paid for through a levy which most producers thought too high. The Committee Chairman, Colonel Wilson, was a great character, himself a producer and member of PIDA. By way of stern reprimand for my presumption, he treated me to a lecture on the importance of the Authority, and directed me then to go back to my members and repeat in detail everything he'd said. So I went back and told them. And of course they were less than ecstatic – and in turn directed me back to the next Committee meeting to press once more for the same resolution.

Well, the Colonel subsequently agreed to meet the Warwickshire members. At the ensuing meeting, he spoke at length – and in terms that were pretty well exactly the same as the lecture I'd been obliged to deliver from him before. Yet he spoke so effectively that from the floor there were hardly any questions or comments!

The following morning, however, Cecil Lees – one of our leading critics of PIDA – telephoned me. He began the conversation with his familiar 'I say,' and continued, 'What *did* he tell us yesterday? I am *still* not happy!'

That was my first lesson in being a representative on behalf of other people's opinions. And most salutary it was.

Whereas 1959 was the beginning of my involvement at NFU headquarters, it was also the end of an era – an era of great wartime and post-war NFU leadership: Lord Netherthorpe retired from spearheading fifteen years of enormous changes in farming history. His successor was Harold Woolley, a well-respected Cheshire farmer, a doughty fighter for his fellow men, and a President very different in temperament and outlook from the man who served in the immediate post-war years. He personified the industry's contemporary attitude as entrenched in a policy that he and the NFU generally believed was the best possible system for agriculture and that at the same time stabilised consumer prices.

From 1961 to 1963, acting in accordance with Woolley's firm conviction and belief, the NFU mobilised all its influence to avert change: it campaigned as forcefully as it could against entry into the European Common Market (then officially described as the European Economic Community). Woolley was the man of the hour in standing firmly in defence of the *status quo* – the Guarantee and Deficiency Payment Scheme, which (it has to be said) many saw as already creaking at the seams as production increased, requiring greater taxpayer support for surpluses.

On reflection, it would have been very much to our advantage if we had been able to help shape the European Common Agricultural Policy (CAP), rather than ultimately having to accept a policy based on French and German grain prices. But then French President de Gaulle said 'Non' to British entry into the EEC – and the NFU was delighted.

This did not mean, however, that the NFU wanted to be isolated, nor that British farmers simply meant to get all they could get while the going was good. Lord Netherthorpe had already realised that agriculture in Britain – the largest importer of food in the world – could not be isolated from agriculture elsewhere. It was he who had launched the International Federation of Agricultural Producers (IFAP) in 1946, and acted as its first President when the organisation was finding its feet. His attitude was not aimed towards producing airy-fairy formulations of resolutions for international debate; it was the hardheaded, ultimately practical kind – the sort that can make the unworkable work.

The NFU continued then, as it continues now, to play an active role in IFAP. Today, more than fifty years later, IFAP represents farm organisations from 80 countries worldwide. I had the pleasure of acting as its President from 1979 to 1982. It was an experience which made me more aware of a world moving rapidly towards globalisation – a world in which more than half of its inhabitants are starving.

I will return to the objectives and impact of IFAP later in Chapter 10.

The first shock to farmers' complacency and the belief that the national system of financial support for agriculture was 'gold-plated' came in 1960, following a Government White Paper. Prime Minister Macmillan made plain the Government's unease at its open-ended commitment to provide deficiency payments if prices fell as a result of markets' being saturated. That year, a domestic surplus of lamb, beef and pig meat coincided with a market marginally oversupplied with imports, which added considerably to the cost of deficiency payments. Together with Britain's application to join the Common Market, it all had the effect of polarising farming opinion, and created a wide division between those who looked forward and those who looked back.

Christopher Soames, an energetic and outward-looking young Minister, was totally committed to the UK's joining the Community. Harold Woolley, however – who utterly refuted any description of himself as either a 'little-Englander' or a 'parish-pumper' – threw his immense weight and prestige behind the party of reaction. In parts of Europe the NFU's attitude was interpreted as a fear of facing competition, yet we prided ourselves on being the most efficient producers.

Times were changing fast. The fact that six nations had pooled their resources, and some of their sovereignty, made it more difficult for Britain to export and stand aloof from food surpluses on its own doorstep. The agricultural revolution in Europe was just beginning, while at the same time the granaries of North America were bulging. The 1960s – a decade that brought problems of many different kinds in Britain – made farmers look to the Government for salvation, and not to themselves. This was inevitable. Under a deficiency payment system, farmers knew where they were. The system had proved itself. It had brought stability to the countryside. It kept food prices down and helped the export trade. It had made British agriculture one of the most efficient in the world. The alternative system under the Common Agricultural Policy in Europe, so the argument went, was going to lead us to dearer food and feedstuffs at home, while British taxpayers would be subsidising backward agriculture in other European countries.

The NFU's chief economist, Asher Winegarten, eloquently expressed such marshalled reasoning many times. A brilliant man, he evinced a most sophisticated approach to agricultural policies worldwide, to the effect that the NFU had no difficulty in showing that the managed market of Dr Mansholt would not make good the loss of deficiency payments, and that it would mean tough times for all producers and growers generally. Whatever pledge the Government might decide to make, such concessions would not amount to the same assurances UK farmers had benefited from through the 1947 Act. It was known and accepted that Asher, in his own persuasive way, had all the answers at his fingertips.

But above all, Asher also knew that the Minister of Agriculture in office, Christopher Soames, was beginning to prepare for changes in the British system of subsidised support in readiness for the country's ultimate entry to the EEC. The *Financial Times* described the NFU's attitude as that of a static mentality. The threat to British agriculture, it claimed, did not arise from a *union with* Europe but from *exclusion from* it. Inside the Community we would be able to work out our salvation with diligence. Outside, we would soon be exposed to the enemy at home, to a demand that recurs at times of economic stress – the demand for cheap food. Shut out from markets in Europe, Britain would not be able to afford a policy for agriculture that absorbed one tenth of total civil expenditure. Nor would farmers long survive under a system that entrenched, every year more deeply, 'Maginots of the mind'.

Sadly, Asher Winegarten did not live to witness the enormous changes, the long and difficult struggle, and the final advance of agricultural development. It was he who persuaded me to stand for the European Parliament in 1979, a decision I will refer to in more detail later (see Chapter 4).

All the reasoning aggressively put to the nation in the early 1960s made us turn our minds to thinking the unthinkable. We had commitments for trade with Commonwealth countries, particularly for butter, lamb and grain. *Could* we turn our backs on our old friends and cousins in New Zealand, Australia, Canada and elsewhere, who fought alongside us in the war against Germany? Couldn't we agree on a quota based on a tonnage of imported products from those traditional suppliers? We were surely not afraid of competition, since we were more efficient than the producers in France, Germany and Italy, for we were farming larger farms. We also believed that we had the finest livestock in the world – our beef, dairy, pigs and sheep in particular.

What an arrogant attitude this was!

Farmers were looking across the Channel through the wrong end of the telescope. Turn the telescope around, and there, between Calais and Paris, are some of the largest and most productive arable farms to be found anywhere in the world. Glance over our hedges and stone walls throughout Britain today, moreover, and you can see more European breeds of cattle and sheep than of our traditional breeds.

Yet it remains true that in the early 1960s there were some 4 million people employed on 2 million holdings in France, and that 75 per cent of the farms there covered less than 50 acres (20.35 hectares). With their families, they represented 23 per cent of a population of 45 million, but received only 13 per cent of the national income.

The Mansholt Plan was to retire one million farmers and move to structural reform. The French Minister of Agriculture of the time, M. Pisani, was a shrewd politician who is reported to have said, 'We can only confront the passions of a protesting peasantry with a doctrine of patience.' A courageous statement to make to 4 million farmers! But French farmers were well aware that under the inheritance laws enshrined in the Code Napoléon, there was no immediate chance whatever of real structural reform. The introduction of Europe's farmer retirement pensions nonetheless started the process and sweetened the pill.

Today there are just over one million employed in French agriculture. Politically, the French farm organisation FNSEA is strong, and there are vigorous marketing co-operatives – but the farming vote is considerably less weighty in the ballot box.

Come 1963, though, it seemed in Britain that the uncertainty of joining the Common Market (the 'Club of Europe') was over. It was my third year as county delegate of the NFU, and I had been elected Chairman of the Animal Health Committee – a job that I thoroughly enjoyed, working closely with the British Veterinary Association and the Animal Health Division of the Ministry.

Then Charles de Gaulle said *'Non'*, . . . and I began to realise that politics was in my bones after all. Harold Woolley announced that the crisis was over, and declared a victory for common sense, a victory over the Common Market, and a victory for the NFU. I didn't have the courage to voice my own opinion in Council. In any case, the decision had been taken – although in my opinion it was a decision that wouldn't hold for very long.

In the meantime, I was able to settle down to problems of animal health and the eradication of several diseases. We had been fairly successful in eradicating tuberculosis through compulsory testing together with a slaughter-compensation scheme. Now we also had a voluntary vaccination programme intended to control brucellosis. The live vaccine for it could be used in cattle only between the ages of six and eighteen months – but the Ministry charged 2 shillings and 6 pence per dose, which could only be administered by a vet. I felt strongly that it should be a compulsory scheme, and that the vaccine should be freely available in order to eradicate brucellosis altogether. Harold Woolley gave me the go-ahead to argue my case in a Price Review, and I was very gratified with what turned out to be a successful outcome.

When I visited the NFU Cheshire county branch and spelled out my victory, though, I was soon cut down to size. One gnarled farmer got up and said sourly, 'That stuff can't be any good – they're *giving* it away!'

But it proved successful throughout the country.

There were other aspects of animal health I was keen to become concerned with. In particular, I thought that there was far too little known by the public about the vast amount of research being carried out in government and private laboratories into the production of drugs promoting animal health – specifically drugs for the purpose of prevention rather than cure. Lord Rank, who chaired the Animal Health Trust, asked me to join its Council.

The Trust had to rely on private funding not only to further its research but even to survive at all, and I was sent off round the country to canvas county executives and to raise funds. I went to meetings with 16 of these in one month, and enjoyed enthusiastic verbal support from most of them. The big mistake I made was in not taking a pile of banker's orders with me to get their signatures there and then! For overall, my efforts were in vain. The Trust decided thereafter to concentrate on treatment for horses, and created a fine veterinary centre in Newmarket.

So at the end of 1963, after a period of fascinating work and active involvement, I was contemplating retirement from the NFU Council. It had been a great experience and I made many friends, but at home there was still the farm to run, three children to be educated, and a young wife who was holding the fort. My expenses far from covered the cost of extra labour needed to keep matters running. Farming 300 acres, looking after the milk production from a herd of 200 pedigree Ayrshires, 50 breeding sows for baconers, and growing 140 acres of mixed corn was a big job, and the farm was in need of a master.

Much to my surprise, my Council co-delegate from Warwickshire, David Darbishire, asked me if I would instead consider standing for the Vice-Presidency. At the age of 38, I felt it would be too ambitious even to try. I saw my chances as nil or, at best, as an 'also-ran' against fifteen other nominees, all members with much more experience. Bob Saunders, an articulate, trustworthy and reliable delegate, was the front-runner. Each of the candidates had his sponsor and supporter, and David had made up his mind. Speaking at the Council meeting, he expressed his amazement that all those who had been put forward were prepared to give so much of their time to the job, as they were either Justices of the Peace, County Councillors, or Chairmen of major NFU Committees. He presented me as a young man with a Kennedy image, and added 'We need young men in the team – and Henry doesn't yet have the commitments that other nominees have, so he will have the time to do it properly!'

'Thrown in at the deep end' again, I found myself elected NFU Vice-President after the Council voted on a short-list of seven possible candidates. I turned out to be the youngest-ever office-holder. Fame, if not fortune, followed via an interview with a farming journalist, whose idea of a punchy headline read HENRY WILL NEVER BE PRESIDENT: HE'S TOO NICE A CHAP! I joined the team of Harold Woolley, who was re-elected President, Gwilym Williams, elected Deputy President, together with Colonel Jock Wilson as Treasurer, and Ken Knowles, General Secretary. The level of support we were given meant that we were well equipped for the battle with the Government on the Agricultural Price Review that was due to commence shortly. Dairy farmers were pushing for an increase on their guaranteed prices, and pig producers also wanted an alteration to the prices due to the overall decline in the number of pigs.

The year 1964 proved to be better for farming, both politically and economically. The aim, as set out by the NFU, was to increase net farm income by 25 per cent over the next three years, and to take the first major step at the forthcoming Price Reviews. There were four major reasons behind such an endeavour.

In the first place, the disparity of real income between farming and industry generally was becoming improbably great. Secondly, the effects of the cost-price squeeze were causing harm to the long-term economic health of the agricultural industry, as was also the Government's refusal to allow producers to retain the benefits of their efficiency. Then, of course, there was a yawning gap between what farmers earned and what they needed for investment, and for labour, management and interest on capital. Last but not least, there was the deleterious impact of standard quantity arrangements on producers' future income-earning opportunities.

All together this was in fact the first major step towards recognition that, in the long run, British farmers would join the European Community, and that farming needed such an incentive in order to expand production. It was equally evident that the corollary to the NFU's political pressure – particularly the annual review of conditions and prospects for farming – was better marketing.

2

FACING CHANGES IN EVERY DIRECTION

OLD PARSON (ONCE CURATE IN THE PARISH):
How do you manage to get on in these bad times?
FARMER: Well sir, last year we lived on Faith; this
year we're a-livin' in Hope; and next year I'm afraid
we shall have to depend on Charity.
(*Punch*, March 20, 1880)

Co-operation

My personal responsibilities as a young office-holder centred very much on our commercial activities and our association with co-operatives and marketing organisations. A large part of the work of our Marketing Development department was devoted to providing information for a Study Group on Vertical Integration, particularly in relation to large-scale intensive production. How far ought farmers to move towards processing and distributing their own products so that they couldn't be dominated by those who bought from them?

The organisation that had led the way in NFU commercial development was created back in 1954 as the Fatstock Marketing Corporation (FMC) to assist farmers in livestock development and to operate a meat wholesaling and processing enterprise. At that time it was founded on bank guarantees, farmer goodwill and a mixed collection of small slaughtering businesses just released from 15 years of wartime and post-war control. World supplies were cheap and ample through much of the 1960s, and although the UK was the only big meat-importing country with a free trade policy, the home industry had to fight hard for its markets against imports, and on several occasions was brought almost to its knees.

David Darbishire – who later became Chairman of FMC – joined me in a study of meat marketing in Sweden. We witnessed a fine example of efficient producer-controlled marketing involving the direct sale of stock from farm to retailer. There were only sixteen slaughterhouses in the whole of the country, and farmers offered their stock a week in advance at an agreed price. It seemed amazingly simple and straightforward, cutting out the middle-man who often adds considerable cost to the animal either on the hoof or in carcass form.

British farmers enjoy the freedom of the market – but I often think of this freedom as an expensive gamble. At the time, there was great concern amongst farmers that vertical integration would take away their control and income. This has now occurred, substantially, in poultry and, to some extent, in pig farming. As we have seen in the USA, it was not the farmers but the processors who took the initiative by extending vertically into production, just as farmers' co-operatives were extending into processing. The percentage of farmers who remained totally independent poultry producers is now greatly reduced, although some use their buildings and labour to grow birds or produce eggs on the basis of contracts with major poultry processors.

In the co-operative field, all were concerned – including the Government – about the importance that efficient marketing would have after Britain entered the EEC. Contract farming, producer groups, machinery syndicates and marketing groups were developing, and there was closer consultation with trade associations. The larger farms were already enjoying the benefit of these schemes, but the smaller farmers still feared for their independence. It was therefore necessary to create the British Agricultural Marketing Development Organisation (BAMDO), consisting of the three farmers' unions, the five Milk Marketing boards, the four co-operative central organisations, four other marketing boards, and the British Farm Produce Council. This great – perhaps ideologically-based – initiative was therefore eventually decided in 1972 and founded on the belief that by co-ordinating our views we could act as a joint negotiator for the whole agricultural industry. At least it brought together both the public and private sectors through the Central Council and BAMDO.

Farmers can co-operate either to buy inputs and services or to sell their produce. In the case of input purchase, the objective of co-operation is to obtain discounts by buying in bulk. In the case of marketing, co-operation can enable farmers to offer a larger volume of standard-quality product and thus obtain a better return.

But by that time, farmers, accustomed to hearing that co-operation would be an answer to their difficulties, mostly remained doubtful whether such advantages could bring more than a marginal improvement to their annual trading results. The problem for many marketing committees was that they were run by well-intentioned farmers with a limited knowledge of the marketing skills needed to match the first-hand purchasers of commodities. Yet marketing projects as introduced by groups and co-operatives were exerting a strong influence on individual farming policies, particularly where marketing groups were striving for uniform production to meet their buyers' requirements.

Meanwhile, the development of buying groups and machinery syndicates enabled farmers to make significant reductions in costs. Once buying groups were established, they were well placed to move into marketing, while machinery syndicates were progressing into the integration of the whole of the growing and harvesting of particular crops. Potato growers, cereal growers and others were beginning to work together: to grow, harvest, store and market their crops on an integrated basis, and to make the use of both labour and machinery much more efficient.

The Government produced an incentive scheme to encourage three or more farmers to share machinery – and I well remember my surprise that it was mainly the larger farmers in East Anglia who took advantage, rather than the smaller farmers in the West, who would have gained substantially from this grant-aided scheme, particularly for silage-making. In 1967, the Government set up the Agricultural Market Development Executive Committee (AMDEC) to administer the grant scheme as a response to the BAMDO initiative. Two years later, this was followed by the formation of the Central Council for Agricultural and Horticultural Development. It provided help and encouragement in unifying the efforts of individual farmers to meet the challenge of an increasingly organised food industry.

I was invited to serve on this body under the Chairmanship of Sir Roger Falk, a businessman who dedicated himself to the service of the agricultural co-operative movement and to further development in marketing and true farmer co-operation.

The year 1967 was also significant in co-operative history for a second reason. The Government passed an Agricultural Act solely concerned with the development of co-operation. Specific objectives relating to farm structure, farm improvements, hills and uplands, and co-operation envisaged various ways to help thousands of small farmers with businesses of less than 600 man-days to co-operate, expand their holdings, or retire.

31

During the 1960s, the path was littered with good intentions. Grants were available to encourage joint ventures and contract farming. Also encouraged were buying groups comprising 20 or 30 farmers who would meet on a weekly or monthly basis and benefit from bulk purchases of farm inputs. But the response was disappointing. And as I hear farmers today claim that the supermarkets are ripping them off, I cannot help but feel it is sad – if not irresponsible – that we missed so many opportunities to get our act together and strengthen our marketing arm 40 years ago. One can take a horse to water but . . . !

Unless farmers increase their co-operative efforts and succeed across the board in creating a strong bargaining position, their profits will inevitably be squeezed towards vanishing-point. Even a so-called 'big farmer' with, say, 12,500 to 25,000 acres (5,100 to 10,200 hectares), is, by himself a sling-less David in comparison with the economic Goliaths of the supermarket world – solidarity and co-operation remain imperative.

In that trading struggle I must say I do not, however, entirely endorse the tactic once (in the days when goods were still weighed in pounds and ounces) adopted by the owner of a small corner-shop against a new supermarket in his area. The manager of the supermarket introduced a 'Bargain of the Week' gimmick as a loss-leader. On the first day, the supermarket's windows were festooned in gaudy posters proclaiming 'BACON £4 per lb'. Immediately, the corner-shopkeeper put a notice in his window 'Bacon £3.75 per lb'. The next day, the supermarket poster read 'BACON £2.50 per lb'. Right away, the corner-shop retaliated: '£2 per lb'. By the end of the week, the supermarket price for bacon was '20p per lb', and that of the small shop '10p per lb'.

The supermarket manager came to see the small grocer on the Friday night.

'Look,' he said, 'This can't go on. This price war is going to bankrupt both of us.'

'It may bankrupt you – and I hope it does,' replied the grocer. 'But it won't harm me. You see – I don't sell bacon.'

Meanwhile, the notion of a centrally-based 'trading business' was developing, having been initially devised by Herefordshire farmer Rhys Thomas, a member of the NFU Council and yet another forceful personality. His concept was sound. It was to provide a centralised buying power for smaller groups – a kind of 'federation' of businesses. Many of the younger business-minded farmers were inclined to follow

Rhys Thomas's lead, with the result that in due course Agricultural Central Trading (ACT) was formally set up.

Sadly, another result was the division of the collective movement, and in such a way as to sap the trading strength of individual farmers and to create tension between Sir Frederick Brundrett, Chairman of the Agricultural Central Co-operative Association (ACCA), and NFU President Harold Woolley. Both were strong characters in defence of their respective empires, but the arguments created further conflict at the expense of the entire farming community.

Joseph Knapp

Many books and papers have been written on the importance of co-operation, some of them by eminent writers – people dedicated to the cause and themselves influential in the wider field of marketing. Joseph Knapp, for instance, was invited in 1965 to write an analysis of agricultural co-operation in England. His remit was wide, but his general instructions were 'to study the agricultural co-operative movement in England and – in the light of its past history, its present development, and the likely future demand by the agricultural and horticultural industries for co-operative systems – to produce recommendations for improving its working methods and its form of organisation'.

Joseph Knapp was administrator of the Farmer Co-operative Service of the US Department of Agriculture, and a long-standing friend of the American Institute of Co-operation. From as far back as the early 1920s he had observed the development of co-operation and marketing by farmers, and had earned a fully justified reputation as the world's most outstanding co-operative research worker. He, like Horace Plunkett (who created the Plunkett Foundation), regarded the English as 'essentially an independent self-helping group of people who are inclined to carry their self-help a little too far'.

Sure enough, the UK has proved to be the least 'co-operative' country in the European Union. But why? History will, I think, show that the reason lies in a combination of the statutory boards set up in the 1930s, and the consequences of the Agricultural Act of 1947. These factors together meant that the marketing of farm produce was guaranteed, with price support through a deficiency payment system. Then in 1973 the country joined the EEC – and came face to face with the self-help arrangements of European co-operation.

In other member states, producers had set up their own off-farm structures invariably linked to a friendly co-operative rural banking system, such as the Rabobank in the Netherlands, Crédit Agricole in France, and Raiffeisen in Germany. Meanwhile, the UK system produced the largest farm size in Europe with the smallest proportion of the national labour force employed in the countryside. It was state support and protection that led to farm business independence in the UK, and subsequently to a sense of security under the blanket of which initiatives to develop markets, and therefore co-operatives, were thought irrelevant.

The series of questions Joseph Knapp then put to the co-operative societies couldn't have been more to the point:

1) To what extent is your co-operative working with other buying or marketing groups?

2) What problems arise?

3) In your opinion, based on the conditions in your trading area, is ACT gaining acceptance as a central servicing agency for groups?

4) Is the group movement sapping or helping the potential growth of societies?

Many large commercial companies were, not surprisingly, dubious about the long-term benefit to farmers of buying groups, and were highly critical of ACT. In October 1962, the National Agricultural Advisory Service invited milk producers in North Warwickshire to form a group for the purpose of recording feed quantities. One month later, a genuine cross-section of the whole farming community – with acreages ranging between 40 and 400 (16 and 160 hectares), and cow numbers between 20 and 80 – agreed to record the amount of bulk concentrates used each month, both purchased and home-grown, and to complete a monthly return of tonnage and cost, the number of cows in milk and dry, and the gallons of milk produced. The group's willing enthusiasm represented a new and modern way of thinking – looking for solutions by sharing the problems.

At that time I was a purchaser of compound feed for both dairy and pigs, and this survey's detailed analysis of my accounts showed that unless I reduced feeding costs by £10 per cow, it would actually be more profitable to grow corn. Like many, I decided to switch from purchasing everything at one large feed supply company to bulk-buying through ACT.

Imagine my surprise when the Chairman of the supply company invited me to dine with him at a well-known temple of *haute cuisine* in Park Lane. Looking me straight in the eye across the immaculate table, he eventually asked, perhaps rather plaintively, 'Don't you place any value on the vast amount of research we do, then?'

'Yes of course I do,' I replied. 'But not to the extent of three pounds a ton.' And it was further proof of the effect of buying groups that it did not take him long after that to offer me an attractive discount.

Knapp's aim was to get to the core of the problem, recognising the divisions between societies, groups of farmers, Plunkett, Central Council and the NFU. In addition, he was aware of the number of private merchants, many of them at that time being bought up by manufacturers or amalgamating, and creating tougher competition. The response that came from many co-operatives to his questions was:

1) Yes, we work with independent buying groups on a limited scale – but we will not trade with ACT. In any case, we do not offer the same terms to groups that we offer to our normal individual members.

2) ACT are undermining the commercial viability of co-operatives and every other form of enterprise.

3) I think ACT is not gaining ground in our territory.

4) Yes, the group movement is sapping the potential growth of agricultural co-operative societies by transacting business on a non-viable commercial basis by which margins are cut to ribbons.

The nub of the argument was the use of the capital involved ('servicing the capital', as resource managers might now say, or 'creating added value') – after all, it was the farmers' capital. But even to ask such questions was a sure way of dividing the loyalties of farmers.

As the NFU became more involved in commercial activities, members and supporters of the established agricultural co-operatives and other groups claimed that they were losing contact with the NFU altogether. And if there were already grave reservations in many quarters about ACT, imagine how much worse the situation became when, in one field of operations, the NFU itself seemed to set up in competition.

That came about as a joint venture with Hurst Seeds – one of the oldest and most highly-regarded seed-houses in the UK, owned by the Balint brothers – by which the NFU established its own herbage seed company. Called NFU Seeds, its products were sold under the slogan 'It's in the Bag', assuring buyers of secure certification and authenticity, as well as guaranteed mixing and varieties. When the first bags of NFU Guaranteed Seeds were delivered at Harold Woolley's farm in January 1962, the NFU President said, 'The farmers now have a real stake in the production and marketing of their own seeds.' NFU Seeds were initially available from nearly 500 reputable agricultural merchants as well as from ACT and independent farmers' groups.

Division amongst farmers nonetheless continued apace.

In December 1965, following disputes between ACT and NFU Seeds, the lack of harmony became even more strident when Harold Woolley put forward a proposal to the Council that Council members felt they could not support. Woolley at once announced his decision to retire from the Presidency. Although he subsequently changed his mind, the damage had been done. On a bid to be re-elected, he failed to get the necessary majority vote of 80 per cent.

NFU Seeds was finally dissolved in 1982–83, by which time it was regarded as having been something of a failure.

As I look back over this period, I must say I wonder how much we have really learned from history. If we have learned from history at all. In the UK there has always been a lack of unity in the commercial field – mainly, I believe, because of farmers' reliance on Government support rather than on the marketplace. The 1960s should have been formative years for co-operatives in preparation for our entry to the Common Market. But while commercial pressures were developing both in the UK and across Europe, we were arguing with each other over responsibilities and about who should do what.

The Federation of Agricultural Co-operatives (FAC) was formed in 1970 to try to ensure that UK co-operatives had an effective voice when British farmer delegates joined the Committee of EEC Farmers' Co-operatives (COGECA) in Brussels. The European organisation worked under a joint Secretariat with the Committee of EEC Farmers' Unions (COPA). The FAC represented the three co-operative central organisations (agricultural organisation societies) of the UK, and did so together with the Agricultural Co-operation and Marketing Boards (ACMS), a producer-controlled organisation established in 1972 to expand the effective share of the market both by representing the English co-operative viewpoint on national bodies to the Government and within the EEC, and by providing information and advisory services to co-operative managers.

To witness the joint operation of COPA and COGECA together in Europe was a salutary lesson for the UK teams, who had tended to think of the UK Marketing Boards as the ideal pattern for the future in relation to all commodities. But the Marketing Boards relied on statutory powers, Government authority wielded with the force of law. And the use of any such powers was now no longer an option, for it was outside the agreed Treaty of Rome to which we were about to be committed. The Treaty thus prevented the establishment of any new Marketing Boards – and was in due course part of the contributory background to the eventual break-up of those Marketing Boards that existed.

However, the FAC did join COGECA (under the 'Knightsbridge Agreement', which provided a means of funding the representation of farmers' unions in Europe), and so, shortly thereafter, did the Wool Growers' Federation thanks to my good friend Eric Wilson who was Chairman of FAC. I believe that this structure worked well, despite its difficulties in representing such wide and often conflicting interests. And I also believe that our entry to the EEC in 1973 was instrumental in bringing our commercial and political interests closer together. The marketing function of the ACMS was eventually transferred to the NFU when the NFU established a marketing division during my last year in office, and the FAC became a representative organisation for the boards and co-operatives.

Britain's entry resulted also in major changes in the Government's agricultural support policy. It was difficult for farmers to adjust to the new situation. Around that time, when I was paying a visit to a local market in the north of England, I remember a farmer poking me without ceremony in the back with his stick. 'I don't *mind* you joining this Common Market,' he said lugubriously as I wheeled to face him, 'as long as you don't hold it on Thursdays so it clashes with ours!'

The changes caused producers to depend more on market prices, following a trend that had already resulted in significant growth in 'farmer-controlled businesses' – a term used to encompass formal co-operatives and other group structures that were farmer-owned, both in the UK and in the rest of Europe.

By the mid-1970s, Sir Frederick Brundrett and I led our teams with enthusiasm, supported by the Central Council, but our organisations still lacked the power and influence that many on the continent already enjoyed. It was a time for reflection – particularly on the subject of what might be done to improve agricultural co-operation generally.

Experience over the years tells me that agricultural co-operation can achieve its aims only if control is in the hands of producers themselves. Enterprises must be run by commercial, not political, operators. Although I am a great believer in the bottom-up approach, there may yet be a case for a central federal body that provides local farmer-controlled businesses with services and goods purchased in bulk. Such a central body should not, however, have any 'controlling' function. It should be a servant to its locally-based masters. This is something the European Union at large might usefully learn too.

But perhaps the greatest challenge for co-operatives is funding and properly rewarding good managers. They are the key to success and must be empowered to take risks. They must also have the confidence of their board and staff, and build up a dedicated team – I say 'dedicated' because the alternative 'loyal' includes some sentimental connotations that are potentially out of place when doing business. What is important, after all, is honouring a mutually accepted agreement between buyer and seller for the conduct of business without unfair strings. Written contracts with societies and marketing bodies, including penalties for breaches on either side, are becoming more and more common practice – and they are essential to guarantee a high quality of product.

The quality and freshness of food, the fair distribution of supplies, the battle against pests and diseases, waste and pollution, and the need for an increased supply of food for a growing world population – all these require an understanding of the true meaning of the word *co-operation*. There is little room for conflicting interests jostling for control. Some people argue instead that 'charity begins at home', that 'God helps those who help themselves': I have no sympathy with that view. During the years I served as Co-President of the Joint Assembly between the European Union and the Africa, Caribbean and Pacific Countries (EU-ACP), agreement on the concept of true co-operation was a major issue in development policies (and to critics, I have much more to say about the matter in Chapter 11).

Co-operation is all the more vital for those who support Western and Christian values – for the men and women who use financial and material resources to foster greater understanding and co-operation and a better world order.

But the real question for us here is, what use do co-operators make of their increasing power and influence in the farming world?

The emphasis today is moving more towards rural policies and away from Government intervention in support of commodities. This represents increased concentration on the marketplace and the use of income support to maintain a living countryside, as set out in the 1996 Cork Declaration (to which I return in Chapter 10). A 'living countryside' requires both social and economic issues to be taken into account. Events demonstrate the importance of caring for our neighbours in the 'global village' if we are to look forward to a tolerable existence on this planet.

'Profits' are an ignoble pursuit in comparison – but farming is a way of life in which we work as though we could farm forever and we live as though we might die tomorrow. These two objectives have to be fused by increased efficiency and greater unity, in the knowledge that the farmer and his family are custodians of the countryside. Certainly, all forms of reconciliation are difficult. Producers need to feel united and satisfied that the application of science and use of modern technology is acceptable to the consumer. But one man's strength often results in another man's weakness – and that is something all forms of co-operation should prevent from happening.

Feather-bedded farmers?

In November 1964, serious attacks were made on the food and farming subsidy system in a BBC television feature entitled *Feather-bedded Farmers*. The programme was, in fact, simply an elaborate montage based on one ill-informed and deliberately offensive jibe made some time earlier by a member of Parliament. Its main emphasis was the size of subsidies – although there was no attempt whatever to quote what the nation received in return. We were encouraged to take pride in the fact that the UK had the lowest-priced food of any industrial nation in the world, and that the farming industry had now made greater progress under our 'costly' support system than at any other time in history. No mention was made of the equally well-established fact that agriculture was simultaneously saving hundreds of millions of pounds that would otherwise have been spent on imports.

Dealing with attacks, whether through the media, at public meetings or in smaller groups, is part of the job. To me, a verbal attack has always represented a challenge. I genuinely enjoy participating in positive debates based on clear-cut facts and figures – as I still do in the House of Lords. So far, I think, I have been able to hold my own in defending my views, from such issues as 'What I Consider a Good Farm' in the early public speaking contest, to 'Price Reviews', 'Matters European' and 'Facts and Fiction in Science', to mention but a few.

In most cases, it was not too difficult to anticipate the kind of attack I would most likely have to face. But there have been some exceptions.

For example, I went to a farmers' meeting in Devon in December 1964. There, right at the back of the hall, was an old country farmer who said he was not going along with some of the other farmers in attacking me. All he wanted was to ask me one question. It was about an NFU advertisement, which proclaimed to the world that during the current decade industry had increased its productivity by only 2 per cent, whereas agriculture had increased its productivity by 6 per cent. The advertisement also stated that, over the same decade, the profitability of industry had increased by 52 per cent, whereas the profitability in agriculture had increased by only about 2 per cent. We had taken a full page spread in one of the national newspapers to get this message across as clearly as we could, so that the public would understand where farming was at in relation to other industries, and to British industry as a whole.

I waited as the old boy struggled to his feet in emotion. He was surely going to make some point about productivity, profitability and percentages, and local conditions. I foresaw nothing out of the ordinary here. I was wrong.

'What do you mean by it, then?' bellowed the old codger finally. 'What's it all about? They tell me that an advertisement in the *Daily Express* costs £10,000! Ten thousand pounds for one day, for one sheet of paper! I'm not against you, I'm with you. But on the other hand, ten thousand pounds would buy my farm. I looked at them words, I looked at them spaces – and *there were more spaces than words*. Now, when *I* go in a field, I plough the bl—y lot. I don't *leave* half of it!'

The year 1964 has been described as a momentous year for the NFU. It was the year in which we saw the first measure taken to raise farm incomes under a three-year agreement with the newly-elected Conservative Government. The future looked highly promising. We published the first comprehensive policy statement for 20 years, calling for further expansion of home production – which would improve the national balance of payments – and launched the *NFU Farm Business Records* book to help step up efficiency. The success of the British Agricultural Exhibition in Moscow, in which we played a major part, opened the way to increased exports in the Soviet Union and Eastern Europe. We also won growing acceptance of NFU policies for co-operation among the major food trading countries. And in October that year, our President introduced the NFU's new policy statement *British Agriculture Looks Ahead*.

By that time the NFU – never anything but non-party-political – had welcomed back Fred Peart as Minister of Agriculture. The Minister's first Price Review, however, aroused a storm of protest. He produced a White Paper packed with ideas for change, including the further reorientation of financial support. The Small Farmer Scheme was to be extended and enlarged. More assistance was to be channelled into the hills and uplands. But these measures might be seen as mere palliatives. What Government had in mind was to set up Regional Development Authorities that had the power to co-ordinate all forms of land use. They would be able actually to acquire land for the improvement of land use and project structure, and for eventual disposal. It was, in effect, the germ of the idea of Rural Development Boards.

Farmers were angry, for the situation seemed to be slipping away from an agreement to make multilateral arrangements for controlling imports in an effort to bring some sort of balance into home and overseas supplies.

The new proposals also contained market-sharing arrangements for bacon, butter and cheese, and minimum import prices for cereals, which put a floor to the market and reduced deficiency payments on home-grown grain. The schedule of guaranteed prices for 1965 left many farmers short of what was needed – or what they believed was needed – to meet the increased bill of costs.

So although 1965 was a bumper year for corn, and filled the shops with some of the best and cheapest vegetables, salads, lamb and pork that housewives had seen in years, the same harvest also produced a crop of roadside posters proclaiming that farmers were in revolt. 'Give farmers a fair deal!' they said; 'Millions spent on foreign food – let *us* grow it!' and 'Don't let them strangle British farming!' Protests were painted on buildings, and for a time there were even heated discussions in the NFU on the subject of possible industrial action.

Prejudice against the newly-elected Minister ran high. Farmers claimed that instead of restoring the prosperity of the farming industry, as he had promised during the election run-up, he had reduced many farmers' income. Farmers' costs in the previous 12 months had risen by £29 million, yet the total compensation the Minister offered the industry was £10 million. Farmers claimed that they were required to make up the remaining £19 million out of their own pockets.

If they had been able to bring themselves to consider not buying machinery for one year, reducing the purchase of fertilizer, supporting a policy of non-co-operation with MAFF, or even withholding supplies to consumers, the farmers might – might – have got somewhere. Any one of these ideas adopted by large numbers would at least have shown a sign of solidarity among farmers. But at the end of the day it was the farmers themselves who were to come off second best.

The 1965 Agricultural Chapters of the National Plan proposed an increase in domestic production of £300 million worth of food by 1970, saving at least £200 million worth of imports and satisfying the increase in consumer demands. We were by then 50 per cent self-sufficient in food and feedstuffs – which seemed good news. There were two conditions that the NFU found difficult to accept, however. The first was that British farms would cut down on already scarce manpower, and do so at a rate of 25,000 workers a year. There was already a drift (if not a push) from the land as technology increased, so this was attainable. But the second condition was that expansion would not absorb an excessive share of other real resources that could effectively be used in other industries either to increase exports or save on imports.

The vibes from Whitehall were coming through loud and clear. Since the failure of negotiations in Brussels, and in the belief that new negotiations were imminent, many officials were saying that the case for deficiency payments was overstated and that efficient farmers were capable of producing more without encouragement from the taxpayer. John Eastwood was proving this with his intensive poultry unit, and horticulture was leading the field in high-quality products without subsidies.

Many felt that farmers were being invited to produce bricks without straw – but it did not pass unnoticed that although the guaranteed price of barley was reducing, acreage and output went on rising, and yields were increasing. The sick joke at the time described the arable farmer's rotation as two years in barley and one in the Costa del Sol. And in some quarters the label 'barley barons' tended to be stuck on farmers generally.

The big change – difficult for farmers to swallow – was that alleged inefficiency, wherever it existed and for whatever reason, must be the subject of remedial action by the state. Similarities with the proposals of Commissioner Mansholt in his European plan for structural reform were obvious to many.

At that time it was difficult to envisage the surpluses we have since witnessed, and the ensuing measures (other than price restrictions) now in place. Minister Fred Peart's plan, or statement of intent, was visionary: it was set out in the form of a complete analysis of the composition of British agriculture together with a programme for structural improvement. Now I have never been convinced, in any analysis, that averages either of farm size or income were the right criteria to work from – but in this case it was the only way to arrive at the 'departmental net-income calculation' from which it was possible to derive a useful idea of the trend of prosperity (or otherwise) when adjusted for weather conditions.

In my opinion there is no such thing as an 'average' farm that represents a nation. I remember taking part in a conference in Japan where we were debating farm structure: I think I might have been the sixteenth speaker. Everyone before me spoke of the average-size farm in his or her country or region. In Texas that meant 10,000 acres (4,050 hectares), in Germany 40 acres (16 hectares), in France 25 acres (10 hectares), and in Luxembourg 3 acres (1.2 hectares). Pompously, I declared that it was not the farm size we should be debating but the size of the business – and I added, 'The only sensible definition of a small farmer is as a chap about 5 feet tall.'

Fortunately, my remark seemed to amuse the Japanese delegation.

In the UK at that time there were 450,000 holdings of one acre (0.4 hectare) and over, of which 25 per cent produced 70 per cent of total output – and that total was being reduced by between 2,000 and 3,000 holdings each year. Today, the total is down to 240,000 holdings of which some 20 per cent produce about 80 per cent of all output, while the rate of reduction was steady at 1,000 per annum over the period 1994 to 1999.

The focus of farming was changing considerably. Consumers still demanded cheap food but criticised factory farming. Farmers felt the wind of change from reduced subsidies as production costs increased. The Government was more attuned to the needs of consumers than those of the farmers.

At the same time, technology was providing innovations intended to increase yields and decrease labour and costs. The early signs of a revolution in genetics were clearly visible, particularly in poultry, pigs and beef lots. Progeny-testing in dairy was based on semen banks and a bureau of performance records: 70 cows a milker was the target of the day. Arable farming was related to size of operation and low-cost-efficiency. Potato-growing was in the process of becoming as completely mechanised as cereal-growing. And the removal of many hedges was recreating the English landscape of the sixteenth century. The economic logic of these changes meant that only the better land would be needed for food production, and only the better farmers would be engaged in it.

Similarly, as time went on, the NFU became more and more involved in European and international affairs. Back in 1966, not only were we full members of the International Federation of Agricultural Producers (IFAP) but we had observer status of the Council of Professional Agriculturalists (COPA). On reflection, this was also the year that contributed to major changes in my personal life. It widened the scope of my already strong belief in prevention rather than cure in both science *and* politics, and led eventually to my active involvement in the European Parliament, in the international agricultural, food and trade organisations, and in Third World development.

The style of NFU leadership was also changing. Many members of the NFU Council were critical of the NFU's increased role in commerce, feeling that we should revert to solely political interests. And Harold Woolley resigned as President, after six years in office. It was sad to see him go. He had been a tough leader and negotiator, totally dedicated to the NFU, and his heart had been in his work. The retirement message he left for publication was typical of his style and approach, and speaks for itself:

A Message from Sir Harold Woolley, CBE

No man can ask for greater good fortune than to be given the opportunity to serve fully a cause that is dear to his heart. As President of the National Farmers' Union for the past six years I have had this opportunity, and I am thankful for it.

The NFU is a great organisation, and it is up to every one of us to do what we can to make it greater still. There can be no substitute for a strong, well-integrated Union serving every section of our industry without discrimination or partiality. The tasks are heavy and the problems do not lend themselves to quick and easy solutions.

My good wishes and loyal support go out to our new President and his colleagues.

I believe we have firmer ground under our feet now, and I will do anything I can to help to build on it.

For all the support I have enjoyed from the Council, the excellent staff at Headquarters, and from our membership throughout England and Wales, and for the tremendous kindness and goodwill shown to me now and at all times, I feel more grateful than I can find words to express.

> To all our members I would say – whatever the difficulties and
> frustrations along the road – keep a steady and balanced outlook.
> Support your Union at all times and give your democratically –
> elected leaders the strength that can only come from your support.
> For all you have given me, please accept my sincere and humble
> thanks.

Gwilym Williams was elected President. I moved up to be his deputy, joined by Tom Cowen, a livestock farmer from Cumbria, who stepped into my shoes.

Tom and I became very good friends. He was thoughtful and intelligent, and had a fine sense of humour. He loved his native Cumberland and told many, many stories of country wit and wisdom. Sadly, he died sitting in his armchair, watching the varsity rugby match between Oxford and Cambridge on TV. We were a good team, full of vigour, and between us we covered arable, dairy and livestock interests in our own farming businesses.

An example of the NFU's change of style was Gwilym's decision to form an 'inner Cabinet' of selected people. In principle this was a sensible idea, but it caused some criticism from the General Purpose Committee.

The standard of living was rising, and the consequences of it for agriculture were evident – food had to compete more with other goods and services making claims on the consumer's pocket. Food production was twice that of the pre-war years, and investment in working capital was increasing year by year. Yet the country failed to understand the historical significance of agricultural development in the past quarter-century. After 21 years of peace since World War II, farmers were asked to undertake a further expansion programme looking to increase the proportion of our home market. The population explosion worldwide, linked to predictions that before long there would be 75 million mouths to feed in the UK alone, became a major issue of concern. Although this prediction turned out to be wrong, the days when farming was considered 'just a way of life' had definitely gone. The emphasis was on business.

Agricultural legislation, temporarily shelved until after the General Election, was now to resume its journey to the statute book. In the Queen's speech at the State Opening of Parliament, Her Majesty said:

> My Government will continue to promote modernisation and
> increased productivity in farming, horticulture and fishing, and

will introduce measures for the longer-term development of agriculture and the establishment of a Meat and Livestock Commission.

The Government will also take action to stimulate progress in implementing the National Plan – and would be ready to enter the European Economic Community, provided essential British and Commonwealth interests were safeguarded.

I saw this latter commitment not just as safeguarding British agriculture but also as giving it an enhanced role in our national and international life. My political responsibilities were increasing, and I was beginning to see more clearly Britain's role in the world and the applicability of the wise words spoken in 1624 by the Dean of St Paul's, John Donne:

No man is an Iland, intire of it selfe; every man is a peece of the Continent, a part of the maine ... and I am involved in Mankinde.
(*Devotions* xvii)

There was growing public awareness of the gigantic scale of the job to be done if the world was to be properly fed. International development was very much to the fore when we hosted the 15th General Conference of the International Federation of Agricultural Producers (IFAP) in April 1966, and welcomed representatives from farm organisations from more than 30 countries.

When I reflect on these years, particularly in the context of my involvement in the EU-ACP Joint Assembly, I often despair of the opportunity, missed at that time, of pressing for more adequate food distribution to prevent famine in developing countries, rather than relying on food aid in crises. Today, the lack of co-operation between the developing countries themselves has made the situation worse, compared with 30 years ago. We only have to remind ourselves of the sombre message from the Food and Agricultural Organisation (FAO) of the United Nations in 1966, to the effect that during the previous twelve months world food production did not rise at all whereas the world population rose by 70 million, and of the equally stark reminder in 1960, alerting us to the knowledge that all predictions and economic theories can be meaningless in the face of tragedy.

Confrontation and active involvement in farming tragedies and disasters became an important part of my life – initially as Chairman of the Animal Health Committee in 1963 at the time of the eradication of tuberculosis, most recently in connection with the BSE disaster of 1996 and afterwards. But in 1967, there was the horrifyingly massive outbreak of foot-and-mouth disease.

Foot and mouth, 1967

Foot-and-mouth disease apparently first came to Great Britain in 1839. Between 1923 and 1924 there were 1,929 individual cases, as a result of which 128,000 animals were slaughtered. At that time (as, indeed, generally today), choices on what to do in the face of an outbreak were limited: either 'slaughter' or 'isolation'. Both my grandfathers had cases on their farms, and had to choose. The one slaughtered his stock; the other (the Plumb) did not. Plumb was wrong – but he was stubborn! Thereafter, legislation demanded compulsory slaughter of whole herds.

The outbreak on grandfather Fisher's farm was believed to have arrived via a letter sent from cousins in Cheshire, who wrote to say that they had foot-and-mouth disease on their farm. My grandmother took the letter to grandfather for him to read while he was milking, evidently carrying not only the news but also the virus to the milking-shed. That is how virulently infectious the disease is.

The 1967 foot-and-mouth epidemic – one of the worst ever experienced – started in Oswestry and spread to the Cheshire plain. Cheshire, famous for its pastoral beauty and for its agricultural pre-eminence, became the main battlefield in waging war against the most wretchedly depressing epidemic of the century. The wholesale massacre of the livestock of those who breed and tend them was a soul-searing experience for farming families. Financial compensation – important, of course, to alleviate the material loss – cannot remove the permanent scars of psychological trauma and anger. Yet common misfortune always seems to tap the reserves of courage and kindness in people, and courage and kindness together amounted to the only bright spot during that dismal winter.

The way in which the farming community faced up to the devastating consequences and set about rebuilding was a fine example of resilient endurance. There were also farmers living in areas of infection who somehow escaped the disease but agonised just as much in long-drawn-out anxiety. Ancillary trades and professions obviously suffered disruption and financial loss, and farmers from all over the country responded by sending in replacement stock when the restrictions were lifted. Many tributes were later paid to those employed in the Animal Health Services of the Ministry of Agriculture: they were a credit to their profession.

To investigate the root cause of this tragedy, and to explore every means of preventing further outbreaks, Minister Fred Peart invited the Duke of Northumberland to chair a Committee of Inquiry. I was invited to serve on the Committee, the only farmer member except the Duke himself, who owned the largest estate in the north of England. It was a well-balanced team from any point of view, and included Professor Sir William Weipers, head of the Veterinary Faculty at Glasgow University, and Anthony Cripps QC from Nottingham.

For more than a year, the Committee met one day a week, taking evidence and studying reports from more than a thousand organisations and individuals. Some of them believed that the virus was spread through the air, perhaps though the use of slurry from cattle. To continue our research, Committee members also travelled extensively, first in Europe and then in South America.

And it eventually turned out that the virus had been transmitted from Argentina, where foot-and-mouth disease was endemic among all their livestock areas. Most probably, our infection had been carried in the bone-marrow of imported carcasses. I spent quite some time in a number of the *estancias* (ranches) and *frigoríficos* (slaughter-houses) talking to the meat men. Any animals that came into the market of Buenos Aires with foot-and-mouth disease were simply moved on to what they called a 'paddock', a field of some 1,000 acres (405 hectares). This, at that time, was their interpretation of 'isolation'.

After receiving considerable evidence and advice from all over the world, we were faced with a decision over whether we should recommend total vaccination (which became the policy in Argentina), should stock up with vaccines for 'ring' vaccination surrounding an infected area in the event of another outbreak, or should rely henceforth on the policy of mass slaughter alone. I was utterly against vaccination other than ring vaccination in the event of an outbreak, knowing that it would be impossible to gather all the hill sheep each and every year, and to be sure that the live vaccine could thus be passed on to the unprotected flocks. It was my strong belief that if the importation of carcass beef were banned altogether, allowing packed meat in in cryovac packs only, the problem would be solved *without any* vaccination – at least until such time as a further outbreak of epidemic proportions might require alternative measures. Anthony Cripps QC was the only Committee member to demur from this view and to write a minority report in favour of vaccination.

Our final decision was clear. In March 1969 we submitted our recommendations to the Government. Following the events of 2001 they make interesting reading.

I [It is recommended] That the slaughter policy, which we consider to be the best method of eradicating foot-and-mouth disease when it occurs in Great Britain, should be continued. This policy by itself should only be adopted if the conditions of meat import policy are such as to reduce substantially the risks of primary outbreaks occurring. If such conditions of meat import policy are not put in force, we would recommend that the slaughter policy should be reinforced by a ring vaccination scheme.

II As the conditions of meat import policy, in our view necessary to permit the policy [for eradicating foot-and-mouth disease] to remain a policy of slaughter by itself, we recommend:

(a) The ban on imports of mutton, lamb and pig meat from countries or areas of countries where foot-and-mouth disease is endemic should continue.

Imports of mutton and lamb offal and pig offal from countries or from areas of countries where foot-and-mouth disease is endemic should be limited to offal processed in such a manner as to destroy foot-and-mouth disease virus.

(b) Because there is a high risk of introducing foot-and-mouth disease into Great Britain by importing carcass beef and beef offal from countries or from areas of countries where foot-and-mouth disease is endemic, on strictly animal health grounds there should be a complete ban on all such imports.

(c) Alternatively if for social, political or commercial reasons the recommendation in (b) is not accepted, imports of carcass beef and beef offal from countries or from areas of countries where foot-and-mouth disease is endemic should be limited to

(i)   boned-out beef; and

(ii) beef offal processed in such a manner as to destroy foot-and-mouth disease virus.

III [It is recommended] That:

(a) Our veterinary staff in South American countries should be strengthened in order that standards of public health inspection acceptable to the British Government can be ensured and so render the retention of lymph glands in boned-out cuts of meat unnecessary, and in order to assist the implementation of the Bledisloe arrangements.

(b) Because some countries in which foot-and-mouth disease is endemic have well-defined areas which for geographical or other reasons are free of the disease and which could be accepted as safe sources for imports of meat, provision should be made to permit imports of meat, under suitable safeguards, from such areas.

IV [It is recommended] That contingency plans for the application of ring vaccination should be kept in constant readiness. They could be put into operation should our recommendations in II not be successful in limiting the number of outbreaks.

V [It is recommended] That the importation of meat and meat products from all sources be subject to revocable conditional licences.

VI [It is recommended] That adequate facilities for the cleansing and disinfection of vehicles and persons engaged in the transport of livestock should be a legal requirement at appropriate points of entry into Great Britain.

VII [We finally recommend] An expansion of research work on foot-and mouth disease, particularly in epidemiology and the use of epidemiological teams in the field.

The Government accepted our views in their entirety. It was estimated that vaccination would cost some £25 million a year at 1967 prices. And because there were no further major outbreaks for more than 30 years, our decision *against* total vaccination effectively saved the taxpayer something approaching £9 billion over that period. Vaccination would have proved a very, very expensive option. It should not be forgotten, moreover, that vaccination is effective only against a specific virus and that the disease manifests itself in the form of various viral strains. Pertinently, the outbreak in 2001 stemmed from an Asian-type strain immune to the specific vaccine appropriate in 1967.

During this difficult episode, there were occasions when I had no other choice than to wear two hats. As a member of the Committee of Inquiry, I was sworn to secrecy until the final report was presented. Half-way through the inquiry, however, I was obliged to take a press conference on behalf of the NFU President. One of the reporters asked me 'What is the NFU line on foot-and-mouth, and what evidence have they been given?'

I was stuck. I certainly couldn't say anything about evidence. But the NFU President must at least have a 'line' on the subject.

'Ban imports of beef from South America,' I replied.

The headline the following day was BUTCHERS SAY: SACK PLUMB FROM COMMITTEE AS HE IS BIASED.

This raised a question and a debate in the House of Lords on 4 March 1969. Lord Royle referred to an article in the *Farmer and Stockbreeder* published that same day. His main question was on how this article could apparently give information about the final Report to be agreed in eleven days' time, on 15 March, at the next meeting of the Committee of Inquiry. The question was in fact twofold. Firstly, had I acted as a genuinely independent member? And secondly, had I blurted out information I shouldn't have revealed?

Lord Royle quoted from the article:

> If the draft recommendations are agreed, it will be a victory for Mr Plumb, the National Farmers Union's deputy president, and the only practical farmer on the committee, who has fought throughout the year to convince his colleagues that prohibition of imports of carcass meat from endemic countries was the right policy. At one time it looked as if Mr Plumb would have to produce a one-man minority report expressing his view. Now, with the Duke of Northumberland himself as the first convert, the majority of the Committee has swung behind his proposal.

When Lord Royle had concluded his eight minutes' speech, in effect saying that I was a man who had approached his task with a mind closed to all persuasion, Lord Beswick responded on behalf of the Government, expressing a different view. I quote:

> Although he [Lord Royle] said that he did not wish to open up a discussion about this wretched foot-and-mouth disease, he is in

fact asking me to comment upon the contents of a Report which not yet has been published. I do not know what is in this Report. Nor does the Minister. And certainly Mr Murray, the author of this speculative article in the *Farmer and Stockbreeder* does not know what is in this Report. No one can object to any active and enthusiastic journalist putting down his own opinions and prophecies . . .

My understanding is that there was no secret about when this Committee met; it was generally known. And indeed, it was not unusual for interested journalists to be around the meeting-place to pick up some unconsidered trifle when those meetings took place. . .

I was rather surprised at the conclusions that [Lord Royle] seemed prepared to draw from the article about the position of Mr Plumb. My noble friend appears to be saying that Mr Plumb has swayed not only the noble Duke, the Chairman of the Committee, but the whole remainder of the members of the Committee to a particular conclusion, presumably against their better judgment . . .

There is absolutely no reason to believe, or for anyone to say, that Mr Plumb is anything other than one effective, loyal and conscientious member among a Committee of eight.

I make just one other comment about this article. It purports to know that at one time Mr Plumb was proposing a minority report. There is only one man who knows what is in the mind of Mr Plumb, and that is Mr Plumb himself.

And I was allowed to continue.

Foot-and-mouth disease had brought the morale of the farming families to a very low ebb. Farmers were running out of money following considerable investment, and even the weather went against them at a most critical stage. During this time of distress, their dream of saving the nation by expanding food production and vastly reducing imports was fading fast. Political and financial constraints imposed by the Treasury made a shortage of men and finances inevitable. The Ministry nonetheless thought that expansion could be obtained on the cheap, that somehow we would find the resources to make agriculture ever more capital-intensive.

Reflecting on those times, it seems inconceivable that 35 years later, despite what was a major catastrophe in the 1960s, foot-and-mouth disease would come back to haunt us.

Over the years, many lessons had to be learned. Bones were excluded in beef imported from South America where, ironically, Argentina claimed until recently that they had virtually eliminated foot-and-mouth from their herds and flocks. The virus we have recently fallen prey to is of an Asian variety but may have come from South Africa. Once again because of waste food ('swill') collected from schools, institutions, airports, etc., and fed to pigs, more than 4 million animals have been destroyed, and the whole of the farming industry and rural community have been made to suffer.

I know from my experiences in the 1960s how difficult it is to trace the disease and isolate the outbreaks as they emerge – how difficult it is to try to 'cure' the problem – but it does seem that we could well benefit from the example of other countries who take more stringent preventive measures than we do. Try, for example, to get through Washington Airport control if you state on the form that you have been on a British farm in the past 24 hours – even without foot-and-mouth! Mind you, all this confirms that communication with the public is important. Closing footpaths, closing markets, stopping hunting, racing and all movement of stock – such measures all contribute to a generally understanding response from consumers. The threat of food shortages, on the other hand, creates panic-buying.

This whole tragic episode raises basic questions: the need to examine the way the food chain works, the question of intensive farming, of farm structure and of moving towards freer trade. It also raises the question of the root cause of cost-cutting on farms – a cheap food policy. But above all, it is more than just a matter of economics and welfare: it is the need to be more vigilant on the implementation of controls on imports of possibly harmful products.

If some of the red tape surrounding the premises of farms, butcher's shops and slaughter-houses were transferred to our borders, we might be able to survive for even longer than 35 years before the next outbreak of foot-and-mouth.

The end of the 1960s

The 1967 foot-and-mouth crisis finally came to an end, and the business of farming went on, amid new considerations of the economic conditions and prospects for farmers. Following the epidemic, with its effects on the countryside, farmers expected that the emphasis of the Price Review would fall on livestock production – especially if imports were to be banned from countries where foot-and-mouth disease remained prevalent. Any change in emphasis on the livestock sector, however, would have a knock-on effect on the arable sector, for with an increase in the livestock population would also naturally come an increase in demand for feed. The question on many people's minds was how much aid the Government would give to the selective expansion programme.

What I did not expect was that talks with the Government over Price Reviews would lead to my again being 'thrown in at the deep end' in another twist to my career.

A few months later, at the request of the Select Committee on Agriculture, the NFU prepared a memorandum giving a detailed commentary on the evidence provided by the Ministry of Agriculture on the implications of EEC membership on food and agriculture. We were also invited to give oral evidence as to the significance of production grants in hill and upland areas, with particular reference to wool.

Throughout the year we kept in close touch with the Ministry of Agriculture, monitoring EEC developments and relaying the NFU's attitude towards them. We did our utmost to ensure that the effects of adopting the Common Agricultural Policy on our own domestic agricultural policy, on our agricultural industry, and on the country's food situation in general were understood as widely as possible – and that those effects would also require certain modifications in existing arrangements. We also kept the Confederation of British Industries and the British National Committee of the International Chamber of Commerce fully informed of the NFU's views, and reached out to the general public through radio, television and other media. Apart from the meetings of IFAP and related international groups, the International Conference at Grenoble was used to explain to foreign audiences the position of British agriculture in relation to United Kingdom membership of the Community. The NFU always impressed upon the Government the need for agriculture to expand in order to save imports, and the equal need for the industry to have the resources to invest in that expansion. Every extra pound's-worth or ton of food economically produced at home directly saved imports, and given the right framework and encouragement, the scope for further economic expansion in production was considerable.

When the Conservatives resumed power in 1970, they were able to assert with justification that the two blueprints for expansion – the National Plan and the import-saving role outlined in the 'Little Neddy Report' of 1968 – had both been introduced without the necessary resources to back them up. We had in effect been marking time for six years, and a great national resource had gone unexploited. Farmers were meanwhile complaining that they were taxed on efficiency, that there was no incentive for expansion, and that 'we have come to the end of the road'.

I wonder how many times I have heard *that*, over the years.

I have always believed that the only way for Britain to compete with other European countries was by expanding. The danger, following a few difficult years, was one of complacency – the belief that we in Britain were the livestock-yard of the world, and that we were much more efficient. This proved to be the myth that by then it was, and today the fields are full of continental breeds of cattle and sheep.

The task facing the UK farming industry, however, took place in a most disturbed and disturbing time, a decade of industrial unrest and occasionally violent strikes. The coal industry was in chaos, as was the steel industry, and farmers became equally militant, demonstrating in the streets of towns and cities on their tractors with their farm equipment. For one thing, the imposition of a levy on farmers for training young people under the bureaucratic aegis of a new Agricultural Training Board was widely perceived as adding insult to injury. It was certainly an issue that generated more heat than light.

On the initial recommendations of the NFU Labour Committee, county delegates were enjoined to emphasise to all authorities the need for a highly skilled and adequately-trained labour force to meet the challenge of increasing technology. The Committee also recommended that Government prices policy should enable the industry to pay wages to attract and retain skilled men, and pointed out the need for a practical wages structure to provide a recognisable ladder of advancement in agriculture.

Increasing technology and scientific development in the production of plants and animals, together with disease controls – while they undoubtedly take some of the drudgery out of farming – require brains rather than brawn. Many businessmen I met at the Rotary Club or elsewhere would ask me if I could find their sons a job on a farm because they were 'not bright enough to go to university'. My answer was always that their sons would need at least two A-levels to work for me – a somewhat supercilious answer from someone who left school at the age of fifteen!

But economic pressures were indeed obliging farmers and their workers to take on routine veterinary work, including artificial insemination, and willy-nilly to become expert mechanics and electricians.

At the time, however, many expressed their reservations about the Government's Agricultural Training Board scheme, particularly because there were very good agricultural colleges around the country. I had considerable sympathy with this view, and argued that responsibility for training might comfortably be left to the colleges without any need for setting up what was no more or less than a quango. The farmers' meeting in 1968, arranged to continue the discussions on a larger scale, was cancelled because of the foot-and-mouth disaster. The NFU remained very much divided on the issue. Some criticism was levelled at the President, Gwilym Williams. To be re-elected to office, he required an 80 per cent majority vote from Council members. He didn't get it.

In the context of today's world, the decade of the 1960s – in which so much changed forever – should be seen as a period of coming-of-age. A high proportion of the new generation of farmers had taken over their businesses from their fathers, and there was no doubt that growth could be justified and resumed . . . but only within the extra dimension of the nine or ten nations that together comprised the EEC.

3

SOME QUINTESSENTIAL PLUMB: THE NFU PRESIDENCY

*The first and most respectable
of all arts is agriculture.
(Rousseau)*

Back home, at the annual meeting of the Warwickshire county branch in 1969, I was asked whether I would allow my name to be put forward for the Presidency of the NFU. I was naturally honoured by the suggestion, but I had already told people that the existing President, Sir Gwilym Williams, wanted to serve another year, and that I was very happy to accept office again as Deputy President.

In any case, I wanted to make my final decision after my national tour had finished – for I was in the process of travelling around the country, attending the AGMs of many of the county branches. Various critics had taken it upon themselves to attack the NFU leadership, saying that it 'lacked fight' and was 'too gentlemanly'. My visits I thought would give me an opportunity to sense the general feeling on the position of office-holders, and to gauge farmers' opinions on the forthcoming Price Review talks.

Tension in some areas was high. On my last visit, to a town in Pembrokeshire, a young man jumped up and shouted, 'We've heard all this tripe before! Let's have some *action*!'

I caused uproar when I responded sharply.

'So you've heard it before, have you? Then suppose you tell me *what* action we should take!'

To be forcefully told that NFU leaders were doing little but sitting on their backsides when in fact I had had only about 10 hours' sleep in four days was not an especially encouraging end to this countrywide exercise. Truly, nerves of steel were required to cope with the tempers of some of the farmers.

They were frustrated and angry, of course, because of the gap between farm-gate prices and the price the consumer paid. We were still the greatest industry in the country – but would not remain so for long if the situation continued. In the meantime, Wallace Day from Devon was leading the militants, and the media soon took to featuring the slogan 'More Days than Knights' – suggesting, with their usual lovable good humour, that the NFU office-holders might be more interested in knighthoods than they were aware of the farmers' situation.

We certainly recognised the malaise – as well as we knew the cure – but we couldn't write the prescription. Farmers didn't want a bigger slice of the existing cake, so it was the NFU's job to try to make the cake bigger. Any policy that involved cutting production would have been wrong, for surplus supplies from Europe and the USA and Commonwealth countries would quickly have found their way to Britain to fill any gaps.

The following week, I found myself elected President of the NFU. I took up office, deeply and painfully aware that I was doing so at a very tense and difficult time. Gwilym Williams – who had been President for four years, and had served as Deputy and Vice-President for eight years – had given unstinted, selfless service, and only his close friends could comprehend the sacrifices he'd made and the pressures he'd endured. His had been a great contribution to agriculture. The change-over was made with goodwill on both sides. Sir Gwilym believed that he had failed to secure the 80 per cent vote because he'd refused to come out into the open and give support to the militant faction.

Farmer and Stockbreeder 3 February 1970

"Hey!—How about waiting for the Plumb Line!"

Farmer and Stockbreeder of 3 February 1970, displaying a cartoon on the previous page, referring to Sir Gwilym as a man who expressed in everything he said his deep confidence in the powers of logical persuasion. As his successor, I was unexpectedly described as someone somehow completely different – as a 'quintessential Plumb' who would not feel uncomfortable handling things if tempers really flared after the forthcoming Price Review, and who could respond appropriately to the ever-shifting feelings of the membership.

Following my election, and joined by Alan Shaw as Deputy and Richard Butler as Vice-President, I was all too conscious of the marathon that lay in front of us. Farmers were planning to invade London at the beginning of our Price Review talks; some were already demanding that I walk out if no satisfactory progress towards a settlement was made by the Minister, Cledwyn Hughes.

There was a weekend left to reflect on the enormous task ahead. I spent most of it walking my few acres and looking at my Ayrshire cattle. Letters were pouring in with messages of congratulation or commiseration – and among them there was one that I shall always remember. It was from Mary Branker, a local vet and President of the British Veterinary Association. It read:

> Dear Henry,
> You are a damn fool, but I always said you would get there.
> Now you *are* there, for God's sake enjoy it!
> Love,
> Mary.

Enjoyment was far from my mind at that moment, but this simple message gave me courage and hope. I had been part of the NFU's top team for six years, so by now I could have no illusions about where the buck stopped! A group of economists led by the formidable expert Asher Winegarten had been involved in talks with Ministry Officials for some weeks, so the NFU case on the present conditions and prospects for agriculture and for the different commodities was well prepared. A new Director-General, George Cattell, had joined our team: he had previously worked for Lord Rootes and then for Barbara Castle while she was Minister of Employment. We were ready for battle!

For the farmers I pledged myself to try to provide the positive leadership they wanted while getting them to see that their leaders were working on their behalf and not for the Government. In particular, I was determined to harness younger farmers into the work of the Union.

Came the day – 2 February 1970 – and thousands of farmers descended on London. There were mild scuffles with police, and the protest brought traffic to a standstill. But it was mostly good-humoured – and indeed, many were chanting 'More pay for the police!' The banners showed the protestors' true feelings, though. 'Unless *we* have the cash, *you* starve!' As mounted police cleared a path to the entrance of MAFF in Whitehall, I joined the crowd – and found myself hoisted shoulder-high, to a storm of cheers. Farmers from north of the border to Cornwall were all there, standing shoulder to shoulder. It was a sight, and a day, to remember.

The day after, I spoke to as many of the police and staff I could see around Whitehall to thank them for their understanding and forbearance the day before. Some of them said they had been terrified. 'Those farmers knew more about handling horses than we did!'

But they were generally supportive and wished us well.

I was tremendously inspired by the reception the crowds had given me, especially since I was well aware that we were going into the most critical Price Review ever. It was a Review that had not only to put the industry back on a profitable footing but also to convince housewives and the people in other industries that the more food we grew at home, the less Government would have to squeeze the economy to keep the balance of payments right.

I made a point of reminding myself of my two mottos. One was taken from the opening of the green booklet on the NFU in the 1970s: 'To shape events, not merely to react to them.'

The other was the utterly frivolous *Nil illegitimi carborundum*, which translates from cod Latin *Nolle permittere illegitimos sub carbundum* as 'Don't let the bastards grind you down.' And I added a mental note that this applied to members of the NFU Council as well as to the Government! I was determined not to be a desk-bound president and simply ask for unity, but to create the conditions by which I and the NFU might deserve it. Finally, I promised myself that after the Review I would get out into the countryside as often as possible to meet grass-roots members and discuss problems at first hand.

And so it was that after having been President of the NFU for only four days, I walked into the conference room of the Ministry of Agriculture and demanded from its highly authoritative occupants an immediate assurance that I wasn't wasting my time. Perhaps taken aback, the Government promised that no decision on the annual Price Review would be made until all the arrangements had been fully discussed. This in itself was no small thing for Britain's 200,000 farmers, whose main concern was to convince the nation that they were really in trouble.

I found that I was actually enjoying the fight to keep my colleagues in business. After all, throughout my life I had become used to being thrown in at the deep end when least anticipating it. I had never actually sought office in the NFU since 1959, when I had been elected a county delegate, had never canvassed for a vote, and had never expected the job I had abruptly been given. But now that I was in that job, farmers could depend on me to battle like a good 'un on their behalf.

As we started talks, many farmers were demanding to see the Prime Minister, Harold Wilson. The doors of the House of Commons were barricaded. The farmers were also in pursuit of the Home Secretary, Jim Callaghan, himself a farmer – who had apparently made a remark to the effect that farms with herds of less than 50 cows were too small to survive. Naturally, he claimed that his remarks had been distorted.

The talks with the Government were to last for one month. After the first day, the Government had given an assurance that no decision would be made about the overall award until after we had ended our consultations and negotiations. It was the wish of the farmers to bring the industry's income to £650 million, which meant an increase of £141 million on the estimates for the current year. Meanwhile, during the discussions at Whitehall, the Permanent Secretary, Basil Engholm, seemed to be doing almost everything in his power to induce me to walk out together with my team and my colleagues from Scotland, Northern Ireland and Wales. In the face of such provocation, I decided that we should stick to our guns and stay talking for as long as it took to get a settlement. And in due course we reached a stage when tensions were running dangerously high, for the Minister, Cledwyn Huges, simply would not disclose his final overall figure.

He invited me 'off the record' to join him and his wife for lunch at his home in Anglesey one Sunday – and while it was obvious that he would be unable to persuade either the Government, the Chancellor of the Exchequer or the Prime Minister to agree on the target necessary, this get-together resulted in a friendly rapport between us that many years later we were to share again in the House of Lords. We often spoke nostalgically there of our days of cliff-hanging and conflict. I am sad that he did not live long enough to be able to read this book.

The cliff-hanging exercise itself was held over until I could talk man-to-man with the Prime Minister. I met him at 8 in the morning in Downing Street before a Cabinet meeting. 'What makes you think that by coming to see me we can increase the offer?' he asked warily.

'Because you wouldn't otherwise have agreed to see me at all,' I replied.

'If we *can* manage an increase, where would you want to put it?'

I knew the answer to that one too.

'£5 million on milk and £5 million on potatoes.'

'Potatoes?' he said in surprise.

'Yes, Prime Minister. Your Minister and officials say there will be no surplus of potatoes this year, so it may actually cost you nothing. After all, the support is only given for a surplus crop.'

'Hmm. And if we do this, will you agree the package?' he then asked, hopefully.

'No,' I said, with matter-of-fact firmness. 'We are still way off the £140 million income objective. But I *will* behave responsibly!'

The Government subsequently agreed, and the Minister announced an £85 million package, including the £10 million for milk and potatoes.

Many years later Harold Wilson remembered his concession and complained that I had 'conned' him. And it is true that that year there was an enormous surplus of potatoes, which ultimately cost almost £20 million in support buying. But it just goes to prove the unpredictability of the weather, which has a greater effect on yield than all the economists and politicians put together.

Much more depended on this Price Review than in previous years. In earlier years the NFU had assembled a great mass of statistics and documentation to support the annual demand on behalf of the industry. Yet this time the whole problem could actually be summed up in just one simple comparison. In the 10 years up to 1969, what the economists called 'real incomes' in Britain had generally gone up by 46 per cent. During the same period, farm incomes had increased by 7 per cent. When this information was published, I was in the midst of negotiations, and the great majority of the people engaged in those negotiations knew precisely how much hinged on the outcome of the talks. Farmers often judged the NFU on the results their negotiators achieved at Price Reviews. Naturally, they were never satisfied – but they could see the result of the annual stocktaking and the subsequent adjustment of price guarantees.

Before the decision was announced to Parliament, I left the Knightsbridge headquarters of the NFU and converged with other NFU Council members on the House of Commons. We carried copies of a resolution of protest that we hoped to present to the Prime Minister, the Minister for Agriculture and George Thomas, Secretary of State for Wales. We were not permitted access to any one of those gentlemen, although we did leave copies of the resolution there. Our protest described the Review as totally inadequate to ensure the industry's income objective, and asked the Government to refer the whole question of farm income to the Prices and Incomes Board as a matter of the utmost urgency. The Minister had described his decision as a four-point plan designed to replenish the industry's resources, to contain and offset costs, to encourage investment for expansion and to help farmers eradicate brucellosis. But the point was that although the money on the table was more than at any earlier Review, farming costs had also risen by £60 million.

There were two other important points. The needs of the industry had never been so great as they were at that time. Cost inflation and falling incomes had bitten deeply into the industry's resources and deprived farmers of the money they needed to carry out investment to maintain – let alone expand – production. Secondly, the total sums that were made available by the Review had also to be viewed in the context of the fall in the value of the currency itself.

The response throughout the country was predictable. The farmers' mood of pessimism turned to anger. Recalcitrant farmers declared that they would take independent action if headquarters were not prepared to lead. After a four-hour meeting, we announced that we disagreed with the Review terms. The real question for producers was whether the combined effects of the package would raise net income in line with the NFU's objective. The answer was that they would not. The measures would recoup the cost increases during the previous year, and would provide cash for capital investment, but they were really nowhere near up to the scale that British agriculture required.

On this occasion the industry needed a significant increase in cashflow to enable it to catch up with the shortfall in the selective expansion programme. Net output was increasing, but because of the inadequacies of previous years' decisions, against the background of falling incomes in 1968–69, the effort required to achieve the programme was even greater. The recovery in net income was unlikely to be sufficient to increase its resources for investment on the scale required to tap its import-saving potential to the full, or meet further cost inflation.

Farmers were also becoming increasingly concerned at the signs of deterioration in the productive quality of the land resulting from their inability to undertake certain husbandry operations and maintenance work because of economic pressures. Land and other assets had suffered a process of depreciation, which represented a hidden cost to the industry. Unless effective measures were rapidly taken, future output might be affected, and to a marked extent.

There was a demand that our case should be put to the Prices and Incomes Board, and that we should force the issue by further demonstrations. Farmers claimed they were being fobbed off by promises, and immediate action was essential. At the post-Review press conference, however, I warned militants that the NFU could not but disapprove of any illegal action, for apart from anything else, it would have a negative effect and alienate the public. Despite a further call for instant militancy at the meeting, our line was to wait for the Government's reaction to the resolution passed. I felt that if I had walked out during the talks, the award would have been lower. The NFU however, having referred to preparation for action, kept a file of contingencies against all kinds of events in a mythical 'Black Box', and set up an action committee to consider every possibility.

It would have been so easy to swing wide the floodgates of protest . . . but I had to consider the end result in the long term, and the effect it would have on future negotiations with the Government. The public were well aware of the farmers' feelings – but I am not at all sure that it made them any more sympathetic to the call to 'Buy British'.

Militant action would undoubtedly be counterproductive and inflict damage on ourselves. One way or another, however, it was imperative to show solidarity. We decided in the circumstances that our usefulness as an instrument for influencing Government should be judged on a proposal to ban any livestock from being sent to any market anywhere in the country.

It is ironic that in the year 2001 the Government has indeed called for just such a complete ban on the movement of animals and the closure of livestock markets, but for a very different reason!

We had the support of the auctioneers – but not the butchers, who pledged unflinchingly solid opposition to any attempt to dislocate markets. Convening a special meeting of the Butchers' Federation to discuss the plan, they condemned our proposed action and instead demanded the disbandment of the Meat and Livestock Commission, proclaimed their indefatigable opposition to the beef stabilisation scheme, and voted against entering the Common Market if its present agricultural policies were maintained.

Another proposal of ours called for a ban on farmers' buying new machinery, suggesting to manufacturers that they might at least keep their prices static for a year. The Agricultural Engineers Association were distinctly less than ecstatic about this, but claimed stiffly that exports were as profitable as home supplies anyway.

Our quarrel was in no way with the general public, which was why the NFU could have no truck with taking the easiest form of protest – demonstrations in the streets and traffic disruption. When I said that banning all movement of livestock would not deprive the public of food, Charles Catlin, President of the National Federation of Meat Traders' Association, described my view as utter rubbish. But I was convinced that our every move must be strictly within the law, and that the programme would enable farmers quite sufficiently to press their point in demonstrating their unity in the fight for better incomes and against the Government's failure to provide justice and set fair prices for the industry.

The ban went ahead – and it was a tremendous success. I remember receiving a telephone call from Shropshire saying 'A huge success: only 2 per cent of stock have been forwarded!' Most other markets were completely closed. This so-called action – really nothing more than a simple display of solidarity – had more effect than any previous demonstration. However, it was a traumatic start to my Presidency, and I was fortunate to have such a loyal team around me.

These events remain so sharply defined in my mind that I have to give a wry smile when people say to me today, 'I bet you're sorry not to be President of the NFU any more! You had it easy in your day!'

My nephew William Antrobus, who was only 14 years old at the time, recently said he had no idea of the level of stress we underwent in 1970. I enjoy talking about the past, as much as I enjoy talking about the future – provided, of course, that the purpose of sharing experiences with other generations is more than merely to make comparisons in terms of better or worse.

Mind you. playing a farmers' generation game can be an intriguing exercise. William's son Charles, for example, who is now 14 years old and every ounce a farmer, came into my office recently to tell me with pride that he had just harvested 110 tonnes of barley that day. I reminded him of the image of harvest that dominates folk memory -- sheaves of corn neatly stooked, sweating men carting and stacking the sheaves ready for threshing, and the womenfolk bringing out drink and refreshment for the harvest teams. I asked him to guestimate the comparison between costs in today's terms if we still harvested the same way.

He quickly scribbled his calculation on a piece of paper and reckoned that 120 tonnes of barley harvested from 40 acres (16.3 hectares) had cost us £1,000 – 40 acres at £25 per acre, involving one man and one combine in the actual combine harvesting, plus one man, two tractors and trailers in carting.

In 1940, the same 120 tonnes of barley harvested from 100 acres (as opposed to 40; 40.5 hectares as opposed to 16.3) would have cost us the equivalent of £10,120, calculated thus:

· Ten days' cutting with a binder into stooks, each day's cost being for six men (four in the field and two on the binder) working 8 hours day @ £5.50 per hour (labour cost historically adjusted) i.e. $10 \times 6 \times 8 \times £5.50 = £ 2,640$

· Ten days' carting, each day involving seven men (three in field, two in the bay, and two carting) i.e. $10 \times 7 \times 8 \times £5.50 = £ 3,080$

· Eleven days' threshing, with ten men, to yield 10 tonnes of threshed barley a day i.e. $10 \times 8 \times £5.50 = £ 4,400$

Total = £10,120

This takes no account of the physical effort of sweated labour as against the skill of today's operation with computerised knowledge and technological competence.

At the start of this new millennium, we are living through a time when many farmers are questioning their future role – and I do not in any way underestimate the problems of the present situation. How can we shape the future, bearing in mind the lessons of the past? What kind of future is there? Is farming going to go the way of mining and the steel industry? Today, the problem lies as much in the market as in the Government – a market that is totally distorted through the low value of the Euro currency, the high value of Sterling, and the dominant strength of the supermarkets.

However, it is often in times of adversity that things change radically. Our 1970 demands for a special Review and for longer-term assurances were given consideration. Spring was springing, and the year's cultivation was beginning on farms. The political scene quietened down.

As I'd promised myself, after my election I toured the country to meet farming families and their workers in the hills and valleys, and listened to their problems in their own environment. I had never met so many generous and hospitable people expressing such a concern for the preservation of the countryside and the conservation of its resources. As custodians they hated the idea of ripping out hedges and felling trees, but were well aware of – and were suffering from – economic pressures.

The structure of farming was changing, and we recognised the need for change in the NFU. Everything was gathering pace in the commodity market. The application of science and technology was rapidly increasing economic performance in farming. Also, the market was changing: it was becoming evident that there would be a greater reliance on support from the marketplace rather than from the taxpayer. In other words, consumer subsidies would decrease.

George Cattell, the recently-appointed NFU Director General, may have been new to agriculture but not to organisation. He brought some revolutionary ideas to the NFU, comparing our organisation with that of the CBI and other industrial bodies.

'With the rate of external change gathering pace – Europe, the flow of new legislation, the effects of the Industrial Relations Act, radical alterations in the support system, pressures from the environmental lobby – we cannot maintain the kind of organisation set up at the turn of the century for the conditions which then prevailed,' he told me. 'I see two basic choices. Either we equip the organisation with the new skills and resources it is going to need, through some form of economy of the internal organisation. Or we think in terms of substantial increases in the money subscribed by members.'

He saw the Union's £24 million income as quite sufficient to service an effective organisation in Europe and furnish an adequate service at home – provided that the organisation was streamlined. He said that during the course of his travels around the country he was amazed to find farmers who seemed less concerned with Europe than with the retention of the domestic branch set-up.

'Their heads are in the sand,' he declared. 'The truth is that unless farmers equip themselves with an organisation capable of taking the lead in shaping European agricultural policy, it will be reshaped with little regard for British farming interests.' These interests could not safely be left to the Government, preoccupied as it was bound to be with enormous problems in other fields. It was up to the NFU to get right inside the European Community agencies – such as the Commission and COPA – to influence policy as and when it was being formulated. This would mean more specialist staff. Brussels must in time become more important than London.

Stressing that he was only putting forward his own ideas – the problem was being tackled by the leadership as a team – George Cattell said he regarded centralised finance as the key. Control of income and expenditure should be from the centre. And he concluded his reasoning with the rhetorical question, 'Are we not a *National* Farmers Union?' But he saw this as a vital issue in the preservation of the present local branch basis involving, if possible, the amalgamation of branches into groups where appropriate. This was happening anyway.

'We must preserve a structure that enables the farmers to meet in some form of local forum, and be able to service them at that level,' he concluded.

It was at county branch level that he envisaged the greatest need for reshaping. Changes in boundaries and a move towards economic development on a regional basis would, he felt, make the old county boundary pattern less and less relevant in the future. With the growing need to decentralise, a regional set-up made sense. Why not form regional councils on the pattern of the Council for Wales, and save six to twelve regions? If finance was centralised so that money passed directly to headquarters, the National Council could allocate a budget to the regions. The precise pattern within the respective regions could largely be left to the operation of the regions themselves. Efficiency and economy would be the ruling factors.

Director General George Cattell's reasoning went further, to examine the problem of fitting the NFU's affiliated insurance society, NFU Mutual, into this framework. Its out-of-town structure was bound up with that of the NFU. Neither the organisation itself nor the NFU staff should suffer as a result of any changes made in the pattern. There was scope also for economies at headquarters – for a start, there were too many committees and most of them were too big. A regional restructuring would mean that the National Council could be substantially reduced. The controlling body should meet monthly, either as an enhanced General Purpose Committee or as a streamlined

Council. Moreover, the Council should work entirely in the interests of farmers. That was its duty, rather than satisfying a small number of farmers who wanted to play an active part in formulating and administering agricultural policies. Members of the National Farmers Union demanded visible results at a price they could afford to pay, which was fair enough.

The Director General then went on to suggest that it was time the Council seriously considered changing the title of the Union. It was the only employers' organisation in Britain that described itself as a 'Union', a term that was not strictly accurate in practice or in law. A change of name might well make the NFU more acceptable in agricultural circles at home and in Brussels. Yes, there was a good deal of sentiment attached to the initials NFU – but was that enough reason to preserve the title?

How did Mr Cattell see the timing of structural change? 'Much the same as EEC entry and transition,' was his answer. 'Start in 1973, and complete in 1978–79.'

It seemed that farming would never pick up again following the disastrous end to the 1960s. The dreary after-effects of foot-and-mouth disease that necessitated the restocking of farms with dairy cattle were particularly felt in the large dairy-farming area of Cheshire. But the unexpected change of Government from Labour to the Conservatives brought a breath of fresh air. The big pay rises won by many people in the six months before the election had led to improved opinion-poll ratings for Labour. Edward Heath, however, in his presidential-style campaign, held the strike-prone unions responsible for rising prices, and the industrial strife had proved a more potent electoral factor than Labour's portrayal of the Tories as 'Yesterday's Men'. Jim Prior's cash injection of some £72 million shortly after he became Minister was a relief to many farmers. Once again, the lights were green for go, and the theme was expansion right across the board.

Sir Emrys Jones, Director General of the Agricultural Development and Advisory Service (ADAS), followed this up with a very clear statement. Speaking in Cirencester, he argued that 'The more food we grow, the less we buy abroad – so down goes the cost of joining the EEC.' He believed that merely by applying the knowledge we had, we could increase farmers' income by £200 million a year. The technical and technological knowhow now available to us through research and development, he claimed, gave us the tools and resources we required. So what were we waiting for?

Sadly, the response was mixed.

I knew Emrys to be a good friend to the farmer and a reliable adviser to the industry. It was only recently that I attended a memorial service to him, which was held in the same Hall at the Royal Agricultural College where he made that famous speech. George Douglas, a Lincolnshire farmer and a good friend of Emrys, in his address quoted some of his grandmother's recollections, including the recommendation that 'If you ever have the good fortune to come across a clever Welshman, beat a path to his door!'

'Don't be nasty to people on the way up,' Emrys himself used to say. 'You may need them on the way down.'

I could have applied this to Lord Cledwyn too!

We had come through a protracted period in which growth was restricted. Indeed, over the whole decade of the 1960s there had been only 2 per cent growth. Now there was considerable concern about possible consumer resistance to rising prices, and farmers were becoming haunted by the spectre of surpluses, butter mountains and 'dumped' produce. For these were the conditions that many farmers saw us joining as we entered the European Community.

Contrary to the belief of some, I have never been a Euro-fanatic. On the other hand, I never believed Britain, as a trading nation, could remain isolated from the European Community. We could certainly have changed the direction of the Common Agricultural Policy had we joined earlier, and I regret that commercially, in co-operation and marketing, we did not become much stronger. We really did miss an opportunity to expand production faster and to control our own markets.

After centuries of dealing in the cumbersome – yet lovable – pounds, shillings and pence, we found ourselves in the second month of 1971 battling with decimal currency. Many mourned the end of the half-crown coin, and found it hard to adjust to the concept of a ten pence coin (which to a good number of people remained a florin anyway). There was some anxiety that shops would use the change in currency to mark up prices. I remember my father-in-law holding out a palmful of new coins and saying to me plaintively, 'Henry, how much is that in *real* money?'

Just as many complain today when battling with their calculators to work out conversions to and from the Euro, people then cursed and wondered dourly what was so wrong with the system we had been accustomed to. The Government additionally announced that in 1973 purchase tax would be replaced by value added tax in order to bring Britain into line with the Common Market. This quickly turned into another issue high on the 1971 political agenda. Psychological resistance to accepting changes perceived as threats to our national identity is an issue I return to later (see Chapter 12).

We had an unprecedented early Price Review that year. Price guarantees for beef, milk, sheep and pigs were higher, and there were token increases for grain. The package agreed was moving towards alignment with the Common Agricultural Policy – the cards were face-up on the table, the light was green, and the 1970s were becoming brighter all the time. Morale among farmers was also high, which in part could be attributed to the exceptionally good weather we enjoyed over the year. But we had a big job ahead of us – probably the biggest the NFU ever had to tackle.

I saw six priorities for the coming year. We had to

(1) continue talks with the Government on the terms of the treaty or treaties of accession;

(2) complete unfinished business on matters like animal health and transport;

(3) forge new links with other farmers' organisations in the Community within a strengthened COPA;

(4) set up a Bureau in Brussels to serve the NFU as well as the interests of British agriculture as a whole;

(5) strengthen the producer marketing organisation and the NFU itself to meet the challenges ahead; and

(6) assure the resources needed for the additional investment in the industry if it was to play an even bigger role as an import-saver.

Sensitive areas of the industry – such as horticulture and eggs – would also have to be carefully watched to ensure that necessary safeguards were in place, for example against the 'dumping' of cheap surpluses.

The transition from guaranteed prices to Community arrangements was of course a highly complex process, and we had to take it stage by stage. Expansion inside the Community was undoubtedly going to be founded on a better basis than expansion outside the EEC, for Britain inside would be afforded protection from the trade pressures being increasingly applied by the big power-blocs outside Europe, notably from the far shores of the Atlantic. Those pressures were already building up alarmingly.

At the same time, unless Government policy ensured that the home market was in a position to expand, Britain would fail to secure the economic advantages of EEC membership, and economic growth might go into reverse. The Government had stated that it expected an extra average growth in our industry of 8 per cent – double what it would have been outside the EEC. A 20 per cent growth was well within the capacity of the industry if maximum import substitution and growth in consumer demand were taken into account. We had our obligations to New Zealand and the sugar-producing countries of the Caribbean, but in most other fields substitution potential was considerable.

In the summer of 1971, I spent a short time in Jamaica opening their National Agricultural show and taking part in a conference of farmer organisations. Part of what I was saying was that British sugarbeet-growers were looking forward to the chance of expanding their sugar production, while recognising Jamaican farmers' ability to expand production of citrus fruits and bananas. This was not a popular message to deliver, particularly as I was being entertained by the Director of the sugar firm Tate & Lyle. In fact, however, Jamaica, together with other Caribbean countries, subsequently gained the wider European market for sugar under the Lomé agreement.

The annual Price Review, crucial as most of them had been since 1947, was even more significant this year. It was not just the farmers' welfare that was at stake but the welfare of our country at large. We were seeking an increase in guaranteed prices that would at least cover increased production costs, and the right to keep the whole benefit of the increased productivity. We needed real price incentives over and above costs, or expansion could not take place. Because the Government's aim was that we should earn our living out of the marketplace, we felt that we in turn were entitled to the right to apply the most effective marketing answers.

I strongly believed that this time the Review team could 'make us or break us' either by launching Britain along the path to expansion or by holding us back from it. If the Government were to fail to deal properly and fairly with the Review, I believed it would lead to a rural recession worse than any since the 1930s. And I did what I could to warn the Government that such a recession would not only involve farmers, growers and their workers, but would also bankrupt many rural-based industries and damage the ancillary industries in chemicals, fertilisers and agricultural machinery. It could mean that the country had to spend hundreds of millions of pounds more each year on food imports – and that, of course, would inevitably lead to an enormous increase, and perhaps a prohibitive one, in the overall cost of entry into the Common Market. A drastic cut in home food production could lead to an explosive increase in food prices to the housewife.

The results of the Review amounted to neither a Government handout nor a wage increase. Nonetheless, NFU committees put in their reports that neither I nor the Minister could have done any better in the economic circumstances. Jim Prior had made a sincere and determined effort to enable the industry to meet its cash crisis, although the price changes fell short of what was needed to provide the boost for expansion. The increase in the guaranteed prices was equivalent to only around 2 per cent of total consumer expenditure on food. The guaranteed prices of the major farm products rose by an average of about 9 per cent over the February 1970 levels to compensate farmers for the record rise of over £140 million in their costs of production.

The Government had put a lot of heart back into the land, but it was no golden harvest.

Price Reviews, whether or not they represent a golden harvest, can of course never be the sole answer to everything. Marketing is of immense importance too, and I warned farmers that in the coming years they would have to become more astute at marketing their products. Crops might previously have been produced in the confident hope that they would be sold at reasonable prices or backed by guarantees, but farmers had now to be aware that if we joined the Common Market, they would face trading with no guaranteed prices – although they would have protection from imports.

There was now an agreement that British participation in the EEC would be on a footing equal to that of France, Germany and Italy. The Government further announced that plans for the transitional period would safeguard the interests not only of British farmers and fishermen but also of New Zealand's dairy industry. The need for co-operation between farmers and growers and producers was vital. I told everyone concerned that this had to become the keynote for the coming years.

Indeed, farmers were beginning to invest in future success, preparing for entry to a new system of protection – protection by which they would be the beneficiaries of direct subsidies through market intervention under a system that no longer aimed to ensure that consumers benefited from direct subsidies even more.

I organised a meeting at NFU headquarters that involved representatives of all the UK farmers' unions, the marketing boards, the co-operatives, the FMC and the NFU Mutual. The meeting identified a formidable concentration of commercial power, which we provisionally called BAMDO, the British Agricultural Marketing Development Organisation. I felt strongly that it was our duty as members of the NFU to be tough in any future relations that we had with the European Economic Community, and that the decision to join the EEC might well turn out to be one of the most fateful ever made in the history of Britain.

Of course, everybody had their own thoughts on the prospects of joining such a Community, and on the overall concept of a Common Market. To me, it was above all a concept that made for reconciliation between countries after decades of unrest – a means of preventing Europe from ever again descending into a shambles.

I had witnessed the total destruction of Coventry during the bombing raids in 1942, in particular the Cathedral, but the true bulldog spirit of the British returned as rebuilding began – it was like the Phoenix rising from the ashes. A small chapel was erected while the new Cathedral was being built. Soon after the war, Marjorie and I listened to an address given by the Bishop of Berlin at a lunchtime service. He reminded us of the importance of our Christian faith and values, and of the similarity between our bitterness against the Germans and the suffering of his people during our bombing of Berlin. I was soon persuaded that the only way forward was through Christian unity and the development of a more united Europe.

The Prime Minister, Edward Heath, signed the Treaty in January 1972. It was to formally come into effect in January 1973. Including Britain, the Republic of Ireland, Denmark and Norway, the Community of Ten would have had a gross 'national' product of nearly £400 billion a year, and 41 per cent of world trade. Norway, of course, in the event did not join, following a negative national consensus, but until that was settled, planning went ahead on the working assumption of a Community of ten member states.

Our main focus was therefore on the theoretical and practical consequences of Britain's entry. I saw the 1972 Price Review as part of the Minister's effort to gear industry towards EEC entry and towards finalising the preparatory marketing agreements. There was a need to set up contractual arrangements, obtain market intelligence and learn about the marketing discipline that we required. The Review was accepted by the NFU with almost unanimous agreement, and we pulled out every stop we could to make ours a flying start into Europe.

Not that we got a real flying start – certainly not the start we would have liked – but we got enough to keep the momentum going.

We were moving away from a policy that protected us as individuals through deficiency payments, to a policy that would protect the industry as a whole through a system of market intervention when the market price of a commodity fell below a guaranteed price, levies and minimum import prices. Old ways of thinking had to be changed to ensure that we retained the biggest share of our own market as well as a chunk or two in Europe. I believed in joining the EEC. My view was that future historians would see us as free men and women moving towards a new kind of political and economic organisation, towards a new way of finding peace and prosperity.

I also firmly believed that agriculture must be taken account of more in planning decisions. With the signing of the Treaty of Accession and the consequent changes not too far away, we had to look ahead as far as possible.

'Let's just think for a moment about the basic meaning of our Union,' I said at the 1972 Annual Meeting. And I went on,

> The NFU is a free association of farmers and growers, of employers and the self-employed, and of owner-occupiers and tenant farmers. Its true function is to serve us in our daily affairs at local level, and to represent our interests as of a strongly-based Union at national and, increasingly, international levels. What we have to do is to help create the best conditions in which we can produce at a profit and expand both our production and our earnings. Within the enlarged Community we shall increasingly rely upon the market for our living. For most commodities there will be no deficiency payments – after the transitional period – while many of the interventions, the buying-in prices, are hardly designed to keep us in business. We are working towards the formation of the British Agricultural Marketing Development Organisation, through which all the major marketing and trading interests in our industry can work together to strengthen and develop produce marketing.

> The opportunities for expansion in the 'Community of Ten' depend on certain key conditions for which we have fought, and for which we will continue to fight – for example, an improvement in liquidity,

more investment in processing facilities, better marketing, the removal of the constraints of the existing restrictive trade practices legislation (which bear more on us than on any country in the Six). And, not least, we need a taxation policy that will help, and not hinder, us in financing the expansion that we want. We will stand on our own two feet inside the Common Market. We will set an example, even more than we have done in the past, that will put this country of ours on the road to prosperity.

The fact that farming was no longer 'a way of life' as such was something many farmers found difficult to swallow. And to accept a new alliance with old rivals was, understandably, even more painful.

I remember that many years later I left Lloyds Bank in Lombard Street and hailed a taxi. 'Take me to the House of Lords, please', I said.

As we drove off, the taxi driver looked up into his mirror and said, 'I know you, Guv'nor. You're that old farmer chap. I used to listen to you at 6 a.m. with my missus and say, "He's looking after his lads, all right!" I learned a lot about farming then. Now you are this big European bloke. But you'll never get anywhere.'

'Why not?', I asked, surprised.

'Because of the bl—y Krauts!' he replied.

I pursed my lips.

'We've certainly fought each other over the centuries,' I said, 'but surely it is better for us to work together now?'

'No,' he said, pained at my denseness. 'It's nothing to do with that. They'll never forgive us for Hurst scoring that goal in the World Cup in 1966!'

If farmers wanted to survive in a changing world, they had to learn quickly how to co-operate in serving the food industry and think seriously about organising their immense potential power as buyers. Consumer influence was about to emerge as a very strong force inside the European Community. Consumers in Britain were used to cheap food prices, and we had an open-door policy on the world's surplus food. This food all too often came in at prices below the costs of production, which meant that our farmers' prices were made up to a guaranteed level by the Exchequer. Basically, we enjoyed cheap food because the taxpayer paid part of the cost.

This policy was now coming to an end due to the high costs involved. Some 90 per cent of the Community's funds were expended on supporting the high prices of improvements needed to sustain life on small farms – and because a major source of the funds was levies and taxes imposed on food imports from outside the Community, Britain would have to face a heavy bill when entering the Community. Britain was, after all, still the largest importer in the world. These price increases would certainly be felt by the housewife.

I believed that our strengths were our stockmanship, our livestock and our grass. It would mean a partial return to our traditional pattern of livestock production from grass, bearing in mind that the practice of hedgerow removal had now peaked and was behind us. But an area that caused greater concern was our orchards, in view of the tremendous orchard surpluses in Italy and France. We had to hang on to the thought that although the Mediterranean climate enabled Golden Delicious apples, peaches and melons to be grown cheaply and in abundance, it does not produce superb apples like the Cox's Orange Pippin or late strawberries.

My noble friend Baroness Trumpington, once a Minister of Agriculture, made this very clear to French apple-growers when she referred to the quality of the Cox in a speech that those who heard it will never forget!

But quality comes at a price, and part of the answer was lying in our own hands, in the improved marketing and advertising of our products. I believed that it was absolutely vital that the whole of our industry should speak with one voice. To both farmers and growers, there was nothing more important than strong producer groups and co-operatives. The Government's Barker Report on contract farming and co-operation took the same line – and it was something the NFU had been advocating for some years. The establishment of the Agricultural Co-operation and Marketing Services Ltd (ACMS) and the involvement of the Government provided the industry with a means to an end. In the background there was also our concept of BAMDO, which linked together in one central service organisation the entire productive resources of Britain's agriculture and horticulture. The importance of marketing and efficiency had to be emphasised to ensure both that existing outlets were serviced by production matched to their requirements, and that new outlets were created.

At the 19th World Conference of farming leaders in Ottawa that year, organised by the IFAP, I made it very clear that our aim was firstly to strengthen the existing world commodity agreements on wheat and sugar, and to conclude an agreement on international dairy products; secondly, to take up the issue of world trade and present proposals for an entirely new approach to the question of agricultural stability; and finally, to ensure that IFAP was the only non-government agricultural organisation that enjoyed consultative status with the UN and other organisations. It was vitally important, therefore, that we as international farmers should discuss our own position and formulate agreed policies wherever possible, so that we remained at the forefront of any changes to the Community.

The explosion of prices in the meat market at that time was yet another illustration of the need for expansion. Time and time again we had urged upon successive governments a policy that would encourage us to produce more red meat. If political leaders had looked into the future more often through the eyes of farmers, we would have had far more home-grown beef. Now we had to face a world shortage. The fact was not only that our traditional suppliers were now eating more beef themselves than they supplied, but that there was greater competition for what was left from consumers in Europe and Japan who were able and ready to pay.

Following a three-day inquiry into beef prices that bore all the hallmarks of political gimmickry, the Minister firmly refused even to contemplate the idea of continuing to ban beef on the bone from anywhere, even from countries where foot-and-mouth disease was endemic. As a former member of the Northumberland Inquiry, I couldn't believe that memories were so short – I had never heard a more wildly irresponsible proposal. In any case, we no longer had the economic power in the world market to attract imports at low prices. In basic commodities we had become part of the residual, rather than the world, market.

The controversy over beef simply reflected that the days of cheap food were over – that we no longer had the divine right to be cheaply fed: an illusion fostered by so many years of industrial supremacy and, over the last three decades, by support from the taxpayer. I believed that the long-term solution was an expansion in the home output of our basic foods, accompanied by international agreements on minimum prices, and stockpiling in times of surplus.

We were thus concentrating all our efforts on expansion. Joe Godber was the Minister of Agriculture, and he took me to see Prime Minister Ted Heath one morning before a Cabinet meeting to discuss progress. The PM had overnight returned from an international summit in Singapore, and was full of a conversation he had had with President Nixon. Nixon had told him that in the USA they were encouraging the expansion of beef lots, because the world would be short of beef for the next ten years.

'Why can't we do that?', asked the PM.

'Because we have a grain-and-grass economy involving many beef animals that live entirely on grass. The Americans implant oestrogens [female hormones] in animals to boost their growth. We are not allowed to do that,' I replied.

'What does oestrogen implantation do, then?', he asked.

Smiling wryly, I said, 'I'm not a scientist, but I'm told it affects your sex life!'

Heath's shoulders heaved in his well-known show of mirth. The meeting ended – but I got £10 million of Government support for the beef industry.

Prior to EEC entry in 1973, it became apparent that a closer relationship with the North American farmers was necessary. Having met many of them at the IFAP Conference in Ottawa, together with the then president of COPA, Carl Knotnerus of the Netherlands, we held the first annual meeting of the US-EC Conference on Agriculture in Brussels in December 1972. Thirteen agri-business and farm organisation leaders representing a cross-section of major commodities and geographic regions of the United States interfaced over two days with twenty-three leaders of farm organisations and co-operatives from the European Community. The conference focused on US and EC agricultural policies, and made a point of identifying the political and social conditions by which they were affected. In 1977, the European co-operatives and their US counterparts joined the talks, which continue today and which have contributed to a better understanding on the part of all sides in GATT and WTO negotiations.

We logged on to the continental system on 1 January 1973.

One immediate effect was a fundamental change in the British tax system, the introduction of VAT, as had been decided two years before. We had been successful in persuading the Government that value added tax should not apply to food, and that farmers should be recompensed for equipment and products used in the farm business. I remember attending a farmers' meeting at which a county branch of the NFU had invited a tax expert to explain the new system. Questioned in fairly pointed detail about its operation, the expert soon realised that farmers were brighter than he had thought, and eventually stamped his foot on the floor in exasperation, exclaiming, 'I came here to tell you how it works – not how to evade it!'

It was a year to remember, particularly in the context of later development and current attitudes towards matters European.

We had already established close and cordial working relationships with our colleagues in COPA, the international NFU, and the institutions of the Community concerned with agriculture. I believed we had a real contribution to make – and five years to prepare for full integration. A neighbouring farmer reminded me recently of a comment I made when we joined: 'It will be good for us for ten years – and then watch out!' But in the meantime, the French and German members had been there from the inception of the Common Agricultural Policy, and the three new members, Denmark, the Republic of Ireland and the UK, were made to feel a bit like second-class citizens. The powerful cereal- and sugar-producers among our new partners saw a ready-made market for themselves in Britain, and had no sympathy at all with our wish to continue to import products like hard wheat from Canada, or butter and lamb from New Zealand.

Nonetheless, we were preparing ourselves to move in six steps over five years to full participation in the CAP, phasing out the former national system of guarantees and deficiency payments. The branches of the NFU in the UK at that time represented around 4 per cent of the working population, whereas in France, Germany, Italy and Belgium the figure was nearer 30 per cent, which obviously gave their farm leaders much more clout. The British Government and Parliament were pressing for immediate changes in the CAP and a restriction on budget spending. The farming lobby in Brussels, however, was too powerful to allow any such thing to happen. We were expanding production and investing in new technology in a way that had never happened before – but so were other European farmers. 'Sit back and enjoy it,' 'Let the French lead,' echoed across the land. But the day of reckoning was coming, as taxpayers complained of butter and grain mountains, and wine lakes.

It is difficult to measure the success of our agricultural revolution and the benefit to the nation of its return on the investment of resources. We certainly made progress in supplying more of our own needs. Yet through the time of increased growth in production, we were also witnessing a growth in population. There were also big changes in the nation's diet and nutrition – a continuing trend that remains significant.

But we had now joined forces with some strong agricultural powers. France was producing about 30 per cent of the total needs of the Community. Next was Italy, and third, West Germany. Together they were producing about three-quarters of consumer requirements for the whole Community. We ranked fourth in the new Europe of nine, and produced only about one tenth of consumer needs. If only we had joined in the early 1960s! We held the competitive edge on farm size, but our land yielded a lower gross product per unit area.

It was a testing time, and the real challenge was one of good housekeeping.

We also experienced some difficulty in adjusting to the rules of the European Club. I invited the French Agricultural Attaché, Pierre Thieux, to speak to local farmers in our Town Hall at Coleshill. The poor man found himself bombarded with questions. Farmers were reluctant to accept that we were joining a club for which the rules had already been set in such a way that there was now little chance of changing them substantially. M. Thieux' English was poor, and our French was non-existent, but his message was clear: 'You can be in *or* out, but not in *and* out!

Today, almost thirty years later, the attempt by some Eurosceptics to revise the Oxford English Dictionary and turn 'or' and 'and' into synonyms is still an on-going battle!

In my speech at the annual general meeting of the NFU that year, I said that when we joined the Common Market, farmers would not benefit from Community prices until they overtook the agricultural guaranteed prices. And I wondered – because the Government had domestic and international reasons for not raising food prices too quickly – where farmers were going to find the cash for investment and equipment. It could only come from higher guaranteed prices – prices that would not only cover increased costs but would also provide a really significant injection of capital. To evade this issue would be to run away from realities – to turn again into the dead-end alley of the 1960s and be given exhortations instead of cash. Farmers needed a taxation policy that would actively help them finance the expansion wanted by the Minister of Agriculture, Jim Prior.

What was needed was a new look at the impact on the industry of existing taxes on capital, especially estate duty and capital gains tax, and at the possibility of changing the methods of assessment of farmers for income tax. However, in my opinion there was no doubt at all that the combined effect of higher central taxation and rating would put us at considerable disadvantage in relation to producers in Europe, and that this European factor would strengthen our case against any re-rating of agriculture.

The industry would provide the Minister with all the extra production he wanted – given the right policies, the resources and, above all, the confidence. These conditions met, we would not only stand on our own feet inside the Common Market but set an example to other sectors of the economy.

It was in that year that the leading seed firm, Nickerson, proudly claimed a breakthrough in wheat yields: their new variety of Cappelle had surpassed an unprecedented 3 tonnes per acre (1.2 tonnes per hectare). The entire Nickerson stand at the Royal Show was one huge advertisement intended to convince farmers that it was this Cappelle variety they ought to grow. I watched as Jim Prior chatted with Joe Nickerson. Jim Prior, himself a grain-grower, warned Joe that unusual weather had the potential to cause a disaster in future years, so it would be unwise to grow only the one variety – and that perhaps 25 per cent of farmers' wheat acreage might be more sensible.

Even as we left the stand, a notice was being put up, saying 'Minister advises all farmers to grow a quarter of their crop with Cappelle!'

Because of the majority support among its members for the principle of statutory producer boards for cereals and meat, the NFU was committed to drawing up the relevant legal blueprints. But it was no good being anything but realistic. Frequent soundings had indicated that the Government would not accept such proposals. Nor could anybody be sure that they would be acceptable to the Community.

One of the advantages of our policy of an annual Price Review of the conditions and prospects for farming during the pre-entry stages to the EEC was the ability to balance the difference between 'horn and corn' – the livestock and arable sectors. Our first year in the Common Market, however, gave corn-growers a better return than those concerned with animal production and dairy, a result that aroused some anxiety among pig and poultry farmers.

I used to receive several delegations at home at weekends, most of them from the Midlands area. They were probably happier to meet a fellow-farmer on his own farm, knowing that he was also hungry. Some six months after our entry into the EEC, a delegation representing about 10,000 farmers from the Midlands arrived at my farm to protest about high feed prices and cost increases. They wanted an assurance that the NFU would persuade the Government to allow food prices to rise. Soaring feed and production costs were threatening to force a cutback in milk and beef output, and would inevitably lead to food shortages. Calf prices had fallen, which meant less for each gallon of milk produced. The demand for cull cows had also fallen.

I have a Giles cartoon on my study wall, signed by him 'With sympathy to Sir Henry'. It shows farmworkers leaving a farm, each one carrying a calf valued at £2.80. That week farmworkers' wages had increased by £2.80. The caption reads: *My Maisie isn't going to like me taking home one of his flaming calves every week in lieu of my pay increase!*

John Lievesley was the delegation's spokesperson, and demanded that the public be told the true facts. If they wanted the food, the producer had to be paid more for it. If that didn't happen, all producers could do was to close down units rather than continue to lose money. Other members present complained that the Government had not taken inflation into account, for the price of corn was the same then as it had been 20 years earlier. In general, they believed that in the existing, more affluent, society, consumers could and should pay more. And they declared that unless the 'cheap food image' was forgotten, there would be less food in this country, because without expansion there was a real danger of a cutback and consequent shortages.

I offered them three suggestions:

(1) subsidising the price of feed, although this might be difficult to administer;

(2) looking to Europe to find a means of shortening the transitional period of full entry to the EEC; and

(3) forgetting the cheap food policy to allow prices to increase.

Milk producers were facing an equally disastrous situation. I had been losing 3p on every gallon of milk that left my farm, and, obviously, I wasn't the only one. Many farmers were forced to slaughter in-calf cows, the amount of milk for butter had fallen by 43 per cent, and supplies of cheese were becoming dangerously low. I promised to urge the Government not to make any agreement with the Community that would prejudice the Milk Marketing Board or its ability to pay a pool price. It was vital that the payment of a price increase be brought forward from the date normally fixed by the Price Review. I gave my personal assurance, and that of my colleagues, that we would do everything in our power to bring the point home to the powers-that-be, and I was supported by Sir Richard Trehane, Chairman of the Milk Marketing Board, and by the Dairy Federation.

As the 1974 General Election was coming nearer, miners' strikes dominated the scene and the country was in turmoil. There was particular concern over the livestock industry, because it was badly affected by increases in food costs. The price upsurge had undermined confidence in the Government's agricultural expansion policy. It had led to a cutback in milk, and threatened expansion in beef and other products. Top priority *had* to be given to agriculture as an import-saving industry. Many farmers who received a monthly cheque for their milk said it no longer covered their feed costs. I had heard rumours that there was to be a certain limit on the price increase for milk. The Minister of Agriculture, Joe Godber, indicated that this had already been broken through. But in looking at the industry as a whole there were considerable difficulties in discerning any form of balance, let alone overall progress.

Concentrating all our efforts on expansion as we were, the bald fact was that British agriculture had become unbalanced. What could be done about it?

It became obvious that Labour could no longer abdicate its responsibility for the lack of a firm guarantee in the market, and that pledges to farmers had been dishonoured. I called on Harold Wilson to make a statement before the Election that should Labour return to power, it would act immediately to honour the pledge Fred Peart had given to the livestock industry. Government policies, despite the expenditure involved, had proved to be ineffective in dealing with the crisis. In view, apart from anything else, of the many personal farming tragedies, I believed that no responsible person could stand by and witness the increasingly rapid destruction of our great livestock industry embodied in the looming threat that many of our cattle might not have enough to eat in the coming winter.

Moreover, the 1974 harvest disasters in the Soviet Union had had knock-on effects all around the world. They emptied the American granaries, which in turn caused the USA to impose controls on exports of soya beans and other products.

On the day of the General Election, the tension on the political scene was felt throughout the country when the result turned out for once to be in the hands of the Liberals. Labour had won 301 seats and the Conservatives 297 – neither party could therefore command an overall majority. Edward Heath was unsuccessful in securing Liberal backing, and Harold Wilson – with whom I had negotiated frequently and often successfully during my four years as NFU President – returned as Prime Minister for the third time.

Life resumed, still very much in crisis mode.

In addition to facing higher costs, we were exposed to the full impact of the weaker pound *and* the price of our products on the farm was held down artificially by subsidies from the Community's Agricultural Fund. We could no longer rely on surpluses from other countries: the Government was obliged to reduce the bill for imported food and to boost production from our own productive soil.

I was convinced that if we could get out of this difficult situation, the future would be bright – we could produce more and save the country's imports. But between January and September nothing changed. I led a protest convoy of farmers round Birmingham's ring road, involving a total of 60 assorted farm vehicles covered in posters asking for fair prices. This demonstration was part of a protest day all over Europe, and in Britain about 50,000 farmers and 5,000 vehicles tried to draw attention to the problems of agriculture in 200 towns and cities.

Fred Peart, again appointed Agriculture Minister, had intended to keep to the 5 per cent price rise agreement for Common Market farmers, which had been agreed at the end of September, but which had been rejected by the West Germans. The Government wanted this agreement to be upheld, but it also wanted a complete rethink on Common Market agricultural policy. A meeting was to be held in Luxembourg, where Fred Peart and James Callaghan, the Foreign Secretary, were to support the West Germans' demands for renegotiation of the policy.

I attended this meeting and discussed the situation. While it was important for Britain's farmers that the EEC talks would result in keeping the farm package deal complete, they were also anxious that the talks should then go on to the subject of a guaranteed price for beef cattle. This was crucial for farmers as well as consumers. It was important that the package went through because, like other European farmers, we needed stability. Uncertainty had caused the loss of farming confidence in the Community, just as uncertainty in the livestock sector had caused frustration to farmers and a cutback in production.

The recession in British livestock farming affected three-quarters of British agriculture. The touchstone was the dairy industry, which was also a source of three-quarters of our home-produced beef. There is no clearer evidence of a lack of confidence in the future than when farmers slaughter breeding stock and cease to breed from what remains. In 1974, the result was that we spent £2,000 million we could not afford on importing the kind of food we could grow in this country more cheaply. In 1975, when the pound Sterling would buy even less, expenditure would be even more.

What had happened to all the new and modernised plants in which the dairy trade had invested so many millions in the expectation of expansion?

Farmers and growers are the first link in the chain that ends up in the kitchen. Rationalisation in the food industry presented us, as producers, with the challenge of organising our production and marketing in collaboration with the processors. It *must* be a question of collaboration, not confrontation. And that question has to be answered with intelligent and sophisticated co-operative action.

If we accept that the food industry is a single chain extending from farm to kitchen, we also have to accept that the interests of those at the beginning of the chain, the producers, are common to those at the end of the chain, the consumers, and of course those between them. Everything has a beginning – and if there is something wrong there, how can the end come out right? The interests of producers, consumers and food industries were inter-dependent throughout the Community as well. Those who couldn't square my concern with incipient disaster in the dairy industry in this country with dairy surpluses across the Channel, ought to have remembered that our own Minister had declared that it was only common sense to reduce our imports of dairy produce by expanding home production.

In June 1975, in reference to the efficiency of our dairy sector, he declared that it was in the interests of the Community as a whole that our milk production should increase, and that the measures designed to achieve a better balance between supply and demand within the Community should not discourage efficient producers. Instead of the 650 million *extra* gallons envisaged in the April 1974 White Paper, we were producing 150 million gallons *less*. Efficient producers were being discouraged to such an extent that they were leaving the industry as never before.

British agriculture needed a coherent national policy backed by an all-party agreement on long-term objectives. In return, the industry would offer the people of this country a food and farm contract geared to providing greater security for the consumer in the supply of food.

I believed our country had a great future, and that the agriculture industry had an even greater potential than at any time in the past for contributing to that future.

4

WEARING FIVE CAPs

If Heraldry were guided by reason, a Plough
in a Field Arable would be the most noble
and ancient Arms.
(Abraham Cowley, 1618–1667)

With the country's great future in mind, and the future of the agricultural industry in particular, I began my period of office as President of COPA in January 1975. All around me there was strong criticism of the EEC Commission's farm price proposals for 1975–76. I remember a note from a good friend, NFU Council member John Hoosen, who believed that I was 'uniquely equipped to galvanise a floppy European situation', which (I think) was nice of him. But he went on more pertinently, 'What has been done in England and Wales, from Penrith to Penzance and from Aberystwyth to Hull, needs doing from John O'Groats to Sicily and from Copenhagen to Nice. The man to find such unity must be a farmer, not a bureaucrat.'

Our full COPA Council met the Commissioner for Agriculture every month, and individual members had regular one-to-one meetings whenever necessary, involving Gundelach from Denmark, Lardinois from the Netherlands, and Dalsager, also from Denmark.

We did some tough talking.

I once complained to Gundelach that he was spending too much time with fishermen while putting together a Fisheries policy. 'You tell me how to keep the fish still,' he said, 'and then I can settle the problem once and for all.'

Lardinois, who later became Chairman of the Dutch Rabobank, was very astute. He would ask me first of all the COPA members what the consensual position was on beef, milk, cereal, wine, tobacco, and so forth. And when I gave him our agreed position, he would then ask, 'Do all your members agree *unanimously* with that – the Italians, for instance?'

The customary reply from my Italian colleagues was: 'Well, Commissioner, we *do* have a special problem . . !'

I told the COPA Assembly in Amsterdam that I considered the EEC proposals to be entirely inadequate and utterly unacceptable. Taking into account the cost increases and non-agricultural earnings for 1973 and 1974, 15 per cent was required and justified for the marketing year of 1975–76. This increase was the absolute minimum necessary if agriculture within the Community was to achieve the essential selective growth in production. The proposals of the EEC Commission clearly did not meet these requirements. The prices announced at Brussels would in any case not mean much unless they were actually received by farmers and growers. Improvement in the market mechanisms was fundamental to price policy – and improvements in this field would have been simplified if the Community had established clearer guidelines for its production objectives.

I would not have accepted the appointment as President of COPA had I not felt that it would also be in the interests of British farmers. Furthermore, I could not believe that our country would withdraw from Europe, for it was surely inconceivable that Britain could become an isolated offshore island following the policies of a bygone age. Such policies reflected a blind belief in the God-given right to cheap food.

The development of the crisis in agriculture could be traced back to the autumn of 1973. It was caused by a combination of escalating costs, falling returns, and political uncertainties, all of which together affected the whole of the livestock sector, including poultry and egg production, and horticulture. Agricultural expansion in the Nine had provided a significant measure of protection against the world food price explosion. But unless the unprecedented inflation in production costs was remedied by immediate and realistic increases in retail prices, neither British nor European farmers would be able to maintain – let alone expand – the output of food.

British agriculture still had great potential, as the country's largest single industry, for an even greater contribution to national well-being. But for this potential to be realised, the Government had to direct its energies to the real tasks.

Our priorities for the year ahead focused on finding out what the Government's long-term intentions were for British agriculture. We needed to know where we stood, in relation to Europe, on our price support system and fair incomes policy. We certainly meant to fight against capital taxes and other measures that would ultimately destroy the structure of British agriculture, and to ensure instead that the system enabled us to produce the food the nation needed. We had shown, through large-scale participation in legal and well-disciplined demonstrations, our solidarity of purpose. There was still a massive amount of work to be done, but we were looking forward and already getting on with it, accepting in advance that there would be some setbacks and disagreements.

At the end of September 1975, some 2,500 farmers and growers staged a national rally. It incorporated representatives from Scotland and from Ulster. But it did more than that, for it was the first time that those not directly connected with the sector – industrial chiefs, representatives of trades unions and consumer groups – had felt so incensed by the unfair treatment of the industry that they had come onto the same platform in support of the farming case. The issue was clearly not just one of falling home food production. It was about the nation's food supply as a whole, about the perilous balance of payments situation, about inflation and jobs – as a statement from all who took part, endorsed by the Council of the NFU, made clear.

I was conscious of the heavy responsibility my words carried at the time, but I believed that improved end-prices for farm and horticultural produce would not on their own guarantee the future prosperity of the industry. National economic recovery and tolerable taxation levels were the overriding considerations for a more optimistic future. The NFU represented the farmers of England and Wales, but were heard by many other ears throughout Britain, Europe and, indeed, the world. We affected household budgets and national policies, and had some responsibility for the retail price of food. Inflation was our concern too, for we suffered from it more than most. And we were entitled to keep a wary eye on Government policies outside agriculture that might add unnecessarily to prices, rates or taxes.

What we did and how we did it could also affect the environment. Care and thoughtfulness on our part could improve the quality of life in terms of the recreational opportunities for millions.

I believed that we could not continue to live in cloud-cuckoo land for much longer. With all the resources available to us, old and new, we should have been one of the richest of the industrialised countries. Our competitors enjoyed a better standard of living all round, because they had learned how to pay their own way in the world and had thus been able to expand their economies at a much more rapid rate. We, on the other hand, since the end of World War II, had not learned the lesson of using to the best advantage the main resource we had in our country – namely, the land.

The year 1975 was probably the most difficult since the end of World War II. Output from British farms had gone down, while what had risen instead were the balance of payments deficit and our indebtedness to the rest of the world. Inflation was approaching a record 22 per cent, and was poised to leap higher, leading to the widespread belief that the Government had lost control over the economy. The pound sank like a stone on the foreign exchanges – to lose more than 25 per cent of its 1951 value, as investors fled from Sterling. Farmers had to cope not only with the extremes of the seasons but also with the inadequacies of Government policy – and with the sheer cowardice of politicians in not acting before the crisis was upon us. Not surprisingly, some farmers had succumbed, and confidence was at its lowest ebb for many years.

It was a memorable year in every sense, for it was the year of The Drought – a summer without rain, scorching the earth and causing crops to be disastrously light in many parts of Europe. On the eve of the Royal Show at Stoneleigh, the Archbishop of York gave a very moving address, at the end of which, before his bidding prayer, he said, 'I've had a strange request on the eve of this great event. I've been asked to give a prayer for rain. So *Let us pray . . .*' Remarkably, and as if in divine response, just as he concluded his prayer, thunder was heard in the distance. No rain fell, however, and the Showground remained as dry and dusty as a desert.

I was President of the Society that year, and one of my tasks was to entertain and take a powerful Russian delegation round our exhibition of science and technology. The exhibition was quite a size, featuring machinery and stock, crop production systems and environmentally-friendly farming methods. And it was so hot there that crowds of people – girls in particular – were lying half-naked on the concourse and around the grounds. After two days' hard work, trying to impress the Russians with British enterprise, I finally felt obliged to accompany them back to the airport. They were still wearing their three-piece suits fully buttoned up. When they started mumbling amongst themselves in the car, I suspected that they might be discussing what they'd seen and, ever optimistic, asked the interpreter what had impressed them most.

'Oh, the women', he said. 'They have never seen so many lying in the sun.'

My face fell.

'Ah, now, that *is* unfortunate,' I said. 'I'm afraid I haven't got any of those for sale!'

The Royal Show always was, and still is, one of the most important annual events for agriculture in Britain. The Show in my presidential year, which was opened by Petrus Lardinois, and the Show the year thereafter, when I served as deputy President to HRH the Prince of Wales, were certainly the most memorable for me personally.

On one occasion, the Spanish Ambassador formally visited the Show. He came up to me and said carefully, 'I see you on TV on Sunday on your farm. You are a very good farmer.'

'I have to be, to be President of the NFU,' I replied.

'But I think you are better actor,' he continued unexpectedly.

Taken aback, I nonetheless recovered well. 'I have to be an actor in my job,' I said.

He reflected on this for a few moments, and in great embarrassment finally said, 'My English is bad – I insult you. I mean you act well for your farmers!'

As President of COPA, I toured several of the drought-stricken areas in Europe with COPA's Secretary General, André Herlitzka, and met many affected farmers and growers. No politician can do anything about the weather, but the tour was a stark reminder that food security cannot be taken for granted, not even in the most developed regions.

One of our halts I remember well. As we arrived in Luxembourg and travelled alongside the River Moselle, an elderly man was scything some pea haulm in a paddock, and a young boy loading it onto a donkey cart. 'Stop, please,' I said to our driver. 'Let's talk to this man.'

After briefly introducing myself, I asked the old gentleman, 'Do you remember a drought like this before?'

'Yes,' he said. 'Back in 1896.'

Astounded, I went on, 'How old are you, then?'

'I'm 94,' he replied. 'Exactly the same thing happened in 1896. The clouds sailed by to the south-east and didn't come back until October – and that's what'll happen this year!'

I remember looking through my office window in London on 11 October and seeing the first real clouds for months. It rained from then until Christmas! We failed to finish harvesting maize silage on the farm that year because of the rain that started when the fields were hard as concrete.

However, it was not doom and gloom at every level of agriculture, and certainly not in areas where our future was reliant on academic research. In September 1975, I was invited to speak at the opening ceremony of the Centre for European Agricultural Studies at Wye College, Kent.

The realisation of the new Centre for Agricultural Studies was a triumph for the British agricultural industry. It was a rare day for me – so rare that I held everyone witness to the occasion when the President of the NFU of England and Wales (me) doffed his cap to the President of COPA (me) and said, '*Now* do you believe we'll make good Europeans?'

In fact, on this occasion I was wearing many caps. Firstly, that of a liveryman of the Worshipful Company of Farmers, a guild that had contributed a great deal to the initiation and establishment of the Centre. Secondly, that of the President of the NFU – and in wearing this cap, I spoke for British farmers who individually and through other agricultural organisations, such as the co-operatives, and not least the Farmers' Club, had contributed to the appeal fund for the Centre. Thirdly, the cap of a farmer, who judged Wye College a good and sound enough place to send his own son. Fourthly, that of a member of the Council of the Centre – and by wearing that one I declared my faith in the Centre's future contribution to the farming community, and in its importance to all those who would be able to use the Centre to increase their understanding of European agriculture. My fifth cap was that of President of COPA, the federation of European farmers' political organisations. My presence there in all these capacities should have gone far towards confirming my earlier remark about the commitment of Britain, and particularly British agriculture, to the European ideal.

It was perhaps no small coincidence that the letters in the word 'cap' were also the initial letters, in English, of the Common Agricultural Policy. It was for the detailed study of this subject and its ramifications for member and other countries that the Centre had been created. If we were to play our part effectively in improving the CAP, then we needed a meeting-place to share a common concern in the land and its industries. This Centre may have embodied an idea that began as a dream, but it had a highly pragmatic and significant contribution to make then and in the years to come.

Of course, at that point the full potential of the Centre had still to be revealed. It was for each of us to decide how this instrument could best be used. It provided a meeting-ground for farmers, industrialists, administrators, academics and research workers. What they would get out of it depended on what they put into it. The Centre would be able to provide information, to organise discussion and to undertake or co-ordinate research, in proportion to the resources which its users and supporters would find worthwhile to devote to these purposes. Its main purpose, however, was to provide an environment which was favourable to the full development and realisation of the power of ideas. Given the mood in the industry, it provided light and hope.

James Callaghan became Prime Minister in May 1976, and his first promise was to halt inflation. One month after his election, the Government was to receive £3,000 million to support Sterling. Most of us were more concerned about taxation in all its forms than about any other Government policy: the NFU doctrine was simple – the taxes we pay must be related fairly to what we earn. They must not destroy our productive assets or our earnings potential. What the Community's agricultural policy required above all was a long-term strategy involving not only fulfilment of the needs of the Community producers and consumers but aid and trade with the developing countries. The CAP could not work as intended until the member Governments of the Community exhibited the will to achieve much closer co-operation, especially in the economic and monetary fields. What we wanted now, in farming and in Britain, was a programme of action – a programme that would inspire us all, and one in which we could believe; a programme with rewards for hard work and the taking of calculated risks; a programme that notwithstanding taxation policies would create new wealth.

We sent an open letter to the Prime Minister signed by Percy Watt, the President of the NFU of Scotland, Robin Morrow, the President of the Ulster Farmers' Union, and myself. We told the PM that British agriculture was a success story in a country badly in need of a few successes. We did not have strikes, we financed our own expansion programmes, and new ventures were the results of our own past effort and risks. We referred to the high import costs of food that we could easily grow in our own country and by so growing reduce the balance of payments deficit (a statement that the PM had himself made in the White Paper 'Food From Our Own Resources'). If other industries had had our track record, we declared, there would have been much less concern over the pound, either real or green (the 'green pound' being the reference rate at which agricultural prices in units of account were converted to Sterling).

We asked the PM why he was not acting to support the success of British agriculture in so far as he had the opportunity and we had the strength and the skills. We wanted him to show us that he meant to give the same priority to home food production as he gave to home energy production, for if he did so we would take the risks and get on with the job. Words, White Papers, Green Papers and green pounds were not enough. Our risks had to be calculated, and we had to be able to rely on a fair price – one that would justify the investment and cover predictably higher costs.

We needed assurances that the PM intended to see that British farmers could base their planning and investment decisions on support prices afforded to other efficient farmers in the Community. The potential of agriculture was not being exploited, profits in real terms were falling, and there was a lack of confidence and a fear that investment in expansion might be undermined by a shortsighted policy toward imported foods. All we wanted from the PM was the assurance that he and the Ministers really meant to back the winners.

The Chancellor, however, had indicated that losing £220 million in food subsidies over two years would raise the cost of living, albeit by less than a quarter of 1 per cent during 1977–78. However, the cost increases that agriculture would have to bear over the period under consideration in the latest Price Review were likely to be the heaviest ever, in that food prices would rise because of the removal of the subsidies.

This was not going to bring any more money into farming – yet we needed extra income if investment in production was to be maintained.

Agriculture was being denied investment resources that we needed at least as much as the industrial sector. If we had had the money, we could have saved the nation an extra £650 million a year off the import bill. At that rate we could have made a significant contribution to paying off the International Monetary Fund loan that was being negotiated!

A nation united behind a united farming industry would be one of the most significant factors in national recovery.

We all knew that the price of food needed to rise, like the price of everything else, and I advised consumers to do some simple arithmetic on the real cost of food. Only a 20th-century King Canute would have expected farmers and growers – faced as they were with a record increase in their production costs – to attempt to reverse the tide of rising retail food prices. Farmers were consumers too, and no one actually relished the prospect of rising food prices. But if customers did their sums, they would see for themselves the gap in the farming industry's housekeeping account.

The equation was simple: our costs were up by nearly 20 per cent in a single year, and a freeze on farm prices – as some advocated – could mean lower production and much higher food prices. Food prices had been held at an artificially low level for far too long. This had only been possible, in part, thanks to the increased productivity of farmers and growers. If farm prices were to be frozen and not allowed to reflect the past year's substantial rise in costs, then those advocating such a shortsighted and dangerous policy would have to explain how farmers could continue to finance investment and production. The overall effect on food prices would have been only 3 per cent compared with the 76 per cent rise in retail food prices since 1974.

The true facts of the farmer's economic plight are borne out by the following typical cost rises over the previous four years:

- · a 115% increase in the price of a leading make of tractor
- · a 57% increase in the price of gas oil
- · a 32% increase in the price of dairy feed
- · a 27% increase in the price of petrol
- · an average increase of 69% in the cost of electricity.

I was convinced that keeping the Common Agricultural Policy afloat was fundamental if Europe was to secure its position as a world power. As Britain took over the EEC helm in the final year of transition, retaining the CAP was essential towards achieving political and economic equality with the United States under its new administration. Any attempt to scuttle the CAP could have signalled the break-up of the European Economic Community.

For it had been clear to me for some time that attacks on the CAP were being made by those who had virtually a vested interest in seeing the collapse of the Community. Under the guise of defending the interests of consumers, workers or food processors, what they were really seeking was a return to the UK's traditional policy of relying upon other countries to supply us with much of our food at prices below those of the Community. They were well aware that without the CAP the EEC could not survive.

Back in 1971 the NFU had concluded that entry into the Community would be in the best long-term interest of our industry – firstly because agricultural prosperity depended largely on the prosperity of the economy in general; secondly, because we saw better opportunities for the expansion of British agriculture inside than outside the EEC; and thirdly, because the EEC had always given a much higher priority to food production than Britain, except in times of war. The Community could not be blamed for the situation that we now found ourselves in. Nor could it be blamed for the fact that although our policy in principle was to produce more food from our own resources, we had in practice become a highly expensive partner of the Community.

Concern with the reform of the CAP was an on-going process in the NFU. Above all, what the Community needed was a long-term policy for food and agriculture in which the interests of Community producers and consumers were integrated into a consistent and developing approach to external trade. I believed the survival of the Community and of the European ideal depended on the survival and the success of the CAP, and I did not believe there could be a viable strategy for British farming without the political commitment that true membership of the Community involved.

The new US administration carried a burden of awesome responsibility, but America needed Europe as much as Europe needed America, and it was also our job to create a Europe that could co-operate with America, politically and economically, as an equal partner. Instead of sniping at each other, the USA and Europe should recognise that they were the two most important trading partners in agricultural products in the world. Speaking in March 1977 at the 75th Anniversary Convention of the NFU of the USA in San Antonio, Texas, I said that in return for Europe's taking US feedstuffs, America should open its markets to the dairy and meat products it had been helping to produce.

I also issued a clear warning that a trade-off between US industrial and European agricultural products would not be tolerated. Just after World War II, when world prices were lower than those in the US, the abolition of quantitative restrictions, as demanded by GATT, would have meant the collapse of US domestic farm policy. It didn't happen then – but, perhaps surprisingly, in the 1970s the waiver still applied, so that the USA could take 'retaliatory' measures against the EEC whereas the Community, because of its GATT obligations, could not take similar action against the USA. In 1975, US exports of agricultural products to the EEC amounted to $5.6 billion, while US imports of agricultural products from the EEC amounted to only $1 billion, leaving a deficit of $4.6 billion. Our exports were being shut out of one American market after another.

The opportunities for product development were what interested us both. We in Europe firmly believed, for example, that with its enormous population, the USA had tremendous scope for raising the consumption of cheese, especially in view of the enormous number of varieties of cheese that we produced in Europe. We believed that far from harming the EEC's own milk producers, the expanded market would be of benefit to Europe – after which we might legitimately buy US soya as feed to produce milk products without creating embarrassing surpluses of butter – which we were not able to export to the USA.

The philosophies of the previous eight years coming from Washington had to give way to an understanding that for the rest of the 20th century the world was going to need the food produced not only in the USA but in the European Community as well – and in increased quantities, if by the year 2000 the entire population of this planet was going to be fed at anything like an adequate level of nutrition.

We needed to work together to see that our governments, after years of bickering and lack of foresight, could at long last put into effect the plans for international agricultural stability – already worked out by us in IFAP and COPA – that were the necessary complement to those we already had for national stability. Our farmers needed stability on both fronts, and the USA and the EEC had a common and major task ahead of them. We had been given some reason for optimism that the new US Administration was prepared to take a fresh look at the whole problem of international agricultural co-operation in the months ahead. And we hoped that President Carter's inaugural references to new opportunities would extend to the aspirations shared by us all to improve conditions worldwide for those working and living on the land.

When I finally reached the end of this speech in Texas, one of the ladies in the audience got up and said brightly, 'You spoke of these nations of Europe joining up. Which nations? And can Texas join?'

'It sure sounds mighty fine!,' she added with an enthusiastic smile.

In Britain there were many critics of the EEC who dismissed the Community as if it were a badly-made machine, operating in Brussels independent of any human contact. They wrongly accused the CAP of raising food prices in Britain, while accepting the humiliating subsidies of more than £1 million a day at the expense of British farmers. They ignored the fact that the goods not covered by the CAP, especially tea and coffee, were the real culprits.

The fact is that in 1977, while the retail food index rose by 21 per cent in 12 months, CAP prices – including increases caused by the transition – contributed only about half of 1 per cent to the retail price index as a whole. The Community all together, and the CAP in particular, needed political support and enthusiasm. Instead of sniping at the CAP, the critics would have been better employed in helping to formulate long-term plans for its integration with overseas trade and aid, and with the international planning of basic farm commodities.

The prospect of a world recession was made more probable by a number of factors. Firstly, the rise in oil prices, invoked by the cartel among oil producers at their OPEC meeting, was a danger-signal for producers, not least for horticulture. I well remember Robin Day interviewing Sheikh Yamani on TV, and accusing him of creating inflation and unemployment in the Western world. Sheikh Yamani replied with firm dignity, 'I have probably 30 years' supply of oil in my country, and intend to maximise the financial return. I will exchange my oil for your rain any day, Mr Day!'

Secondly, a series of Russian harvest failures together with the political mismanagement of the British economy at home had produced a currency crisis and inflation upon which the anti-Europeans mainly relied for their ammunition. The CAP was the victim, not the culprit, because as long as the disparity in exchange rates and inflation remained, the CAP would not work as it was intended. Until countries were prepared to balance strong and weak currencies – as the British Government at that time refused to do – wide variations in returns to farmers would continue. The £500 million worth of dairy products imported in 1976 into the British market could, and should, have been supplied instead by home producers. This was not the fault of the CAP. The policy was introduced at a time of relative economic stability. It was a victim of the cat's-cradle of monetary and economic chaos and of the failure of member Governments to back their membership up with a far greater degree of political commitment.

To farming this meant that the achievements of the last 25 years were in grave danger of erosion. Increased production from British farms over a generation had, by 1976, enabled the industry to make a significant contribution towards easing the UK's recurring balance of payments problem. Widespread uncertainty about the future, lack of confidence and a lack of cash were now undermining the ability of the industry to make an equally effective contribution to the national good in the years ahead.

And then there were the climatic disasters. The severe snowstorms and the flooding in February 1978 provided an example of such always-possible but never-expected blows, at that time for farmers in south-west England and Wales in particular. They suffered a devastating loss of livestock due to the inadequacy of sea defences. I visited the area by helicopter to examine the extent of the damage, and I met farmers in Dorset, Devon and Somerset, then crossed the Bristol Channel to visit Pembrokeshire, Carmarthen and Glamorgan. I also looked in on many of the intensive fruit-and-vegetable-producers in south-west England who had been hit badly by the storms. As we landed on the north Somerset coast, above lashing waves 30 feet (9 metres) high, the pilot said, swooping down a stone's throw from a farm, 'Now we'll see some really angry farmers.'

'Leave it to me,' I said confidently, and stepped out of the helicopter.

I was at once confronted by the farmer, whose evident fury turned, on seeing me, to astonishment.

'Oh my God!' he exclaimed.

'Well – sorry, no.' I replied. 'Just the President of the NFU!'

I asked for an early meeting with John Silkin, the Minister of Agriculture, and called a special meeting of the NFU General Purposes Committee to discuss ways of providing help.

It was quite obvious that there were three main areas of concern: structural damage, loss of milk, and livestock losses, particularly sheep. The Minister shared my concern. I nevertheless took the opportunity to impress several points upon him. One of these was that the NFU was quite prepared to take the initiative in evolving a method of self-help within the agricultural and allied industries, but for this to be a success the Government must be equally prepared to make a no less positive contribution towards repairing the damage sustained by farmers and growers.

During my tour of south-west England and South Wales, I learned that the EEC intended to give no financial help from its disaster fund to redress the storm damage. I was certainly not going to let that be the end of the matter, for we were to continue to impress upon the Government the necessity for substantial financial help from the EEC as well as from national sources. One knacker's yard in Devon had already dealt with 1,000 dead sheep and could take no more.

We set up a self-help fund to aid farmers as quickly as possible, on the clear understanding that the Minister of Agriculture, the statutory bodies

– such as the Milk Marketing Board and the Meat and Livestock Commission – and other organisations connected with agriculture, would follow suit. I telephoned every organisation and prospective supporter I could think of. Within a week our appeal raised £1 million. Although this was far from the full recompense for all that farmers in the disaster areas had suffered, I believed that it would be a real help, and I confidently expected that the Government would now be able, for its part, to make a very substantial contribution.

A few months later, the British Government added £3 million – part of a grant made available from the EEC Disaster Fund that we had helped to establish. We were able to provide compensation at the rate of £20 a sheep and £70 a beast. Although I had only one letter to say 'thank you', it was a magnificent example of an entire industry doing something practical and worthwhile to help individuals who were in trouble.

But whereas this compensation package proved that the farming industry was prepared to help itself, a self-help fund available on an *ad hoc* basis for specific disasters turned out to be only a short-term palliative measure. We relied on the Government too much – and Government intervention had (as it still has) its limitations, usually in terms of the strings attached. With hindsight, a statutory levy on all products sold off farms, controlled independently by a Farmers' Trust, might have acted as an insurance policy against the potential disasters that are always at the back of our minds in the hazardous business of dealing with living and growing plants and animals. Many countries operate such a scheme, to the benefit of their farmers. And as we in Britain are now moving away from the end-price subsidy towards income support for rural development, it becomes even more imperative that self-help is established on a more permanent and formal basis, to avoid the accusation of continuing to run cap in hand to the Government or of relying on the nanny state!

We could, for instance, build up a fund to help compensate in the event of such multiple disasters as we experienced in the spring of 2001 with the foot-and-mouth disease that for many followed the tragedy of swine fever or BSE ('mad cow disease').

5

'WHERE THERE IS NO VISION, THE PEOPLE PERISH'

> What greater gift or better can we
> offer to the state than if we teach
> and train up youth?
> (Cicero)

As we reached the end of our transitional entry into the Common Market in 1978, we were starting to see signs of radical change in the Common Agricultural Policy. Farmers were beginning to realise that unlimited expansion could not go on unchecked for much longer. We were facing a period of recession. Demand for scarce resources nationally and in the EEC was pressing in on all sectors of industry. There was much talk of tighter market management control since production could not go on increasingly unaccounted for. Specific prescriptions and rationalisation proposals were emerging week by week, and the decision we had to face became very clear. Was it to be substantial price cuts or quotas?

Already Europe produced 40 per cent of the world's butter and half of the world's cheese. The day of reckoning over the future of the CAP was upon us! From a situation in which cynics could say 'Farmers have never had it so good' in the mid-1970s, this was going to mean hardships for everyone, and cuts in 'nominal support prices'.

The large cattlemen might say they preferred price cuts rather than quotas; the smaller producer could see quotas as some sort of safeguard. Price cuts might have been acceptable in the UK, but they were certainly not on the Continent – and so it became obvious we were moving towards a managed market. If EEC prices were to be reduced substantially, the countries most sympathetic to farmers would simply substitute another form of support, leading to a huge re-nationalisation of agricultural-support spending. This would, quite definitely, not apply to the UK.

We had to face the continuing problem of the 'green currencies' – the rate at which EEC agricultural prices were converted into real currencies – and the adjustment through the currency mechanism that they made necessary. Equally, we had to face up to the realities of the world market and our commitment to traditional suppliers like New Zealand. It is often not understood in Britain that we still, today, import more than 76,000 tonnes of butter and 11,000 tonnes of cheese at a preferential rate from New Zealand every year, as well as 220,000 tonnes of lamb. In 1999 the New Zealanders were actually unable to fulfil their lamb quota of 220,000 tonnes, and only 53 per cent of shipment came to the UK.

But the point is that when Britain joined the EEC, the door was opened for New Zealand to trade with the other European countries. Following the adoption of the Euro by eleven (plus Greece) out of the fifteen EU countries in January 1999, New Zealand exporters and importers are already changing the way they trade with this region.

Hans Pauwels of importer Richmond Europe recently stated that, from his perspective, trading will be made a lot easier when the Euro currency is introduced in January 2002. 'We can reduce the number of clearing accounts, and will be pricing, marketing, buying and paying staff in euros. It will bring us important savings in administration costs, banking fees and exchange rates,' he said. He added that such 'price transparency' will represent an important development in view also of the company mergers and acquisitions currently taking place in the retail sector across Europe.

Europe is an extremely important region for New Zealand:

In 1997, more than 10 per cent of New Zealand exports – 1 billion euros ($NZ 2 billion) – went to Euro-participating countries – 'the EU-11' – while more than 13 per cent of imports (over $NZ 2 billion) came from those countries. By the end of 1998, the EU-11 was New Zealand's third largest export market during the year, with 1.23 billion euros ($NZ 2.4 billion), 11 per cent of the total.

Farmers in Britain in 1978, having slogged through the five years of transition, expected now to reap the benefits of common prices in a bigger market. Yet common prices were as far away as ever, and our markets were threatened by unfair competition such as no other industry had to put up with. It was not the fault of the Community system. 'Europe' had been many times cited as a scapegoat, and EEC rules and regulations manipulated to serve many purposes. Farmers had been the victims of a political strategy that sought to secure the benefits of club membership while avoiding the full subscription.

I believed that the difficulties in the farming industry demanded an all-party, rather than a partisan, approach. This was a time when the expansion of our food production had a vital role to play in underpinning the nation's economic recovery and safeguarding consumer supplies.

The exchange rate of the green pound and the problems caused by the EEC's subsidy on exports (the MCAs, or monetary compensatory amounts) were at the bottom of the serious disparity between UK and European prices. EEC Commissioner Finn Olav Gundelach was in the process of preparing a report on the MCAs for the Council of Ministers, while the NFU had already put its own evidence to the Commission. As for the reported bilateral deal between France and the Republic of Ireland on a levy-free lamb supply to France – that, if true, was a situation Britain could not possibly tolerate. We made very strong representations to the Minister, and he responded promptly, emphasising his own opposition to any arrangements discriminating against the UK.

We were to continue to press very strongly to ensure that the Treaty of Rome was honoured in this matter.

The time for talking was over. Our home market was already subject to free and, in some cases, subsidised competition from Europe. Our co-operatives could match the continentals in marketing expertise – Lingarden was actually exporting daffodil bulbs to Holland, after all – but although much had been done to improve the structure of co-operation in the years since 1972 when ACMS was set up, we had barely scratched the surface of what still needed to be done.

We were again debating our future in a setting in which the outlook for even the strongest political lobbies was far from promising. In the interests of farmers and growers, the NFU sought to secure and sustain a satisfactory financial base for the industry as a whole and for its different sectors, now in the European dimension. And of course it also had to protect the individual interests of all those who subscribed to it. I believed that British housewives would have had no objection to paying European prices for their food, had their families enjoyed European incomes after tax. Britain certainly could not go on being a reluctant member of a Common Market while avoiding common prices, because industrial over-manning and low productivity would inevitably result in low incomes. Neither would we cure inflation nor increase our prosperity by interfering with market forces, inhibiting the successful, or cheating the farmers.

Of course the critics would say that this is what free trade is all about. In industrial competition, this is what the capitalists who do not win must suffer when they lose – except for capitalists in the steel industry, where the price of failure is a £520 million bill to the taxpayer. But what we were looking at was not just straightforward industrial competition. Our industry was being forced to compete with foreign industry *plus* their Government, plus *our* Government. It was a combination that would defeat any industry, however efficient or productive it might be – and that such a situation should ever be allowed to arise, let alone prevail, was a clear and damning indictment of the British Government's neglect of its agriculture.

Those most affected by the green pound – the pig, beef and dairy producers – sought no more than a straight contest with their competitors for the favours of the consumer. They naturally accepted that their customers were entitled to the best product at the most economic price.

A primary aim of farmers was to sustain and improve farm incomes. If we could not achieve it through support policies or lower costs, then we were obliged to strive to achieve it by all other means at our command. Already we were putting more effort into representation – not so much in relation to prices, but in respect of retaining earned income and accrued capital. We had had a measure of success in the form of relief on capital transfer and capital gains tax, in the avoidance of rating on farm buildings, in disease compensation payments, and in the abolition of the three-months' delay in other areas, such as the payment of capital grants – to take but a few examples. I believed our efforts would soon be rewarded by further gains in the areas of direct taxation and tax spreading.

But we also had more hazards to face by way of a threatened wealth tax and of land nationalisation.

Our professional strength had to be developed still further, so that owners and occupiers of agricultural land might prosper through investment financed by reasonable prices in the markets for farm output. It was those market prices – established to an increasing extent by the success with which we were able both to meet and to create demand for our products – that were most likely to determine the size and shape of British agriculture in the years ahead.

All we needed was the will, the determination not to be pushed around on account of our position as small buyers and weak sellers. I believed that our political and economic interests and our commercial activities were complementary – but that we should keep them separate. From our relationship with the Government we needed political goodwill in order to establish the framework within which we could develop all the commercial opportunities open to us. On the other hand, the European governments needed us too. They needed our expertise, enthusiasm and hard work – particularly for bringing in the harvest when conditions were 'impossible' – a task for which certain other political systems found even the machine-gun an inadequate piece of farm machinery. They needed our capacity for cherishing the countryside and contributing to national life. *They needed our efficiency and our proven productivity.*

To obtain common pricing for agricultural products within the Common Market remained the underlying objective of NFU policy for many years to come. Without common pricing there could be no true common market, and producers and consumers of food would not benefit from one of the underlying principles of the EEC – that output should be concentrated in regions where production was most efficient.

Through the device of the green pound our farmers had been deprived of resources. Food outputs had tended to stagnate, and in 1977 we produced only as much as we had in 1974. Yet there was no doubt in anybody's mind that sustained expansion of food from the resources we possessed in Britain would boost economic growth and provide jobs for many more people. To those who feared the effect of a green pound devaluation on food prices I offered the reassurance that there was no danger that the kind of immediate devaluation we advocated would have a deleterious effect upon any incomes policy. A devaluation of 10 per cent would have raised food prices by about 2.5 per cent, and the overall cost of living would have gone up by less than 1 per cent.

In fairness, we did not think our producers – already penalised by a 'green pound gap' of nearly 30 per cent – could be expected to suffer more. This was why the NFU advocated that Government policy should also include an immediate commitment to reduce this large gap to more manageable proportions. It was a realistic attitude, which indicated a willingness on the part of the NFU to overcome some of the difficulties that confronted us at home and in Europe. For us to do the job properly, financial penalties upon home agriculture – such as the MCA rates, which were undermining our own products on our own market – had to be removed. That was particularly true for beef, and for pig meat, in respect of which the whole of the industry – producers as well as processors – was under great and unwarranted pressure from EEC-subsidised imports.

There was no doubt that the agricultural situation in Britain did not conform to the principles and objectives of the Common Agricultural Policy. I believed that trade distortions, caused by the operation of the EEC agri-monetary system, were impinging upon the economic future of the UK. It was a pity that the Government had not woken up to the danger before the problems reached such proportions.

The Government had given a false impression by pointedly saying that more than 70 per cent of the total EEC budget was used for agricultural support. But what else *should* the bulk of the Community budget be spent on when agriculture was the only major common policy of the Community?

I hoped we would not fall into the tempting political trap of looking at agriculture in the short term, and forget that ours was essentially a long-term operation. The EEC farm price support system was designed to ensure continuity of food supplies to consumers, and to secure a fair standard of living for those who worked in agriculture. The simple object was to take produce off the market whenever there was over-abundance which threatened to reduce farm returns to uneconomic levels. The surplus could thereafter be released in various ways, but always making sure that a prudent reserve was retained – a principle adopted with some success by the Biblical Joseph in ancient Egypt, through the seven fat years and the seven lean years. Because of the British Government's failure to devalue the green pound steadily and effectively, there had been a transfer of resources from this country to elsewhere in the EEC.

The object of the CAP was to make the best use of the Community's resources, and Britain had lower unit costs than most other member states. Any transfer of resources for most major commodities should have been towards Britain rather than the reverse. The effect went further than farming. Every tin of ham, every packet of butter, every item of food we imported unnecessarily had to be paid for by some export.

British troops in German army bases ate Irish bacon rashers because European farm subsidies made them cheaper than UK supplies. We knew that the NAAFI (the National Association of Agriculture, Family and Industry) would prefer to buy British bacon, as it did before we entered the EEC, but because of the considerable price advantage in relation to Irish supplies, both the NAAFI and the Ministry of Defence felt that the taxpayer's money must be seen to be used economically. Consequently, the British bacon industry, which was actually able and willing to produce the goods cheaper than its competitors, had not been given a chance to compete to retain this account.

I couldn't think of anything more ridiculous.

The price advantage on Irish bacon worked out at 9p per pound (0.45 kilogram) because of the unfair calculation of the monetary compensatory amount (MCA). The Danes received a similar handout – and the Dutch did even better, receiving as much as 12p a pound back on bacon. All of this was galling to British farmers and curers, who were quite capable of turning out high-quality bacon at lower cost than their competitors. The only thing that stopped the British farmers from meeting the challenge was the unfair MCA calculation. In the long term this was bound to speed up the decline in the UK bacon industry, which in 1978 was recording an output still 12 per cent below 1974 production levels. For the consumer that meant ever-increasing reliance upon imported bacon. For the industry, meanwhile, there was the prospect of further factory closures, so that even if our farm production did recover to any extent, there would no longer be the processing capacity to handle it.

Another example was what happened to the Marketing Boards, and the Milk Marketing Board in particular.

I gave notice to anyone in Europe who was tempted to try in any way whatsoever to undermine the operations of the Milk Board, that the NFU would defend it to the limit of its resources – and that we would be no less active in the defence of the prerogatives of Britain's other Marketing Boards. Any attempt to change their constitution or to reduce their powers in such a way as to prevent the boards from carrying out their functions in the future as effectively as in the past, we would resist.

In the meantime, I went to the Ministry of Agriculture and delivered a petition signed by 200,000 people asking the Government to halt its plan to phase out supplies of unpasteurised milk by 1980. If the ban went through, an important consumer demand would be frustrated, and many of the 3,700 farmers who produced and sold this kind of milk could go out of business. The Government based its policy on the belief that the drinking of untreated milk was a risk to health. I believed that the risk was in truth no greater than the risk involved with the consumption of any other untreated food, and that the health record of untreated milk – seen from its proper perspective – was good.

The EEC Commission came up with a report on proposals for an EEC milk regime in September 1978. It outlined a range of options, all of which would require careful appraisal. I felt that the NFU must not rush to comment in detail, particularly on any of the mechanisms put forward by the Commission for a restraint on European producer prices. We had to deliberate on such proposals in the context of two main features that dominated our thinking.

Firstly, the NFU had long accepted the principles of free trade and fair competition within Europe, and therefore believed that any Community arrangements that might be introduced must give scope to the continued economic and technical efficiency of the UK industry. Secondly, we had been emphasising that the UK producer already suffered a penalty in comparison to other member states through the operation of the green pound mechanism, which depressed UK support prices by more than 20 per cent. The consequent MCAs (subsidies) on imports undercut our market return from dairy products.

As for the other elements of the package, we continued to believe that the main thrust and vehicle for the restructuring of the European milk industry must comprise a really effective non-marketing scheme. A reduction in the Community milk herd was essential – and we noted the support for the existing scheme contained in the Commission's report. Any future scheme had to be sufficiently attractive to yield positive results.

The NFU had strongly supported capital grants for agriculture, and we needed to oppose the suspension of national and Community aids. It was important that milk producers increased their efficiency so as to keep pace with technological improvements, to the benefit of consumers and producers alike. We welcomed the Commission's intention to continue the measures to maintain or increase the placing of milk products. Whatever proposals were to be finally adopted, we were most concerned to see that the supply of calves to the beef rearer was safeguarded as far as feasible in any attempt to reduce the Community milk production. In this context we noted a mention of the possibility of a grant for suckling cows, which might assist in the matter.

In consequence, the NFU staged a Milk Marketing Board poll. The results demonstrated the depth of support among British dairy farmers for the Board. There were approximately 48,000 dairy farmers in England and Wales, and they kept 2.6 million cows. Through our county and local branch structure, every dairy farmer in the country had been approached personally to gauge support during the three weeks before the poll closed. It was a tremendous achievement for all NFU members and staff who took on the enormous job, and I was proud of them.

The vote in favour of retaining the Board was massive – more than 97 per cent of all votes cast. The NFU was confronted with a major issue, and the fact that we had the ability to canvass support through an unrivalled organisation was of vital importance. There had been some who had expressed real surprise at the size of the vote, and of the majority. I felt that we had now demonstrated the determination of the NFU and the farming community to preserve our own institutions from whatever quarter came the opposition. And although the statutory powers of the Board were eventually removed, I still believe that producers would have supported the same powers on a voluntary basis without dismantling the essential marketing instruments.

The consumer-orientated, largely free-trade-minded British public had accepted the principle of producer marketing boards for more than 40 years. It was not entirely surprising, if rather ironic, that the criticisms of our Boards came from the continentals, who tended to favour state-directed or regulated economies. Without the marketing organisations operating as they do now, the European Community would look a very different proposition to us.

A policy of incomes restraint could not be a permanent feature of British industrial life. The alternative was a policy to increase productivity. Farmers became sick and tired of industrial disputes and the wrecking tactics of politically motivated militants. This was not because of a 'holier than thou' attitude but because we knew that our record was second to none in terms of productivity and also in labour relations.

It sometimes escaped the notice of others in British industry, and in the Government, that Great Britain was still an agricultural island. Agriculture was the largest single industry, and just as farmers and farmworkers had been key members of society before the Industrial Revolution, so they were in the late 1970s. We had survived the lean years, and a succession of depressions, because the agricultural industry was well equipped to fight through the kind of trouble that was destroying other sectors. We had raised our productivity level – sometimes quickly, sometimes more slowly – but we had done it year after year. Our rate of increase over the past 15 years was precisely twice that of the national economy as a whole: 5 per cent compared with 2.5 per cent. Our labour relations were still a model for others, despite occasional disparaging remarks. We had nothing to be ashamed of, in the way our workforce was paid or in their conditions of employment, and I believed the results, of which we were all duly proud, showed that.

We only once experienced the threat of a farm workers' strike, mostly centred on potato- and sugarbeet-growing farms in East Anglia. My herdsman was secretary of the local farmworkers' union, and I discussed the situation with him.

'Would you join the strike?' I asked.

'Solidarity is our theme-song,' he nodded, 'so I'd have to.'

'Does that mean I'm going to have to come home and milk 150 cows every day?' I yelped in dismay.

'Oh no,' he said comfortably. 'I'll be getting up a bit earlier and doing the milking, have a bit of a strike in the day, and do the milking again in the evening!'

The key to all this was not the level of wages, nor the margin of profit, but the one fact every farmer knew – that the more you take out of any business, irrespective of the ability to pay, the deeper is the ruin. The NFU supported private enterprise. British industry was founded upon the work and dedication of the individual with freedom to operate. The only way we in Britain could now retain that freedom was by raising the productivity of our manufacturing industries to the levels achieved by British agriculture. If we did that, then inflation would become a bad memory.

At the Lord Mayor's Banquet in London, in November 1978, James Callaghan, the Prime Minister, said that the way the European Community funded its farming needed a thorough review. He then went out of his way to say that he agreed with the principles and objectives of the CAP – but the cost to Britain of its operation was giving cause for concern.

We thoroughly agreed.

One of the CAP's key purposes – perhaps the fundamental one – was (and is) to make the best possible use of the agricultural resources of the Community. This meant free and fair competition. And that, in turn, should mean the eventual phasing out of the artificial green exchange rates and the associated MCAs (subsidies) that had done so much to distort competition.

The damage already done to our own livestock industry, and to processing industries with which it was associated, was a classic example of the consequences of such distortion. We could not be expected to compete – and in competing, realise to the full our own acknowledged efficiency – when we were penalised by a monetary gap of some 30 per cent in the prices we received.

I shared Mr Callaghan's concern about the funding of the EEC budget – although, as I've already said, since the CAP was the only really 'common' policy in Europe, it was hardly surprising that it took up so much of that budget. Given that Britain was a relatively poor country and that we received comparatively little aid from Community sources, it was time to ask whether the cost of price support for commodities in structural surplus should continue to be entirely funded from the general Community budget. Community aid in other areas was contingent upon aids also being supplied by the individual member state – and perhaps this principle should now be extended.

What could not be denied was that farmers must produce for consumers, not for the intervention store. The NFU had always recognised that agricultural policies, both at national and at EEC level, must be designed to achieve a sensible balance between supply and demand.

The 1978 figures indicated a gap of about 40 per cent between the prices determined for Germany and the low prices set for British farmers. But as experience over the years had shown, it was extremely difficult to derive truly common European farm prices while the individual currencies of member countries fluctuated. The European summit talks in Brussels failed to reach agreement on an overall European monetary system. I felt the national interest would suffer once again if Britain were to remain behind while most European countries decided to join.

History was repeating itself, for we were depending on a cheap food policy in order to try to make ourselves competitive in world markets. It was not working, but we clung desperately to it, nevertheless, and remained entrenched and intransigent while the rest of the EEC moved away from us. In those areas in which we could show most of our competitors a clean pair of heels, our lead was being nullified by political policies that seemed designed to depress agricultural returns so that food could flow in from overseas. The situation was being compounded by inflation, and masked by the benefits of North Sea oil. The day had to come when we would have to pay a delayed bill for such 'cheap' food, which never really existed.

This was why we were prepared to look ahead and support moves – such as the introduction of the European Monetary System (EMS) – which although they might not produce immediate benefits for farming, could help Britain to improve its position in relation to the other members of the European Community.

My views on Britain's role in Europe and in the world at large have never changed. I still feel that it is better to shape events rather than react to them. Similarly, I believe that a national policy on long-term agricultural objectives should have the full backing of an all-party agreement. And in my view, the importance of the current debate over whether Britain should join the Euro currency – and if so, when – is such as to merit all-party agreement yet again in support of the final decision.

In 2000, I witnessed the nationwide launch of the 'Britain in Europe' campaign. A cross-party initiative, its objective is one that I support because I believe that the level and depth of our involvement in the European Union is too important to be used as a party-political football or a vehicle for winning elections. Standing there at its inauguration, I remembered the French diplomat's words about the impossibility of being both *in* and *out*. Since so many apparently intelligent people nowadays seem to think it is possible for Britain to turn its back on the commitments and agreements made in the context of its international relationships, campaigning for 'Britain in Europe' makes sense only if campaigning for 'Britain *out* of Europe' or even '*outside* Europe' has to be taken seriously.

It is my strong belief that the establishment of Economic and Monetary Union (EMU) was a huge step forward for the twelve EU member states who agreed to participate from 1 January 1999. In principle, a single currency reduces the cost of trading between member countries. Today, businessmen in France can trade with their German counterparts without any need to take the risk, or to insure against the risk, that the value of one currency will move adversely against the other between agreement on a price and completion of the deal. This advantage is now available to the majority of those who agreed with the principle of the single currency.

The negative attitude in Britain would seem largely to be based on a number of psychological factors and fears – for example, fear of the loss of sovereignty – to which I refer again in Chapter 12. Mind you, at a superficial level it is easy to understand such fears. The European Union has undeniably interfered in some relatively trivial issues – such as weights and measures – in a way that appears still to upset many of my fellow countrymen and women in their daily lives.

I believe that the balance of advantage for the UK is in favour of joining EMU, and that our involvement in this now central feature of the EU would give us greater power, not less, to argue against any future proposals for legislation that would have a detrimental effect on the UK.

In considering the UK's entry into EMU, the exchange rate at which the value of the pound would be fixed against the Euro is of course a major issue. At the outset of EMU, the general feeling in the UK was that an exchange rate of around 73p to the Euro would be acceptable for most of industry and commerce (i.e. DM 2.65–2.75 to £1 Sterling).

Since then, the value of the Euro has dropped dramatically against the pound, so making the terms of international trade much tougher for virtually all British manufacturers and services because they have faced competitively priced imports and have found it difficult to compete on export markets. There have been protests from manufacturers and exporters – but in the vibrant UK economy they have knuckled down, adapted and cut costs, and the fittest have survived.

The Confederation of British Industry suggested that by the end of the year 2000 most UK businesses could cope with an exchange rate of 64p–65p per Euro. It would appear in any case that since 1998 or so, significantly greater productivity gains have been made by UK businesses than by their continental competitors, and they are now better placed accordingly for the future. Concerns persist about the attractiveness of the UK to inward investors (e.g. Japanese car manufacturers), but these anxieties probably relate more to the volatility of the pound as an independent currency than to the actual value of the pound against the Euro.

For farming, however, the value of the pound relative to the Euro has a greater impact. The Common Agricultural Policy was designed from the outset to stimulate trade in agricultural goods within Europe, and Britain has been subject to the CAP since 1973, albeit with a 5-year transition period to 1978. The EU is Britain's most significant trading partner by far in relation to agricultural commodities and processed foods, and a major net importer of foods as a whole, which makes food prices in Britain highly dependent on the Sterling-Euro exchange rate.

This is particularly true for milk products, meat, vegetables and fruit. It is also true for grain, in which the UK is a net exporter but competes with France and other Euro-based economies. Such a high dependence on trade with the rest of the EU gives UK agriculture an advantage when the pound is weak against the Euro, and puts the UK at a disadvantage when the pound is strong. Any such currency-related advantage or disadvantage is compounded by the fact that the various support payments – which all EU farmers receive – are determined in Euros. Farmers in the member states outside 'Euroland' are then paid in the local currency at the prevailing exchange rate by their own governments.

This dependence of UK farmers' prices on the pound-euro exchange rate has led to steadily falling incomes and steadily increasing trauma for UK agriculture since the introduction of the Euro and its subsequent dramatic weakening against the pound. For farmers, therefore, the pressure to increase productivity, shed labour and amalgamate has been even greater than for business generally – and these processes are having major negative impacts on agriculture, the countryside and rural development.

There are no valid statistical figures available on the attitude of farmers in 1998 as regards Britain's joining the Euro, but a significant proportion seem to have been opposed. These farmers may have been swayed by a general mistrust of EU institutions and by doubts that the UK Government would ever be sufficiently committed to Europe to be able to influence its proceedings. British farmers' attitudes have also been influenced by such events as the French reaction to UK beef exports after the BSE crisis.

Logically, farmers should have been strongly in favour of the UK's joining the Euro at the outset. If the UK had joined then, our farmers would now be prosperous, with prices and support payments some 20 per cent higher than they actually were at the end of 1999, and with lower interest rates. Now that the UK is clearly outside Euroland, however, it is fully understandable that farmers would not vote to join, at the current exchange rate of a strong pound against a weakened Euro. They would surely benefit if the rate rose once more to 70p per euro or higher – but few people would bank on farmers' voting in favour, even if that rate did return.

The fact remains that in 1979 the NFU did regret that the heads of the EEC Governments had been unable to agree on a currency stabilisation scheme to which it could subscribe. But if British agriculture was not only to withstand the growing challenge from other Community countries but also to increase its share of the market, we had to get on with the job and work on improving the prospects for farmers and growers for the years ahead. British agricultural industry was about to face an extremely serious cash crisis.

I was deeply concerned by reports about the monetary proposals the Commission was to present to the Council of Ministers during the 1979 Price Review. The Green Pound was, after all, now back to nearly 30 per cent – the level at which it stood when the House of Commons demanded a 7.5 per cent devaluation in January 1978.

By its attitude to agriculture, the Government had put the food chain under increasing pressure. In 1978, farming increased its output to the tune of an extra £350 million saving on the balance of payments – yet farmers had to borrow an additional £400 million to keep going. Just as farming needed food for its animals, it also needed incomes to feed future investment, and to maintain and increase the nation's food supply.

The CAP was designed to give just the sort of long-term assurance of income that we needed, but political and economic forces had prevented it from working as was intended. As a result, in an EEC that was supposed to have common farm prices, and that had a farm policy designed to promote the efficient production of commodities in those areas best suited to them, the UK farmer received less than the average of his European competitors, and had to fight for his own food market against subsidised produce from less cost-efficient producers.

The immediate solution to the economic problem was devaluation by the British Government of the green pound to narrow the 30 per cent gap between our prices and Continental prices. We were not asking the Government to enrich the British farmer – we were imploring it to safeguard the nation's larder.

I felt that the day had come that I would not stand for re-election as NFU President in January 1979. I had been an office-holder for 15 years, nine of them as President, and I thought it was time for a change. The decision was one I took with reluctance, but I believed that our farmers might benefit from a fresh hand at the helm.

On the day I was first elected NFU President, the industry was in serious disarray. There was militancy in the air, and we had banners and demonstrations at our own annual general meeting. Many things had changed since then, but there were also some disturbing similarities between the situation that faced me on the first day of my Presidency and what we saw as the position at the conclusion of my NFU career. Nonetheless, the NFU was in good heart – perhaps better than when I had taken it over – and I could with every confidence hand on my job to Sir Richard Butler, who had been my loyal deputy and good friend over eight years. We wouldn't win every battle, but it was the NFU's job to defend farmers' interests effectively, and I knew it was as capable of doing that as it had ever been.

I had been fortunate to be the leader of a good team. Moreover, the Council members truly represented the wit and wisdom of so many farming characters throughout England and Wales.

One such character was Ronnie Farqueson, a large arable farmer from Dorset and for many years Chairman of the NFU Cereals Committee. He collapsed one morning as he arrived at the railway station in London, and was immediately taken to see a very eminent doctor in Sloane Street, one Dr Abel. The good doctor diagnosed a major problem with his teeth, and sent him to a colleague in Harley Street for dentistry. After removing all Ronnie's remaining teeth, the dental surgeon was making impressions for a set of dentures when Ronnie mumbled 'How much?'

'Around £100,' said the dentist, as casually as he could.

Ronnie exploded, stuttering, 'I can get a set for half a crown at the Dorchester market!'

Subsequently, both the dentist and the doctor were regular guests for a day's shooting on Ronnie Farqueson's estate!

I had been re-elected without opposition every year by a Council who could be highly critical when it wanted to be – so my team must have done a good job and said what the Council wanted us to say. In Europe Britain nonetheless had a long way to go before farmers could speak effectively with one voice.

We had made speeches about marketing so many times. Marketing meant more than just product promotion, although that was important, especially as our competitors made such a feature of selling their own branded products in our country. First of all we had to get supply and demand right for the commodities we wanted to produce in this country. We produced for a market, and no market supplier can work in isolation. A sensible agricultural policy was necessary for the well-being of us all.

Two very important questions we faced focused on animal welfare and the ownership of land. Few other nations in the world were as susceptible to emotive propaganda about animal welfare as the British: we have long been a nation of animal lovers. I was proud of the fact that the NFU had done as much as anyone to further the cause of animal welfare, but I was afraid we might sometimes have got carried away and lost our sense of proportion.

The first office I held in Agriculture House was Chairman of the Animal Health Committee, but I think I could claim that my anxiety for the welfare of animals dated back far earlier – right back to my first memories of farm stock and working with cattle, sheep and pigs. I would never condone cruelty to animals – or to people, for that matter – in any shape or form. I had done my share of sitting up through cold winter nights lambing ewes, farrowing pigs or calving cows. I well remember going to a dinner party at the home of my farming friends Tony and Mary Gatling, when at midnight they'd had to call the vet to a difficult calving. The vet, Alisdair Steele-Bodger, was President of the Royal College of Veterinary Surgeons that year, and there is an amazing photograph of the two Presidents – of the Vets and of the Farmers – stripped to the waist, calving that cow in the small hours of the morning.

I sincerely believed, however, that not only was the banning of live animal exports unnecessary, but that it would also be a retrograde step for the cause of animal welfare. No fewer than three major Government enquiries over the years exonerated transporters from causing unnecessary suffering or economic damage on each occasion. And frankly, long before a ban ever became even a matter for debate, Parliament should have given us a firm, clear assurance that the trade could continue, subject to welfare safeguards, so that we could get on with the job unmolested. For the weight of the advantage to the UK, not just to farmers and exporters, lay in continuing the trade. The trade was in fact worth £33 million a year, and had been shown to maintain a high standard of welfare. It was also providing an increasing level of emphasis on the protection of animals in transit. Conversely, the ban could not and did not increase the sum total of animal welfare, and its enforcement placed an unnecessary and unfair burden upon all engaged in it.

Legally, it was actually very difficult to ban animal transportation under EEC law, and although the reports made useful suggestions on the welfare aspect of the trade, it was quite clear that there was no justification for it either. The NFU wanted to support all reasonable measures, introduced on expert advice, to further safeguard the welfare of animals in transit.

I respected the views of some of the critics of the trade as being honestly held, but every shred of evidence available showed that they were based upon lack of real knowledge. Well-meaning concern was a virtue, but not when emotion was allowed to displace expert scientific and veterinary advice.

In the meantime, the way to deal with the problem of maltreatment when it occurred was to weed out the odd offenders, not to apply blanket restrictions to the whole trade. Intensification of livestock units had also drawn some ill-informed criticism. I hoped, as I stepped down from the NFU Presidency, that we could continue our efforts to acquaint the objectors with the facts about what was going on and the reasons behind such developments. If the nation wished to enjoy good food at its lowest cost, it could not at the same time deny to the farmer the most efficient and humane means of producing it. I supported the rules and the strengthening of them wherever necessary, and I was sure that we would never tolerate cruelty or unnecessary suffering in any degree.

The other issue that continued to crop up was the ownership of land, particularly the proposals for public ownership. The NFU was to use all of its power to resist any proposals for any form of land nationalisation or compulsory public ownership, direct or indirect.

My final Dinner as NFU President was an occasion I shall never forget – and in my speech I tried as best I could to convey my feelings, which was perhaps the most difficult task I ever had to face. My past was not just flashing before me. That evening, I was surrounded by it. I was very proud, obviously, that our guests included not only the Minister of Agriculture and some of his colleagues, but also all the ex-ministers with whom I had had to deal, and the past Presidents of the NFU. Together with a glittering array of men and women from almost every sector of the agricultural, horticultural, and food industries, they made as worthy a company of friends and allies as I could have dreamed of under one roof. But above all, my family and many close friends were with me.

In my speech I said that my fifteen years as an NFU office-holder was hardly a lifetime, but confessed that it had often felt like it. I had spent some time clearing out my office, and I collected all my old diaries which I intended to keep as a record of a marathon. I would not have missed that race for the world – but I would have been hard pressed to repeat it. It was a test of strength and endurance in more ways than one.

Today I find myself reliving those years, and sympathising with Ben Gill, the current President, who is weathering the storm like the great trooper that he is. Tough it might be, but there is some satisfaction in fighting for the families of the land. Farming is more than raising wheat, cattle, pigs and sheep. It is also raising scientists, statesmen and humanitarians – a great forum of people uniquely endowed to give more than their share to preserving the countryside. Even with a few language problems, farmers the world over are on the same wavelength.

But meet someone who lives in the same street or in the same block of flats in London, and they act as if they are from a different planet altogether.

The perception of farming held by the general public had become – and remains –strangely distorted, informed by sensationalism rather than by facts about such issues as BSE and foot-and-mouth disease. The truth is that the farming industry has been driven down a side-road to more industrialised production through the demand for cheap food. There is an old saying among farmers that you grow mangolds to feed cows, to make muck, to grow mangolds.

Another old saw goes that farmers are never really satisfied. It is like the old farmer who took his cow to market. When he got home, his wife said to him 'Did you sell the cow?'

'Yes, I sold the cow,' he said.

So she said, 'Did you get what you expected?'

And he said, 'No, I didn't get what I expected. But then I didn't know what to expect!'

Today the drive for cheap food has forced farmers to work harder, for longer hours, for less income, merely to stay in business. The outbreak of the dreadful and much-dreaded disease that we are currently experiencing is a stark reminder that food does not just appear by magic on the supermarket shelf or the butcher's slab. It is bred and nurtured on the farm by a farmer, by a carer for its welfare.

At a rough guess, during my time as President I travelled about 1 million miles (1.6 million kilometres) on NFU business. Much more frightening was the estimate – and this assumed only a moderate intake on each occasion – that I had eaten more than three tonnes of food at official functions – including a few working breakfasts. Without actually being too aware of it, I had certainly done my bit to reduce surpluses . . .

At the Dinner, I promised one thing – namely, that my diaries would never be published . . . although I thought I might get round to my memoirs sometime. Applying the rules for cabinet papers, what I had said to Ministers and the like at critical times might one day be revealed. I was taking my nine diaries with me. Here I recalled Moses, who came down from the mountain with ten tablets – he had the advantage of me by one, but another advantage he enjoyed was a very clear course mapped out for him by the Great Election Agent.

There is more than an element of sadness in leaving any organisation after such a long time. It was deepened for me, and for everyone that evening, by the fact that one man who had been by my side the whole time, was not there. Asher Winegarten had been so well known, so well loved and respected, that I was at a loss for something adequate to say. The NFU had been his life, and the debt we all owed to him was immense and could never be repaid.

Asher and I had led a team in Europe, and I knew that he had been as sad as I that we had not made more progress in the EEC. The positive line that Britain had once taken as a nation, back in the 1960s, had not been continued. I believed that the best thing for Britain in the face of that defeat was to renew the European commitment and to press forward once again. We missed the boat once, and we had been trying to catch up ever since. Time was running short in which to avoid missing out again, and we now needed an honest display of our good intentions in order to regain some of the goodwill I feared we'd lost. If the British had lost their way in recent years, it might have been because there was no signpost, no vision towards which to strive. We were still a strong, proud and capable people, but strength became brute force if it was not used wisely and with compassion.

Since I had been NFU President, I had preached a sermon or two – and although I had not intended to add to that number at 'Plumb's last stand' (as I found out later some had been less than awe-inspired enough to call it), a text that used to be popular with the old-time preachers who toured the rural circuits sprang to mind for the occasion.

It came from Proverbs (Chapter 29, verse 18) and reads, 'Where there is no vision, the people perish'. In Europe, and at home, we needed some kind of political leadership that would give us vision – vision not only of the better future I was sure we would find in the Community if we looked enthusiastically enough, but also vision to help our people give the agitators and the wreckers permanent notice that, despite their opposition, we did not intend to perish and we *did* intend to look for fulfilment of our hopes and dreams.

Sooner or later the wise man forms a strong bond with his neighbours. We learned that a long time ago in the NFU, and despite the problems of fragmentation and diversity that separated us in the physical sense, we British farmers had the most effectively united lobby group in Europe – the only one, according to an acknowledged expert, to compare with the great political lobbies of the United States. Our problems had not prevented us from forming a real Union of the independent and hardworking people who ran the kind of individual businesses that were the backbone of Britain.

If we British farmers could preserve the family feeling in agriculture, surely we British people could all preserve it throughout the UK?

It has been said that optimists and pessimists are basically the same people – except that the pessimist's glass is half empty and the optimist's glass is half full. We had seen troubles enough, but after 15 years I was still an optimist, for agriculture, and for Britain.

There was much to work and hope for, and I believed there was little we could not attain so long as we never lost sight of our vision, or forgot the purpose behind our high endeavour. I hoped that whatever happened thereafter, I would be able to continue serving the British people, agriculture, and the NFU in some way or another.

6

A NEW DIMENSION

I am not a politician, and my other habits are good.
(Artemus Ward [Charles F. Browne], 1834–1867)

It was only natural that my interest in the tremendous changes taking place in agriculture – the many research programmes for further agricultural development, increasing production, and the food safety associated with that production – all in time got me more and more involved in agricultural politics.

It had started way back in 1959 when I became representative for Warwickshire on the Council of the NFU, then to be appointed to the Vice-Presidency in 1964, and the deputy Presidency in 1966. And the politics involved were specifically 'agricultural politics', because I always felt, as President of the National Farmers Union, that it would be wrong for me to be affiliated to – or even known to favour – any particular political party. So I never was, during that period of time. After all, in my job it was essential that I could work with *all* parties.

There are farmers around who will say even today, 'You know – some of the best times we had in agriculture were under a Labour Minister, rather than a Conservative.' I'm not sure that that's true, especially if you look into the overall effect of levels of taxation and the myriad other outside effects that agriculture experienced, in common with other industries in the country.

The notion of my entering party politics, rather than continuing to represent 'sectoral' politics on behalf of, and within the agricultural industry, was sparked off by the opportune timing of the first direct elections to the European Parliament in June 1979. Some six months earlier I had announced my intention to step down from the NFU Presidency, and I had since then been earnestly wondering what to do next. In fact, I had drawn up a sort of short-list of possible activities involving a range of options – not at all unlike the story of the policeman who took a promotional exam and was faced with the question:

Consider the flowing scenario and state in not more than a hundred words what you would do, and in which order:

(1) You arrive at the scene of an accident.

(2) There is a car overturned in the ditch.

(3) The driver is standing by the car, looking distressed.

(4) Inside you recognise the wife of your Inspector.

(5) You notice a bus coming towards you travelling on the wrong side of the double white line.

(6) You see a man coming out of a crowded pub opposite, drunkenly walking towards his car.

(7) You perceive a dog walking up the road without a collar.

The policeman's answer was straightforward: 'I would take off my uniform and mingle with the crowd.'

One day I talked the situation over with my son John, who was carrying on the day-to-day management of the family farm. When I asked him what he thought I should do, he replied at once, 'Since you're always complaining about the state of the yard, you could make a start by sweeping it!' At that moment I decided to present myself as a Conservative candidate at the polls in June!

On a more serious note, it was my good friend Sir James Spicer who persuaded me to put my name forward as a candidate. He was himself deeply involved in political representation, carrying the dual mandate of Westminster and Brussels, and he convinced me that it would not be unduly onerous or time-consuming. This, of course, turned out not to be the case.

The transition was easily made, since many of the issues I was interested in were also of acute party interest (and were to become increasingly so over the years). I had been astonished once, during my NFU days, to be accused by a Minister of ganging up with other farmers to 'paint all the fields blue'! There was of course no truth in it, for in keeping with the traditions of the NFU, my original political school, I had never declared for a personal party colour. But it was certainly the case that I did not believe in the nationalisation of anything – whether of oil or onions – or indeed in some of the other tenets of traditional socialism popular at that time. For me, only the Conservative Party was promulgating the policies capable of achieving the goals I wished to see realised – a sound free-enterprise economic policy, an emphasis on the responsibilities and liberties of the individual, and an effective and credible defence programme.

And as for Europe, which I was interested in generally as well as deeply involved in professionally – wasn't the Conservative Party 'the party of Europe', looking back to the post-war vision of Churchill, the travails of Macmillan and the eventual success of Heath? To me the Community provided the framework for the only credible role for my country, in answer to former US Secretary of State Dean Acheson's famous dictum about Britain's post-imperial dilemma ('Great Britain [...] has lost an empire and not yet found a role', 1962).

I had been delighted by the 2-1 positive outcome of the 1973 Referendum. The approach of the ageing Harold Macmillan, as he outlined it in a broadcast just before the vote, seemed to me to focus on the key issue in a way that remains valid today. During the campaign there had been considerable debate over agricultural supplies and prices – much of it ludicrous to anyone who knew anything about the realities of the world food market. I could hardly believe my ears, for example, when Peter Shore solemnly assured the nation that abundant cheap food could be grown on what he called 'Britain's other farms in Canada, Australia and New Zealand'!

Macmillan opened his broadcast with the words 'I am not here tonight to talk to you about the price of butter. I'm here to talk to you about the map of Europe.' And he went on to give a masterly geo-political lecture on the continental context of British national interests.

I met him only once during that campaign. We came away together from a rally at which Christopher Soames had given a rousing pro-European speech. I expressed my admiration for Soames's rallying-call, and especially for the wonderful rhetorical phrases he had used.

'Wonderful phrases . . .', mused Macmillan slowly. 'Hmm, yes, indeed. They were mostly *my* phrases.' Then, throwing back his head, he gave one of his rare guffaws.

My experience in matters European had, of course, a great deal to do with the price of butter, since at that time – and indeed at the European elections of 1979 – there was no doubt about the Conservative Party's vision of a Britain at least being able to play an enthusiastic and leading role in the development of the EEC. The Thatcherite tragedy lay in the future. I call it a 'tragedy' advisedly, for I believe that Margaret Thatcher's mistaken attitude to Europe not only led, indirectly, to her own political downfall –sad enough in itself, given her outstanding achievements in other fields – but its baneful consequences are still with us today, in both party and country.

In April 1979, at a time when I was still President of the IFAP (International Federation of Agricultural Producers) and had to start campaigning for the European Parliament, I found time nevertheless to go to the 23rd IFAP Conference which, that year, was held in Italy. National farm leaders from fifty countries and representatives of twenty international organisations concerned with farming and food problems took part in the week-long talks of this unique world parliament of farmers. The programme featured discussions on three major issues. Firstly, the impact the GATT multinational trade agreement (then nearing completion of the first round) would have on farmers worldwide. Secondly, the input farmers should make into the forthcoming World Conference on agrarian reform and rural development. And thirdly, a programme of action on farm commodity markets, which itself comprised preparation for input into the 5th United Nations Conference on Trade and Development.

Immediately prior to this conference, farmer representatives in their various groups had held discussions on specific commodity sectors. The group focusing on grains, for instance, had reviewed the situation on the world grains market following the failure of governments to negotiate an international grain arrangement, and had looked into the costs of grain production around the world. The group on sugar discussed the market outlook and the international sugar agreement covering trade.

Sugar is one of the world's key crops – and high on the list as one of Europe's most sensitive topics. Although it is still in its early stages, many people believe that in not too many years' time sugar will replace petroleum as the major source of fuel for motor transport and for the feedstock industry.

There was also a group concentrating on dairy products. Their particularly controversial topic was butter, which they discussed at length in relation to the world butter market. But they also considered dairy products in relation to international food aid, and the new proposals for an international dairy arrangement worked out within the GATT negotiations. These proposals in fact mirrored the terms of a draft agreement put forward by IFAP as early as in 1971.

The group on meats and feedstuffs examined the revised version of the world's meat producers' charter, and looked at the overall prospects for the livestock and meat sectors in the key producing and importing countries.

Farmers travelled from all over the world to the conference, many under their own steam and using their own funds, prepared to pool their thoughts and ideas, to learn from each other, and to actively co-operate.

IFAP is an organisation whose members may have widely differing beliefs, but they share first and foremost a strong notion of fair competition for all countries. The organisation was established in 1946, and was the creation of one of my predecessors in the National Farmers Union, Lord Netherthorpe. For years it was the sole worldwide farmers' organisation, the membership consisting of sixty national-level farm organisations spread across six out of seven continents. Representation stretched from the subsistence farmer in Niger and Indonesia to the large producer in the United States and Argentina; from sugar-cane cartels in Australia and Jamaica to the small dairy farmer in Scandinavia; from members of agricultural co-operatives in what was then Yugoslavia to wheat-pool members in Saskatchewan, Canada.

IFAP's many activities cover all types of farms and farmers. Regional Committees meet in Europe, North America and the Pacific area to look after the more political interests of farming groups. Various Committees on Agricultural Co-operation within the developing countries get together on a fairly regular basis. The Committees themselves may pool information and resources. By the year 2000 IFAP incorporated 84 different organisations all over the world.

The experience of taking part in these forums opened my eyes not only to the complexities of the food chain and its economics on a worldwide scale, but, more parochially, to the increasing opportunities for British producers to participate with greater energy in international trade. Traditionally an industrial nation that imported a significant percentage of its food, the United Kingdom had never seriously explored the possibilities of value-added agricultural products and their exportation. I could also foresee that there would be a burgeoning need to export agricultural knowhow to many developing nations, particularly in Africa, to help them feed their ever-expanding populations. In some of these countries today, despite infant mortality rates higher than 25 per cent and, in more recent years, the ravages of the AIDS epidemic, demographic growth can be as high as 3 per cent per year (as it is, for example, in Malawi).

I was enthusiastic about furthering an international approach to all these problems, and saw the EEC as a key element in the search for solutions. Despite British reservations about the Common Agricultural Policy, I believed that we should participate in it to the full. We should also review the CAP itself, for even by the end of the 1970s it had begun to be a victim of its own success: most commodities were being produced in quantities not just enough to secure supplies but in abundance, which led on to problems of costly storage and wasted expenditure.

It was natural that when I came to present myself as a candidate in the European elections in June 1979, people should think of me primarily as an agriculturalist. This was actually far from being an advantage in the constituency of the Cotswolds where I decided to make my bid, for although there is a certain amount of agricultural activity practised in that delightful area – indeed, the Royal Agricultural College is situated in Cirencester, one of the main towns of the constituency – it is not an essentially agricultural region in the way that, for example, parts of Lincolnshire and East Anglia are. The towns of Cheltenham, Gloucester, Stroud, Tewkesbury and Whitney were far more influentially represented on the Conservative Euro-Association, the body whose duty it was to select the party's candidate.

Lord Blake was Chairman of the Interviewing Committee. I came through the early rounds of the selection process without incident, but faced stiff competition on the final short-list from other candidates, including Sir Guy Millard, a former British Ambassador in Rome, and Richard Simmonds, who had been the head of Ted Heath's Private Office in the 1960s (and who would later become an MEP for another constituency, and a close friend and colleague of mine).

The most gruelling part of the selection procedure – apart, of course, from having to wait for the final decision – was the ten-minute 'pitch' each aspiring candidate was invited to make.

I decided on a frontal assault.

'Many of you will think of me as "the farmer's friend",' I began. And as I paused for effect, I sensed an expectation among my audience that I would go on to say, 'But . . .'

Instead, I simply said, 'And so I am.'

The tension was broken at once, and I do believe that that was the moment which swayed things in my favour.

I was delighted to obtain the nomination as Conservative candidate.

All the same, had I been a true born-and-bred politician, my 'pitch' might have been far more closely geared to the thoughts and expectations of my audience. It might perhaps even have reflected something of the methods of a Frenchman who was one day in the future to become a colleague of mine. He, in France and a Frenchman, was known to enjoy whisky more than cognac – and was questioned about this issue as the elections approached. He thereupon wrote to all his constituents:

Dear Elector,

I had not intended to discuss this controversial subject at this time. However, I do not run away from controversy. I will take a stand on *any* issue, at *any* time, regardless of how controversial it may be. You have asked me how I feel about whisky and I will tell you.

If, when you say *whisky*, you mean the devil's brew, the poisonous scourge, the bloody monster that creates misery and poverty, and literally takes the bread from the mouths of children ...

If you mean the evil that topples Christian men and women from the pinnacles of righteousness and from gracious living and brings them down to the bottomless pit of degradation and despair, shame, helplessness and hopelessness ...

Then certainly, I am against it with all my power.

But **if**, when you say *whisky*, you mean the medium that is the lubricant oil of conversation, the wine of philosophy, the ale that is consumed when good fellows get together and that puts laughter on their lips, the warm glow of contentment in their eyes ...

If you mean the drink that enables a man to increase his joy and his happiness, and to forget if only for a little while life's great tragedies, heartbreaks and sorrows ...

If you mean that same drink which pours into our Treasuries millions of Francs that in turn provide tender care for our little crippled children, our blind, our deaf and dumb, our aged and infirm, and allows us to build highways, hospitals and schools ...

Then I am certainly in favour of it.

This is my view, and I will not compromise.

For me, the election campaign, which lasted for three weeks, was a distinctly strange experience. Because the election was the first of its kind, there was no form-book and no party had given much thought as to how to communicate in the new constituencies, each of which contained an electorate of approximately half a million. Fortunately, from a Conservative point of view, our main opposition – the Labour Party, who had been opposed to British membership of the EEC – had been almost completely demoralised by their defeat at the hands of Mrs Thatcher in the General

Election only weeks before. Indeed, some Conservative candidates concentrated exclusively on energising party workers to get the voters out, and made no attempt to contribute to, let alone stimulate, public debate.

A fellow candidate of mine, Eric Forth – who later made a fine Ministerial career for himself at Westminster – even went so far as to forbid his agent to do anything at all to put his name in front of the public, on the grounds that it might actually alert Labour voters to the existence of the elections.

That may have been good party tactics, but it was scarcely good for democracy or the cause of Europe.

Campaigning, too, was a strange experience. With an electorate of 500,000 scattered over a constituency of some 1,500 square miles (3,885 square kilometres), where did one begin? A central feature of my campaign was factory visits. One of these in particular stands out in my memory.

The manager of an engineering factory in Cheltenham had given my team permission to try our luck at attracting and holding the attention of the workforce during their afternoon tea break in the canteen. Opposition and heckling would have been fun – their general apathy was more difficult to deal with. It was hard going. We were expending a lot of energy and getting virtually no response at all. One group of card-players at a table was pointed out to me as being the hardcore militant-left shop-steward leadership. As I passed them on our way out, one of them shouted to me, 'What yer going to do in this Eurothing for *me*, then?'

'Damn all,' I replied.

'Hey!' he said to his mates, 'I might just vote for this geezer. He speaks our language.'

Despite my feeling that I wasn't really getting to grips with the electorate, or the election, thanks to the good work done by our loyal party supporters, and the reputation the party at that time enjoyed as the one with the sensible policies on Europe, enough people did vote for 'this geezer' to see me on my way to Strasbourg, Luxembourg and Brussels, the three 'workplaces' of the European Parliament.

Top Left: On Shanklin Pier with parents
Top Right: With calf in show ring
Bottom: With 4 grandees outside church

Caption: Family holidays in the Isle of Wight and local pride at the
Midlands Show. From muddy boots to full rig with four former presidents of the
NFU, Ken Knowles, Lord Netherthorpe, Lord Woolley, Sir Gwilym Williams.

Top: World Food Conference 1988
Bottom Left: With Ray and tractor
Bottom Right: With Cattle in market

Caption: Talking food and doing agriculture, linking the statesman, the farmer and the price of cattle. With Kenneth Kuanda in Brussels in 1988; with Ray Price, head tractor driver on the farm at Coleshill, 1973; and admiring cattle in the local market.

Top: Tractor: £600 million in the red
Bottom Left: With Fischler
Bottom Right: At Royal Show

Caption: Speaking up for farming: demonstrating by tractor at Haverford
West with John Davies in 1970; arguing with Commissioner Fischler in Brussels
in 1983; and receiving the RASE Gold Medal at the Royal Show for services to
agriculture, Stoneleigh 1983.

Top Left: With Whitelaw & Pym
Top Right: With Reagan
Bottom: Election in European Parliament

Caption: As NFU President petitioning Conservative Shadow Ministers
William Whitelaw and Francis Pym in 1974. With Ronald Reagan in the White
House in 1987, and elected President of the European Parliament in Strasbourg
also in 1987.

Top: With Thatcher
Bottom: With Conservative MEPs

Caption: More hand to hand than eye to eye with Mrs Thatcher, on her visit to the European Parliament in 1989; but proud to serve with the Conservative MEPs in 1994: (*front row, from left to right*): Anne McIntosh, Caroline Jackson, HP, Tom Spencer, Sir Jack Stewart-Clark, James Provan. (*Back row, from left to right*): Brendan Donnelly, Giles Chichester, Robert Sturdy, Brian Cassidy, James Moorhouse, James Elles, Edward Kellet-Bowman, Edward McMillan-Scott, John Stevens, Graham Mather, Roy Perry, John Corrie.

Top: With Kohl
Bottom: With Arafat
Caption: With Chancellor Kohl, the architect of the new Europe, in Bonn
in 1988, and flanked by Rudi Arndt, a leading German MEP, receiving Yasser
Arafat on a peace mission to the European Parliament the same year.

Top: With Major
Bottom: With Pope

Caption: Happy times with John Major at a European Parliament
reception in Brussels 1992, and a privileged moment being received by Pope
John Paul II in Rome in 1988.

Top: With Africans
Middle: In China (duck)
Bottom: In Mauritania (traditional dress)

Caption: The well travelled international statesman: in Burundi and Rwanda with Glenys Kinnock MEP in 1994, inspecting the duck for dinner in Beijing in 1988, and in traditional dress in Mauritania in 1995.

7

THE NEW EUROPEAN PARLIAMENT

> This is not the end. It is not even the beginning of the
> end. But it is, perhaps, the end of the beginning.
> (Winston Churchill)

The British press devoted very little by way of serious coverage to the opening of the new, directly elected European Parliament, which met for the first time in Strasbourg in July 1979. There was, it is true, some comment in the broadsheets on the election as President of Simone Veil, a French Liberal and ex-Minister of Health, who had for several years topped the political popularity polls in France. Because she was also a survivor of Auschwitz, her election seemed to have an extra symbolic significance as a sign of a happier Europe.

However, the fact that Ian Paisley, elected as one of the three MEPs from Northern Ireland, was able to point out on a point of order in the plenary that the Union Jack hoisted alongside the other national flags outside the Palace of Europe was being flown upside down – technically a sign of distress requiring assistance – attracted almost as many column inches.

Such trivialisation was to be the hallmark of most of the British media's coverage, with the singular and honourable exception of *The Financial Times*, for the next 20 years. I suppose it was merely an extension of the underlying attitude in Britain to the European Community as a whole – as though somehow Britain hadn't quite joined the strange, foreign enterprise, which was consequently not to be taken too seriously.

On the other hand, 'knocking' copy was of course always given prominent coverage: olive oil scandals, Commissioners' personal expenses, a rumour that production of the traditional British sausage was to be prohibited by Brussels, and suchlike. But the bare fact that the United Kingdom was an integral part of a continuing operation aimed at European integration remained shrouded from the average newspaper-reader.

Nor was the fundamental importance of EC membership or of the European institutions likely to be pointed out by our national political leaders, least of all by Mrs Thatcher, who had assumed office just before the Euro-elections. She had not by that time revealed, as she would several years later, her visceral objections to the whole European enterprise, but even at the most superficial level of image politics she was keen to demonstrate her policies as quite distinct from – if not ultimately opposed to – those of Ted Heath. And hadn't British membership of the community been her predecessor's finest achievement?

Of course, the political neglect of European affairs was not just down to Mrs Thatcher. It resulted more from what I think might be termed the 'Westminster is the centre of the universe' syndrome. The uniquely dominant role Westminster has enjoyed in our national life over several centuries has been of immense benefit to our society and democracy, giving a comprehensible focus to our affairs and constituting a universally-accepted forum in which the great issues of the day can be thrashed out in public, the laws of the land determined, and the Government – itself drawn from the Parliament – held to account.

In no other major European country does the national Parliament occupy a stronger position in public opinion. However, there is a downside in the modern world to this Westminster-centric aspect of British public life. It is that the news media, in covering political affairs, focus much too closely on the national Parliament, with the underlying and largely unchallenged assumption that what is not on the agenda at Westminster cannot be too important.

That does not mean that European affairs are altogether neglected. On the contrary, they sometimes fill the headlines – but rarely as European developments *per se*, and almost always as viewed through the prismatic lens of Westminster.

This problem is further complicated by the simple fact that while national parliaments will continue to have an important role to play, major legislation and policy determination will more and more take place at the European centre. That is one of the inevitable effects of the European integration process – and it is, institutionally, a bitter pill for any national Parliament to swallow in the interests of pooled sovereignty. For a Parliament as proud and strong as Westminster, it is a most unpalatably bitter pill to swallow. This explains why there has been a general tendency to play down the full significance of British membership of the (as it has now become) European Union.

Interestingly, it is a tendency that is not so much marked in the House of Lords, which I have always found to be much more aware of, and indeed positively disposed towards, matters European than the House of Commons.

One recurring item of negative comment about the European Parliament, which dates from its earliest days, refers to the so-called 'three workplaces'. It is a criticism with which I wholeheartedly agree – and I believe the reasons for such a nonsense should be understood by all, especially by the European taxpayers who have to foot the bill and who should be encouraged to press for change, not only in the interests of simplicity and (sacred buzzword of the 1990s) transparency, but of budgetary savings.

The position is this.

Strasbourg is the official seat of the European Parliament, which now has a Treaty obligation, since Amsterdam 1997, to hold twelve 'part-sessions' in that city each year. In practice, one is held every month except August, and the one missing is compensated for by holding two part-sessions in October. A part-session technically lasts from a Monday afternoon until the next Friday mid-day, but whether a shorter part-session would be compatible with the treaties remains an issue still to be put to the judicial test – as I expect it soon will be.

In addition to the Strasbourg part-sessions, additional plenary sessions are held – typically for one full day and two half-days – in six weeks of the year in Brussels. Again the limit on the number and duration of these Brussels plenaries has not been tested in the European Court of Justice. It is in Brussels that the twenty or so Standing Committees hold most of their meetings for two weeks every month. Likewise, the political groups usually hold their monthly meeting in Brussels in the remaining week of the cycle, although they occasionally hold this meeting elsewhere in the EU as 'study days' – a frequent embarrassment for northern Puritans – about which more later.

To add to the complication, the seat of the General Secretariat (i.e. the Civil Service) of Parliament is in Luxembourg, thus condemning many officials whose work relates to a direct parliamentary service to shuttle between Luxembourg, Strasbourg and Brussels, and the taxpayer to bear the extra cost.

Why this 'geographical dislocation' (to use the Euro-jargon for this state of affairs)?

The original reason was that when the EEC was being set up, there was an understandable desire among its founders to spread its physical institutional presence in order to raise the profile of the new enterprise in as many member states as possible, and to avoid the impression of over-centralisation. Smaller states were also to receive special favour – hence the choice of Brussels and Luxembourg as sites of important institutions.

Strasbourg enjoyed a special symbolic significance as the capital of Alsace, which had for centuries been something of a political football between French and German territorial claims, passing from one jurisdiction to the other no fewer than five times in even fewer centuries. Now that the ideological bedrock of the new Europe was Franco-German reconciliation, what better place to house one of the new institutions than a pleasant French city on the very borders of Germany, a city in which the local *patois* was essentially Germanic, and of which the university had been the *alma mater* of Wolfgang Goethe, the German Shakespeare?

Symbols are, however, not always comfortable in practice. The abiding drawback to Strasbourg – despite its charms and the ceaseless efforts of its authorities, citizenry and innkeepers to be impeccable hosts – is its lack of size. With a population of a little over a quarter of a million, the city was never going to have the transport services – particularly air links – to the capitals and major regional centres of even the original six member states, let alone the current fifteen and the likely twenty to twenty-five of the early decades of the 21st century.

For example, whereas flights between London and Brussels are virtually hourly throughout the day, flights to Strasbourg are limited to one or two per day, and direct links between Strasbourg and regional airports outside France are almost non-existent. I believe this transport handicap may prove fatal for Strasbourg in the long run, despite the extraordinarily vigorous efforts in defence of the city's interest mounted by successive French governments.

Strasbourg's handicap is made worse by an attraction from another direction, for it is Brussels where the lion's share of business is conducted by the European Commission and the Council of Ministers. And as the role of the Parliament becomes more and more directly focused on that business, the desire of MEPs to have a fixed institutional abode – with all the necessary attendant facilities – in the same city is bound to increase.

I also believe that the bringing of the activities of the Parliament in Brussels together with those of the Council and Commission would help project a better image for all three institutions. On the doorstep in my own constituency I found myself frequently reproached for all too apparently 'jaunting about at taxpayers' expense'. The fact that the decision on the Parliament's seat lies not with the Parliament but with the governments of the member states was small consolation to me, and none at all to my constituents.

Removal of the 'geographical dislocation' would not only bring savings of around £85 million per year – a small sum perhaps in the context of the EU's gross 'domestic' product, although one that could undoubtedly be put to good productive use – but would significantly increase the efficiency of the Parliament as an institution, and of its individual members (not to mention the European Commission and their personal staffs, who also have to trek to Strasbourg for at least part of the Strasbourg week, as do the Ministers of the member state currently holding the Presidency of the Council, which changes every six months.)

I had an inkling of all these problems in that very first part-session in July 1979. My flight from Birmingham to London was late, I missed the connection with the 'members' flight' to Strasbourg, and I then had to wait hours for another one, bouncing off Lille. In Strasbourg members from other countries complained of similar vicissitudes. Such laments were to become part of the monthly ritual.

Once I was into my stride as an MEP and had survived a few part-sessions in Strasbourg, I would sometimes ruefully reflect – as I went to bed exhausted after a 16-hour day – on the disparity between the popular image in Britain of an MEP's life and the experienced reality. Perhaps because of our insular geographical position, and our history as a nation that therefore spread its business across the high seas and throughout the big wide world, we have tended to associate neighbouring continental France with frivolity, levity and leisure-time activities. Newspaper photos of the fulsome buffet in the Members' Dining Room or of the annual asparagus festival organised by the Strasbourg authorities as part of their charm offensive, serve only to reinforce this image.

The reality, alas, is very different.

The average MEP, who has spent the weekend, like his Westminster counterpart, attending activities in his constituency – which in my case covered a total of seven national constituencies – must get up well before dawn and face the rigours of two flights before arriving in his office in Brussels or Strasbourg. Waiting for him will be a great pile of papers, mostly relating to his work in two Standing Committees, the facts and details of which he will have to master as quickly as possible, with the help of background and advice papers from the Committee secretariats, his political group and his own research assistant, who will have assembled information from a variety of sources. During the day he will, as well as attending his Committee meetings, meet several visitors, a number of whom will be from industrial or commercial sectors likely to be affected by proposed legislation and who come to lobby in favour of their point of view.

Such lobbying, incidentally, may appear on the face of it to be opening the door to allowing 'undue influence' to be brought to bear, but I believe that most MEPs, and certainly the Commission, would agree, on balance, that the easy access the European system offers to virtually all comers is not only a democratic plus but a source of very useful information and advice from real practitioners – information and advice that can help towards improving European policies and, in particular, legislation. It does mean, however, that the conscientious MEP is obliged to devote a great deal of time to listening to and evaluating such advice.

But back to the daily grind.

There is often a party political meeting to be fitted in at the end of the MEP's day. Only on rare and cherished occasions did I manage to have the sort of leisurely supper of *fruits de mer* or *turbotin aux poireaux* in one of Brussels' excellent restaurants that my constituents no doubt fondly imagined was part of my daily routine. I kept a small flat a short walking-distance from the Parliament's main building in Brussels, and it was usually a case of leaving it at 7.30 in the morning and not getting back to it until around midnight.

Once a month the British Conservative MEPs met for three days in London, usually in hired rooms in Church House, which ostensibly gave our party colleagues at Westminster an opportunity to liaise with us. Few did, although we frequently managed to arrange for a Minister to brief us on some topic of current interest. It was not for many years, and following persistent pressure on our part, that MEPs were eventually granted better-than-public entry rights to the Palace of Westminster – and that, I may say, was symptomatic of how we, and indeed the Labour MEPs, were viewed by the political establishment.

After every such meeting in London, it was necessary to put all our group and personal papers into large steel boxes that were then sent overland by lorry to be delivered to our offices in Strasbourg. All this packing and unpacking of multifarious files, reports and papers was a dreadful bore and a terrible waste of time – but it became part of our routine, repeated several times a month.

As British Conservatives in the European Parliament, we had a different sort of 'group life' from that of most other representatives of major national political parties. That was because initially, and indeed until the arrival of the Spaniards in 1986, we were virtually alone, having only two Danish Conservatives and one Ulster Unionist for company. The political groups in the European Parliament are really rather loose coalitions of basically like-minded national parties – Socialists, Liberals, Christian Democrats, and so on – and in order to encourage transnational bondings, the rules governing the setting up of groups lay down a minimum number, which decreases on a sliding scale as more nationalities are included in the group. Because we Conservatives were by ourselves already 63 in number, thanks to the first-past-the-post electoral system in force in the UK, we could, if we'd wanted to, have comprised an official group just by ourselves.

Some feelers were put out towards, and from, the Christian Democrats, who sit in the Parliament under the (to English ears) slightly confusing label of 'the European People's Party'. But quite a few of our number were put off by the excessively federal rhetoric of some of the CD leaders, even as some of them – especially the Belgian and Dutch MEPs drawn from trade union backgrounds – harboured grave reservations over people whom they saw as Mrs Thatcher's disciples.

A different possibility, and one desultorily canvassed by the more Francophile of our members, would have been an alliance with the Gaullists, many of whose policies were in fact similar to our own. But their wily leader, Christian de la Malène, while unfailingly friendly towards us, was not keen to become a junior partner to the British, and preferred instead to remain the senior partner in an alliance with the Irish Fianna Fáil representatives who, in turn – because of the way it would inevitably be construed back home – could not be seen even to contemplate being in coalition, however loosely constituted, with the Tories.

We had a problem regarding our name – more for semantic than ideologically substantive reasons. 'Conservative' translates directly into the major European languages, but in general has a distinct tinge of 'reactionary' in its meaning (just as, paradoxically, 'People's Party' to English ears is somehow more redolent of Erich Honecker than of Helmut Kohl). So we called ourselves the European Democratic Group

... and set about the business of influencing the development of Europe according to our particular lights.

At any one time in the European Parliament there are seven or eight political groups, and usually between fifteen and forty-five non-attached members who either cannot or do not wish to join in the activities of any of the groups on offer.

There are several advantages in being part of a group. Firstly, in terms of resources, the Parliamentary budget makes available to each group, in proportion to its numerical strength, an annual financial allocation for its political activities and information campaigns, plus support staff who are directly answerable to the group. In political terms, the leader of each political group is an *ex-officio* member of what is nowadays called the Conference of Chairmen (or Presidents). This meets once or twice a month, under the Chairmanship of the Parliamentary President, to take the more politically sensitive decisions on behalf of the institution as a whole – for example, as regards agendas – although the right of ultimate decisions in fundamental matters is jealously reserved for the House in plenary session, to which the Conference of Chairmen can, of course, make influential proposals.

Within each group, spokesmen or co-ordinators are appointed to take responsibility for specific areas of policy, usually related organisationally to the work of the sectoral Standing Committees of Parliament. Within the larger groups, each national delegation may have its own spokesman. It is by means of the regular reporting of these spokesmen via briefing documents that an individual Member can keep himself abreast of what is going on across the whole spectrum of parliamentary activity. He can then be advised, through the party or group 'whip', on how he should vote on particular issues in the light of overall policies.

Because 'proportionality' is a key concept within the European Parliament, the bigger the political group the bigger the clout, not only in resources but in speaking time and influence generally. The obverse of the coin is that within either of the two major groups – the Christian Democrats and the Socialists – each national party delegation is in competition with the other components of the group for posts of responsibility, speaking time, and so on. But on balance I have always favoured being part of the larger entity, and I rejoiced when we were joined by the Spanish Alianza Popular. It might be easier to reach agreed group positions in a smaller group in which the British Conservatives dominated, but the discussions lacked the bite of the international exchange of ideas, and ultimately there was a feeling of isolation, not always splendid in nature.

The Right–Left divide in the European Parliament has never been a simple matter to calculate because some of the smaller groups and national party representatives within groups have tended to vote one way on one set of issues and another way on others. For example, the Italian Communists and the German Greens could occasionally find themselves, to our considerable mutual embarrassment, supporting a British Tory point of view on budgetary matters, whereas on such matters as European defence issues, or energy policy, they would be poles apart from us. In general, nevertheless, the overall balance of voting power lay with the Left, taking all its components into consideration, throughout the period 1979 to 1999, and swung in favour of the Centre-Right only after the European elections in June of that latter year.

On the Centre-Right, the four groups – the Christian Democrats, ourselves, the Liberals, and the Radical Alliance (of which the Gaullists were the main component) – did their best to co-ordinate their positions through regular meetings of their sectoral spokesmen and monthly meetings of their Chairmen. I have to say, however, that although I never felt satisfied with the degree of coherence this achieved, it did on occasions save the day when concerted efforts were made by the Left on some particularly thorny issues, such as the deployment of Cruise missiles, or, in another category of importance altogether, support for Arthur Scargill's miners' strike in 1984–85.

Matters of lesser ideological significance in the fields of logistical organisation and staff matters are dealt with by another centre of decision-taking, the Bureau of Parliament, which is made up of the President, the fourteen Vice-Presidents and five (non-voting) Quaestors. This last category is one 'inherited' from the practice and custom of Parliaments in southern Europe. The Quaestors' main function is to monitor all matters that affect the day-to-day activities of individual Members, and to arbitrate in such matters as disputes over allowances and privileges. In other words, they are shop stewards on the works council.

A third forum in which decisions are taken is the Conference of Committee Chairmen, which meets monthly, largely to facilitate planning of the longer-term parliamentary programme of legislation, session by session, and of such other activities as Parliamentary Hearings, to which outside experts, as well as representatives of the

Commission and Council are invited to provide a European-wide focus on specific topics of interest.

Each Standing Committee is constituted on the d'Hondt system of proportional representation, which means that in theory it should politically be a microcosm of the House as a whole. In practice that is broadly, but not exactly, true, since, unsurprisingly, agriculturalists tend to make a bid for membership of the Agricultural Committee, feminists for the Womens' Rights Committee, lawyers for the Legal Affairs Committee, green ecologists for the Environment Committee, and so on. However, the fact that all important reports from Committees eventually come to the floor of the House, where they can be amended, largely corrects any political distortion that may have taken place at Committee level.

Each MEP is normally a full member of one committee and a substitute member of another. Appointments to – and removals from! – committees are in the gift of the group Chairman, who also exercises a minor amount of patronage through the appointment of group representatives on the European Parliament delegations to other parliaments worldwide.

Among the Standing Committees, undoubtedly the most influential are the Budgets Committee and the Budgetary Control Committee – for the obvious reason that they play a key role in one of the Parliament's major spheres of influence. As in many national parliaments there is frequent tension between these 'moneybags' and the other Standing Committees – and indeed between them and the other two power centres of the institution: the group Chairmen and the Bureau. Even after twenty years the European Parliament has not fully succeeded in defining clearly who decides what, and perhaps such an ideal can never be realised. I personally believe that the situation could be much improved, perhaps by means of a thoroughgoing examination of the problem in all its aspects by a body made up of representatives of all the fora involved.

Each legislative period of five years is divided into two halves. At the beginning and after two and a half years all the posts of responsibility in the three main spheres – the Bureau, the Conference of Group Chairmen, and the Committee Chairmen and Vice-Chairmen (and the Chairman of Chairmen!) plus the lesser offices of Delegation Chairmen and Vice-Chairmen – come up for election. In reality, the results of most of these elections simply reflect the relative strength of the groups, the number of national delegations within groups, and the political clout of individuals within national delegations.

All together, the MEPs elected to these posts of responsibility constitute the fifty or so 'big men on the campus' who largely determine the general thrust of Parliament's business. To appreciate the importance of this nucleus of decision-takers, bear in mind that – unlike a Westminster-style Parliament – there is no government, no Cabinet drawn from the ranks of the European Parliament that might otherwise provide leadership. In that specific respect the European Parliament is more akin to the House of Representatives in the United States as part of an overall institutional system of checks and balances. Mind you, the European Parliament obviously has a long way to go before it achieves the political power of its US counterpart.

The European Democratic Group confronted this new and complicated world with enthusiasm. Looking back, I realise we were a very mixed bunch indeed.

Some, like our leader Sir James Scott-Hopkins, and Sir Tom Normanton, had attended Westminster for years and had even had ministerial experience. Others, such as Dame Shelagh Roberts and Lady Elles, had had distinguished careers in local government. Yet others brought with them their experience of non-political public life, such as Sir Fred Catherwood, past Chairman of the National Economic Development Council (commonly known as NEDDY), and Sir Fred Warner, a former Ambassador to Japan and an expert in international relations. There were big businessmen too, such as Sir David Nicholson, Chairman of Rothmans, and Boz Ferranti, head of the electronics firm. Ideological homogeneity was definitely not our strong point, which frequently irritated the party managers in London, but we were united by a belief in the importance of making the European Parliament – and the European ideal in general – work in practical terms, and in the importance of injecting as much as possible of our British Conservative values into the process.

Believing that I should start by trying to do what I know best, I managed to be nominated as a member of the Agricultural Committee. I then endeavoured to become its Chairman. My interest was not just in agriculture as such, or in the Common Agricultural Policy – which I thought was clearly in need of radical reform – but in the wider aspects of how European farming related to such other issues as the environment and the development of Third World economies. In short, the *leitmotiv* of my political and professional activities was 'world food and how it is produced'. Such highfalutin ideals very quickly collided with bare-knuckle politics in the background manoeuvrings surrounding the decision on the chairmanship of the Committee.

The d'Hondt system of proportional representation and the known priorities of the political groups soon made clear that the choice lay between myself and Michel Debatisse, a French Member who had been Chairman of his National Farmers Union and whom I had known well for many years. I soon discovered that the French considered all to be fair in love, war and politics, in that they attempted not only to boost their man – which was fair enough – but to denigrate me in an altogether outrageous way.

It was reliably reported to me that Jacques Chirac, who at that stage already had behind him a two-year term as Prime Minister of France, was telling rallies of farmers and politicians that I must be stopped at all costs, on the grounds that I represented only the interests of the landed gentry. To this he apparently added many colourful pointed details. I was said, for instance, to make a weekly tour of my tenants to make sure that my estates were being kept in the manner required by my feudal principles – a picture that would have amazed my friends and neighbours in Warwickshire, but which may well have seemed plausible to some Continental ears, ever eager to believe the most outlandish tales of old-fashioned eccentricity among the English.

In the event, this knavish trick came to nought and I became Chairman.

At the first meeting of the Committee, before business had begun, Debatisse warmly congratulated me. Then Chirac entered the chamber, threw his arms out wide and cried, 'Henry, I come in peace' – and without the slightest embarrassment, embraced me in the manner of a President of the Republic bestowing the insignia of the *Légion d'Honneur* on a national hero. Although taken aback at the time, I must admit to an abiding admiration – and, indeed, a liking – for Jacques Chirac as an engaging personality and a courageous politician.

Once we got down to work, my impressions of life in the European Parliament – shared, I believe, by many of my colleagues – were diverse to the point of contrasting. On the one hand, the direct contact with the elected representatives of the other eight member states was extremely stimulating and intellectually rewarding. We quickly came to appreciate the unique value of this democratic European forum, which every day made possible a blending of international experience and viewpoints over a vast range of subjects in a way that could not otherwise be arranged. Our discussions with our counterparts from the other countries rapidly led us to the conclusion that if the European Parliament had not existed, we would have had to invent it.

On the other hand, there were many frustrations.

When I entered the European Parliament, it was not my intention to get too involved. I was, after all, looking for a break from leadership responsibilities and from farming politics. But the challenge from Debatisse – my colleague and often *bête noire* in COPA as President of the French Farmers Union – was one I just couldn't resist.

The all-party Agricultural Committee was very diverse in representation. There were five ex-Presidents of Farmers Unions, members of the German Green Party, and those who wanted to scrap the Common Agricultural Policy and cut subsidies to agriculture. Barbara Castle, Joyce Quinn (later Minister of State for Food and Agriculture) and Madame Edith Cresson sat in the front row, each in turn giving me problems.

Barbara Castle continually complained that her English translations of official documents were not ready. Edith Cresson – who later became Prime Minister of France after being Minister of Agriculture – was aggrieved that I had not given her a *rapporteur*-ship. I gave her the Report to prepare on swine fever.

One member of the Committee was a French aristocrat, a wine-grower and owner of Château Ormesson: Olivier d'Ormesson. He told me in strict confidence that Madame Cresson 'had worked very closely with François Mitterrand'. When the French Socialists won their national elections in 1981, the closeness of this relationship was confirmed by her appointment as Minister of Agriculture. (She was subsequently – and fatefully – to become a Brussels Commissioner, again as Mitterand's protégée.)

At the end of the first year, the Secretary of the Committee, Martin Schmit, was moving to another post. I decided that we should give him a farewell party from the Committee. Naturally, on the day, I said a few words of appreciation and thanks. But much to my surprise, and his, Barbara Castle also stepped forward to publicly add her thanks. I say 'surprise', because she had long been critical of him – and of me.

Before responding, he gave Barbara a kiss. So I stepped forward and said, 'What's good for the secretary is good for the Chairman!'

As I moved towards her, however, she quickly moved back a pace and said, 'Oh no! There *are* limits!'

Since those days I have always had the greatest respect for Baroness Castle (which she hates being called). She is a doughty fighter for just causes – her latest being a fair deal for pensioners – and still makes a forceful contribution in the House of Lords.

At that time there was growing anxiety about surpluses of butter, wheat, beef and other commodities, and criticism of the waste of so much money. Taxpayers were subsidising cheap butter for Russia, enabling the Russians to spend their money on the arms race instead! I was then a Knight of the realm, called by many of my Continental colleagues 'Sir Plumb'. Both these notional strands came together in the nickname I soon found had been created for me: 'Sir Plus'.

Although the European Parliament had many of the essential characteristics of a modern democratic parliament, it had them in a strangely muted form. The experience of an MEP was at one and the same time therefore both tantalisingly promising and deeply disappointing. In broad principle, the Parliament – together with its role as a forum in which European public opinion could make itself heard (in itself a useful and novel function) – had the powers to pass laws, to allocate huge budgets and to scrutinise anything it wanted to examine. Superficially, that was an impressive list. But the reality, involving the highly specific limitations placed on those powers, was far less satisfactory.

As regards legislation, not only did the power of initiative rest solely with the Commission, but the role of Parliament was purely consultative. So although we worked assiduously at improving the draft legislation texts placed before us, when necessary by preparing copious amendments and explanatory texts, Parliament's role was limited to a single reading, after which our opinions and suggestions were merely forwarded to the Commission and Council, whose only obligation was to 'consider' them.

Indeed, it took a decision by the European Court of Justice (in the so-called 'Isoglucose case') to ensure that even this perfunctory requirement was at least formally fulfilled. At its worst, this state of affairs meant that when decisions came to be taken in Council on a piece of legislation, so long as the Parliament's amending proposals were made known and some formal reference made to them in the record of the meeting, the Ministers from the member states could totally ignore the European Parliament's position.

It was not always the case. Sometimes we did succeed in putting forward proposals that found their way into the final legislation texts. But the system certainly seemed to us to be a hit-or-miss affair, unworthy of a Parliament's operations.

In the budgetary sphere things were a little better. The Parliament was at least, with the Council, one element of the joint budgetary authority

– even though, again, the original proposals came from the Commission. The European budget for any one year was not valid until it had been passed, on a Second Reading, by the Parliament normally in the preceding December session – the First Reading having taken place in the month of October – after a series of inter-institutional exchanges concerning the proposals and Parliament's amendments.

But although the procedure formally ended up in Parliament, the President's signature being the ceremonial seal on the document, the joint budgetary authority was not a partnership of equals. In procedural terms, the background to this was that the budgetary lines were divided into two categories: 'compulsory' and 'non-compulsory' expenditure. And 'compulsory expenditure' related to those items of expenditure that flowed from already existing 'common policies' and the financial obligations attached to them.

For this category, in the event of disagreement, the Council had the last say – and because in the early 1980s the Common Agricultural Policy accounted for over 70 per cent of the total budget, the Council in reality wielded the lion's share of the budgetary powers. My personal frustration in this respect was particularly acute, for it was precisely in the realm of the CAP that I believed substantive savings could be made, to the benefit of the consumer, the taxpayer and the farmer.

As for the scrutineering powers of Parliament vis-à-vis the Commission and Council, the situation was once again one of promising appearances and disappointing results. Using virtually set-piece declarations, the President of the Commission and individual Commissioners, as well as the 'Presidency-in-Office' comprising a national Prime Minister and his or her ministerial team, would always pay extravagant lip service to the role of Parliament – which they spoke of in tones usually reserved for motherhood and apple pie – and solemnly undertook to improve the flow of information to Parliament, the degree of consultation with its Committees, and the accommodation of its considered points of view.

Again, reality was different. Logistical and timetabling problems (the alibi of the 'three workplaces', for example) frequently meant that Commissioners and Ministers could not attend vital Committee meetings. They sent officials who, understandably, kicked for touch ('I would have to refer that question to my Commissioner/Minister, since it is a matter requiring a political decision') once questioning approached the nub of any controversial matter.

We did manage to have a regular Question Time in respect of both the Commission and the Council, but it was a pale shadow of, for example, its Westminster counterpart. Rarely was the Commissioner or Minister present in person. More often delegated to make a reply was the individual directly responsible in the Directorate General or Ministry appropriate to the Question. And all he or she did was to read out a usually overlong, circumlocutory answer in the monotones of the shipping forecast on a calm day. Any lively supplementary questions were parried with a standard 'I will take that point up with my colleague, who will no doubt write to the Hon. Member in due course.' Since the Question had probably been tabled three weeks previously, and the letter concerning the supplementary points could take up to five weeks to arrive, the notion of accountability did not look as if it might ever become more than notional.

Another factor that dulled the parliamentary impact of Question Time was the language barrier. The Parliament's teams of interpreters are among the very best in the world and perform miracles in enabling Members to follow in every detail the proceedings of all official meetings in the language of their choice. But the slight time-gap between original and interpreted comment, and the absence sometimes of direct colloquial parallels between languages, inevitably mean that the dramatic cut-and-thrust of Question Time in the House of Commons will always be impossible to replicate in the European Parliament.

Very occasionally, it must be said, the interpreters yield to the all too human temptation to improve the atmosphere of a debate by personal intervention – which is, strictly speaking, against professional etiquette.

I remember on one occasion a British Member, fond of literary quotations and addicted to puns, had made a speech which was full of both – witty to English ears, but virtually impossible to interpret. On my way out of the Chamber I met an Italian interpreter whom I knew well. I asked him how he had coped with one particularly abstruse wordplay.

'Oh,' he replied, 'it was no problem. I just said to my Italian listeners, "The Hon. Member has cracked a funny but impossible-to-translate joke. You know my livelihood depends on it, so please laugh heartily on the count of three. One, two, . . ." – and they did.'

At the beginning of every Presidency of the Council, the Prime Minister of the member state concerned comes to Parliament to outline the priorities of the six months ahead. Then following each European summit – one of which occurs at the beginning of the Presidency – he reports on what has been achieved. Similarly, the President of the Commission annually presents a proposed work programme for the year ahead. Following consideration in the Standing Committees, there is a plenary debate on its contents. These wide-ranging set-pieces are often not as useful, however, as the more detailed exchange of views and information that take place between the other institutions and Parliamentarians in the framework of the Standing Committees.

In European legislation, as elsewhere, the devil is very often in the detail – and at Committee level it was easier for us to make an impact on a Commissioner or Minister . . . whenever we managed to get hold of one.

Within our power of scrutineering we had only one real sanction available to us: that of dismissing the entire Commission. But that was a bit like having a nuclear deterrent, in that it was an indiscriminate weapon of mass destruction that everyone knew could be deployed only *in extremis*. Until the debacle of the end of the Santer Commission in 1999, its use was only ever seriously threatened once – in 1984, in the context of a temporary impasse over the annual budget. At that time, in my opinion, it was not taken seriously enough by its intended victims.

Even in the early 1980s it was obvious that a far more effective power – and one that will have to come eventually – is the prerogative that would enable Parliament, under an established procedure, to dismiss an individual Commissioner. The struggle to acquire that power continues to this day, and the understandings reached in late 1999 between the President of the Commission Enrico Prodi, his Commissioners and the European Parliament, based on the notion that individual Commissioners have pledged themselves to accept the President's invitation to resign should they lose his confidence (and the indications of Parliament's confidence would be a significant factor in that), no doubt foreshadow what must surely become enshrined in the Treaties in a future constitutional revision.

8

EUROSCLEROSIS

Good statesmen, who pulled ruin on the state,
Good patriots, who for a theory risked a cause, . . .
Now may the good God pardon all good men!
(Elizabeth Browning)

The early 1980s are nowadays referred to by the pundits as a period of 'Eurosclerosis'. And that is a fair description, up to a point. Following the entry of Britain, Ireland and Denmark into the EEC, and the transitional period during which most of the tariffs were dismantled and the newcomers fully assimilated into the existing system, a wider 'Common Market' had come into existence, in the sense of an advanced customs union. But for a while there appeared to be a distinct lack of a European dynamic to carry the enterprise forward to its next stage.

Most of the news out of Brussels was dominated by the long-running saga of the British budget rebate. It was an episode that came to be encapsulated in many cartoons of the day, depicting Mrs Thatcher as a handbag-swinging housewife demanding 'her' money back. I firmly believe that she was fundamentally right.

And yet, of course, if we step back and view the matter in its historical context, beginning not with the UK's entry into the EEC in 1973 and the terms and conditions negotiated at that time, but with Britain's shortsighted refusal to become involved with the preparatory work leading up to the Treaty of Rome in 1958, we can see that the Original Sin in this matter was our own responsibility. Sadly, our national record in respect of European integration has been one of tardiness, for which we have paid a heavy price through being absent from the formation processes.

As we shall see, it is a sin that still besets us.

But in the context of Mrs Thatcher's premiership, she was right to insist on reforms in the way the Community raised and spent its money, and, in particular, on an equitable basis of national contributions. She pursued that goal with vigour and persistence over almost five years. It was a campaign that has been meticulously chronicled by Sir Michael Butler – who, as the UK's Permanent Representative in Brussels, was one of her principal aides – in his book *More than a Continent*.

The matter was finally settled (in so far as budgetary matters are ever definitively resolved) at the European summit at Fontainebleau in 1984, by means of a deal that has been of great benefit overall to the United Kingdom, and one that really did represent 'fair play'. (It must be said, however, that from a British farming point of view, some aspects of the settlement, relating to agri-monetary exchange rates, are currently to our disadvantage.)

Whether Mrs Thatcher could have achieved that settlement by patient, quiet diplomacy, without the histrionics and the sometimes excessively belligerent vocabulary, must forever remain a matter of speculation. What is certain, however, is that her tactics and the attitudes she struck profoundly alienated continental opinion at almost every level, from Prime Ministers down. Furthermore, her budgetary success seemed to convince her that the only way to deal with the Europeans was to thump the table, if not indeed the Chairman, at every turn. By the end of her premiership she had almost fewer friends in Europe than in her own Cabinet. Her partners certainly respected her resolve (all the more on account of her spectacular victory in the Falklands War of 1982), but they came to suspect that British interest in Europe was at best lukewarm. That suspicion has still to be completely dispelled.

Paradoxically, British influence was a major factor in re-energising the European enterprise through the promotion and realisation of 'the next big idea' – the Single Market. Success has, of course, always had many putative fathers, and there is nowadays no lack of politicians and economists who claim to have played a decisive role in this stage of European development. And one could argue that to move on from a customs union, in which tariff barriers had been abolished, to a single market in which non-tariff barriers to free and undistorted trade would equally be removed, was such a logical step to take that it was virtually a self-defining plan. Nevertheless, such a plan required not only to be promoted politically but to be worked out in detail and applied, above all through binding European legislation.

Within the European Parliament a great deal of pioneering work was carried out by British Conservative Members in co-operation with our EPP allies and, it must be said, some German Socialists, such as Dieter Rogalla.

As well as promoting movement within the framework of Parliament's reactive role, those who favoured active progress in this field formed a ginger group (officially called an 'Inter-group' since its membership straddled several segments of the political spectrum), which bore the name of the 'Kangaroo Group' (the PR image being of the animal bounding over the obstacles of various trade barriers). The EDG Members, led by Boz Ferranti and Fred Catherwood, played a major role in the propagation of this idea and in pressing for action to be taken. We were fortunate that several positive strands came together at the same time.

In London, economic, trade and industry ministers could see the advantages for the UK as a trading nation of the proposed internal free market – the Single Market, as it came to be known. The possible longer-term constitutional implications of the completion of the Single Market had not yet come to trouble the minds of the Euro-sensitive members of our party.

So British Government support for the project was strong. And at the all-important Commission level – for it was from that institution that the detailed proposals for implementation would have to come – there was a fortuitous partnership between two truly remarkable individuals, Jacques Delors, its President, and (Lord) Arthur Cockfield, the British Conservative Commissioner and a Vice-President of the Commission, whose responsibilities made him the key player in the Single Market game.

Delors, despite his technocratic image as a banker and economist, also had the political capacity to inspire when with great lucidity and passion he put across his vision of the development of Europe. (After all, he was credited with having converted the TUC in a single speech at their Bournemouth Conference on 8 September 1988 – a missionary exploit that must rank with those of St Augustine.)

Arthur Cockfield was equally lucid, but with his pedagogical style of speaking, combined with his rather owlish appearance behind thick horn-rimmed glasses, he was less charismatic than the President. However, his great talent was precisely what was needed: he brought together an unparalleled grasp of the details of the changes necessary in European legislation and a dogged persistence to see the programme through. Few could have drawn up so meticulously and accurately the list of 282 legislative instruments to be enacted in the years 1986 to 1992. Personally, I don't think anyone else on the European scene at that time could have done it.

One of the little ironies of the Cockfield success story was that although he had been, and for a time remained, one of Mrs Thatcher's favourite politicians – indeed, he had been her appointee – she later came to view him as having 'gone native' once the full impact of what he had achieved for Europe began to sink in.

The immediate politico-constitutional consequence of the drive towards the Single Market was the treaty revision necessary to provide the European framework within which such a deepening could take place. It was to culminate, in 1986, with the curiously entitled Single European Act – the first major overhaul of the fundamental text of the Community since 1958, and therefore a milestone on the path of European integration.

The European Parliament from its earliest days in its directly elected form had been pressing for such a reform, although its main interest had originally been in bringing about changes that would enhance its own role as a parliament within the inter-institutional relationships. Such attempts to catch up, institutionally, after the first two decades of the Common Market in which trade and commercial concerns had dominated and parliamentary control had been held at a distance, would, in isolation, undoubtedly have taken a very long time to come to fruition. It was the harnessing of the economic imperative to Parliament's politico-institutional ambitions that brought success.

Not that this 'success' was – in the eyes of the more radical constitutionalists among our membership – anything more than partial, if not paltry. For there emerged at that time a pattern that has since been repeated three times and is now entering a fresh cycle.

The European Parliament, in terms of the integrational process, has by and large consistently been at the federalist extreme in its vision of the European future. Indeed, it has adopted a self-appointed role as the driver of 'the ever-closer Union', and has not hesitated to formulate – on its own initiative, if necessary – detailed proposals for the implementation of its vision. Its critics may point out (with considerable justification) that such visionary activities are all very well for those who do not have the task of grinding out the day-to-day results, often with great difficulty at inter-member-state level. But in the overall system of checks and balances I believe it is useful that the constant pioneering enthusiasm of the Parliament should be, and invariably is, tempered by the practical caution of the Commission, together with the occasional agnosticism of some of the member state governments.

The pattern that has emerged in these inter-relationships within the framework of constitutional reform has been

· for the Parliament to advance its 'ultra' position;

· for the Council to set up an inter-governmental conference to study the need and potential for reform (to which the European Parliament again makes a detailed input); and at the end of the day – the day being anything up to two years long –

· for compromises to be hammered out at a two-day summit between the heads of state and government.

Only then do new texts emerge that represent an overall treaty revision.

It can be argued that the final stage of the horse-trading that takes place at the summit – witness Maastricht and Amsterdam – is necessary in order to achieve negotiating breakthroughs. But it has always struck me as strange that after so much careful preparation over such a long period, the future constitutional shape of a continent is decided within a few hours by fewer than a score of men and women driven to conclusions as much by exhaustion as by conviction. If I could believe that the hours spent at the crucial summit represented for these same men and women the culmination of long months of reflection and preparation on their own part, my reservations would be less discomforting. But that is simply not the case.

However unsatisfactory – and messy – these treaty revisions have been in their final textual form, those of us involved have been able to draw consolation from one basic fact: that each successive revision is merely provisional. There will be further opportunities to make improvements and to break new ground. The European Parliament's unwritten strategy has been, and remains,

· to push for a maximalist position, in the knowledge that only modest gains will in the event be achieved;

· to criticise the shortcomings of the revised treaty – but to pick up and encourage the use of whatever elements in it suit Parliament's cause; and

· to begin at once to agitate for the next stage of reform and development.

As early as in the long run-up to the Single European Act, the European Parliament adopted its first maximalist position. The Institutional Affairs Committee even went so far as to produce, in the Spinelli Report, a draft federal constitution for the 'Vision'. The report was adopted, with a sizeable majority, in the Strasbourg plenary of April 1984.

That event produced one of the great moments of the European Parliament, when Arturo Spinelli – the grand old man of European federalism – made the closing speech in favour of his Report, drawing a literary parallel with Hemingway's *The Old Man and the Sea*. Parliament, like the old man, must strain every nerve to bring this great fish of the draft treaty into our boat, lest it escape and forever swim away.

Throughout its passage, the Spinelli Report posed particular problems for the EDG. Many of our natural and regular allies in the other groups were passionately in favour, and there were elements in the Report's push for reform with which we were certainly in sympathy. But there was much in it that Spinelli and his supporters considered to be fundamental, which to us seemed either too far-fetched (was Europe really ready for 'Union'?) or downright unwelcome – particularly its overtly federalist philosophy.

My memory of that period is seared with recollections of endless debates within the group, sometimes fuelled by contributions from Spinelli supporters from other groups, over how we should try to amend the text, how we should vote, and so on. We knew that for the time being the European Parliament's Resolution by itself was not going to bring about constitutional change. The positions we now took were nonetheless going to be of importance vis-à-vis the party at home and in the way we would be perceived in future public opinion. In the end we largely abstained, although some individual members voted against the whole Report all down the line.

Normally I eschew abstentions as a cop-out – but on this occasion I feel it was an accurate reflection of where I, at least, stood.

My objection was not so much to the adjective 'federal' as to what I considered to be the unrealistic leap into an unprepared future, which the Spinelli text represented. Both aspects are worth examining in some detail, because I believe they touch upon something that must be understood in relation to different political experiences and cultures – something fundamental to even a Europhile British approach to the integrational process on the Continent.

Firstly, the concept of what is and what is not 'federal'.

In the vocabulary of modern English politics, 'federal' – despite its dictionary definitions – is frequently associated with the notion of a 'super-state', involving all the connotations of 'Big Brother' which that concept evokes in its turn. In the popular press and in popular opinion it is deemed to be A Bad Thing, and should therefore be resisted in favour of what is popularly perceived as its opposite: the individual sovereign national state.

Due to historical experiences, however, the word 'federal' strikes quite a different chord in other countries, especially in Germany. After the centralisation and totalitarianism of the Nazi period, Germans rejoice in their own federal constitution, which to them is a guarantee against precisely the overbearing 'super-state' that so many of their British neighbours imagine to be the end-product of federalism. In the German Republic the citizen lives — apart from in his city or local government area — essentially on two political levels: that of his *Land*, which enjoys autonomy of roughly similar degree to that of post-1999 devolution in Scotland, and that of his federal Government in Berlin. Political power and budgetary resources are divided equally between the two levels, which co-exist in a constitutional balance. For a German, a federal future for Europe is therefore no more than an extension of what to him represents democratic normality — a very different vision from the one of popular British imagining.

I take a pragmatic view of this question. Aren't we moving towards a 'Federal UK'? We have a Parliament in Scotland, Wales and Northern Ireland, and an elected Mayor and Assembly in London. How long before the demands increase for these in England? To me 'federalism' is not an absolute but a matter of degree. Once we strip away the high-flown rhetoric of Utopia and the correspondingly unrealistic prophecies of totalitarian doom, federalism for me refers, in practical terms, to an element of central organisation between states in the interests of overall efficiency and for mutual benefit.

Thus it already exists in Europe to a certain degree — actually, to quite an advanced degree. To what degree it should further develop in the first years of the new millennium or at some future date is, I firmly believe, a matter not for constitutional pipe-dreaming but for constant review in the light of changing needs and changing opportunities.

And that is precisely my objection to 'Spinelli-ism' in its various forms, in 1984 and ever since. I recognise the need for imaginative and constructive thinking about Europe's future, and in contrast to the British experience. But I do *not* believe that in terms of the European treaties we can, or should, proceed by way of theoretical constitution-building. I also recognise that in several continental countries — such as Italy, France and Spain — the national constitution has been produced all of a piece according to a blue-print. I make no apology for maintaining the archetypal British approach (once described to me in pejorative terms by a Frenchman as revealing a 'treasure-hunt mentality') by which we keep on going in one specific direction but proceed in stages and only when it is necessary, practical and beneficial so to do, and when we have already made a success of the current stage (i.e. 'solved the clue' in the treasure-hunt analogy).

I was convinced in the 1980s – and I remain so today – that regardless of any such differences in approach resulting from varied historical and cultural backgrounds, *it is in Britain's interest to engage constructively with our neighbours in helping to organize and shape the future of our common continent.* Never to be a positive player in the constitutional process is a huge mistake. We should *always* be an active participant in that sphere, as well as in the economic one. Our traditions, historical experience and pragmatic approach will often lead us to see things from an angle different from that perceived by our partners. But so long as we genuinely participate, our counter-balancing contribution will be of value – to ourselves and to the other Europeans.

In advocating this approach I am not falling into the error of imagining that those who adopt a more visionary approach do not really mean what they say, and that they will not work (differently from the way I work) for the realisation of their vision. That was, I believe, Mrs Thatcher's mistake. It was one shared by many in British political life – as was evident in the period leading up to, and indeed including, the finalisation of the Single European Act. As I have already said, the economic objective of the creation of the Single Market was one Mrs Thatcher heartily embraced, but psychologically she chose to ignore the fact that others saw in this next step not only the necessity, but the opportunity to integrate further the political entity of Europe, not least by increasing the power of the European Parliament.

Take, for example, the Solemn Declaration of Stuttgart, 1983.

Many of Mrs Thatcher's true-blue disciples have since been astonished to learn that she put her signature to a document which declared that

> in order to achieve ever-increasing solidarity, the construction of Europe must be more clearly oriented towards its political objectives, more efficient decision-making procedures, greater coherence, and close co-ordination between the different branches of activity and the search for common policies in all areas of common interest, both within the Community and in relation to third countries
>
> (art.1.3)

and which spelled-out the need 'to promote the objective of a Europe speaking with a single voice and acting in common in the field of foreign policy' (art 2.2.3). One of the specific goals for the future set out in the Declaration was the 'Approximation of Laws' (art.3.4) – which meant bringing the legal codes of the member states more into line with one another.

Mrs Thatcher herself stated later that the full political implications of the Single European Act were not apparent to her at the time. What are we to make of that? Was she too tired or too pushed to read the papers? Was she tricked by duplicitous Euro-fanatics?

No: the answer, I believe, is more straightforward. She simply didn't take the non-economic bits of Eurospeak seriously enough. Like her predecessors who turned down the invitation to attend the Messina Conference, she just didn't believe that the Europeans 'would get down and do it'. They have never, it is true, managed to 'do it' in the timescale forecast, or in exactly the form as originally outlined. Yet the history of the last four decades shows that the process of European integration in both economic and non-economic terms does sooner or later advance, more or less as foreshadowed.

We in the United Kingdom should – however late in the day – take that lesson to heart. This is how I believe Conservatism should distinguish itself from Thatcherism.

The gut reaction of most people to Mrs Thatcher as a person, and/or to 'Thatcherism' as a political creed, tends to be extreme, ranging from unquestioning idolatry to unrelenting opposition. I find myself torn between strongly contradictory opinions of her.

On the one hand, I acknowledge that she was one of the most influential political figures of the 20th century, not just in the United Kingdom but in the wider world. Whatever else history may come to say about her, I believe she will be remembered for three outstanding achievements:

> 1) she succeeded as no politician before her had done in convincing the electorate at large that all government actions have a price-tag, and that the public must cease to believe in the economic magic peddled by the other parties, who were subsequently obliged to take over vast parts of Thatcherite policy territory;
>
> 2) she broke the political economic stronghold of the TUC barons and of 'nationalised' thinking through her trade union legislation and her policy of privatisation; and, on the wider scene,

3) she played an unswerving role as a Cold War Warrior in helping to keep Europe on side with the United States – especially as regards the development of cruise missiles on this side of the Atlantic in the mid-1980s – and was undoubtedly a major factor in the collapse of the Soviet Union's empire in Central Europe.

Any one of these triumphs would have crowned the career of most political leaders.

And yet, . . . and yet, . . .

The darker side of Mrs Thatcher was not just the *hubris* that overtook her in the latter years of her premiership – many, if not all, politicians who have been at the top for a long time fall prey to an overconfidence and a loss of objectivity that in the end brings them down – but the amazing blind spot she had regarding 'Europe'. Pundits have been startled at the well-documented tales of her famous seminar, organised with Nick Ridley, on 'What Makes the Germans Tick'. Those of us who saw her at close quarters on European affairs over the years were not in the least surprised by such revelations. A starting-point of 'let's examine Johnny Foreigner' as though our neighbours were worthy subjects of anthropological, if not indeed zoological, interest, was not just in character – it was the *leitmotiv* of much of her thinking.

It is true that many of her generation who can vividly remember World War II have built-in mental reservations about all things continental, whereas others – notably Ted Heath – have brought from that experience a determination to see an integrated Europe. What is extraordinary is that someone of Margaret Thatcher's breadth of education and experience should be so deeply tainted with this corrosive Europhobia.

As leader of the British Conservatives in the European Parliament for eight years, I naturally had to transact business with her during that time. Well, not all that much business in point of fact, for neither she nor the party whips, nor Conservative Central Office, ever really got to grips with what the relationship with their own MEPs should be. Her initial electoral victory in June 1979 had been followed only three weeks later by the first direct elections to the European Parliament.

Those who won seats as MEPs were almost to a man and woman from the earlier pro-European Tory tendency. And they went on to exploit a moment of inattention and indifference in London by mounting a significant little coup: they elected their own leadership without reference to the Party at home. So the situation was that the 62 Conservative MEPs were largely autonomous, financed from the European budget and essentially in favour of further EC integration, while the Party at home was now in Government, and was already Eurosceptic in its mood. Indeed, it was not at all in favour even of the existence of the European Parliament (which Mrs Thatcher resolutely continued to call 'the Assembly' for many years to come).

There were, of course, frequent contacts between Party, Government and us MEPs, especially on specific issues – such as crucial votes in the defence, security and budgetary fields – but there was also an unmistakable *distance* between us.

Once or twice a year (usually after the date had been changed umpteen times by Mrs Thatcher's office), the Prime Minister would receive the entire group of British Conservative MEPs at Downing Street. These were always embarrassing encounters. The prevailing atmosphere was one of a meeting between a maiden aunt and a gaggle of rascally nephews who had clearly been up to mischief on a school trip abroad. On our side we tried to prepare for these meetings by letting Mrs Thatcher's office know in advance what points we wished to raise. Our policy spokesmen (and women) put a great deal of effort into working up papers and in presenting them succinctly at the meetings.

All in vain.

Apparently, no such preparation was considered necessary on her side. We were frequently subjected instead to a dress rehearsal for a forthcoming speech on a topic that might or might not have any relevance to the European Parliament. Her responses to points raised by us were all too obviously off the top of her head. And if she interpreted any comment of ours as being to the slightest degree hostile to her point of view, she would invariably preface her reply with the put-down, 'Well, in politics in the *real* world, . . .'

Clearly, as far as she was concerned we were in neither. I wish I could say that it is some comfort now to know from many sources that towards the end she treated her Cabinet in much the same way.

In terms of my personal relations with Mrs Thatcher, I have no complaint at all about the level of civility and courtesy in our exchanges. But regardless of the specific context of our meetings, she would eventually bring the conversation round to agriculture, and would invariably preface her questions with flattering remarks about how much she valued my expertise in these recondite matters. I think she did so for three reasons.

Firstly, I have the vanity to believe that she did consider I knew a thing or two about the subject – and it was a subject about which she herself had little direct knowledge and suffered from a great deal of contradictory official advice. Secondly, 'agriculture' meant to her the Common Agricultural Policy and therefore 'Europe', on the subject of which she could thereupon launch her latest anti-Brussels verbal missiles. And, thirdly, talking agriculture with me spared her the necessity of dialogue on other political issues on which she knew that my fellow Conservative MEPs and I did not see eye to eye with her at all.

One incident nicely illustrates her general attitude. It happened at a grand reception at Downing Street in honour of the King of Spain. There was the usual presentation line-up, with Mrs Thatcher very expertly giving His Majesty a rapid thumbnail sketch of each guest by way of introduction. When my turn came, she said, 'This is Lord Plumb, who was for many years our farmers' leader.'

The King – who had met me on several occasions in the European Parliament context – replied, with a twinkle in his eye, 'I think my friend Henry has done a few other things since then.'

The Prime Minister flashed the smile of the synchronised swimmer and stared over my shoulder at the next in line.

The Party was never very comfortable about the involvement of the EDG at the annual Party Conference. Even before the stage in which 'Europe' came to trigger an automatic reflex of hostility amongst many elements of the Party, our very existence was an unwelcome reminder of a policy domain the leadership would have preferred to pass over in near-silence. So there was always a great deal of programme-shuffling to make sure that our MEPs did not feature too prominently during the week.

It was hard to get across the message that we were representing our constituencies, and putting forward Conservative policies, in the European Parliament in the same way that our colleagues were doing in Westminster. By some we were regarded as operating behind enemy lines, by others as potential – if not already actual – conspirators involved in a plot to take away Britain's nationhood. What struck me forcibly, in listening to the debates, was that frequently social or economic problems of widespread concern could be examined without reference to how these issues were being treated in the other European member states.

A case in point was the drugs problem.

It so happened that the European Parliament's *Rapporteur* on the subject was Sir Jack Stewart Clark, a member of the Bureau of the EDG. He had done a most thorough job in not only comparing how all the member states were tackling the problem, but in surveying the various links in the baneful chain – from the farmers who grew the narcotic plants, the gangsters who organised their refinement and international transportation, the distribution networks at national level, the pushers, the users, the health victims, to the medical carers and the law enforcers. He painted a comprehensive picture on a vast canvas.

Some weeks before a Party Conference, David Mellor – who was getting into the subject at the Home Office – came to Brussels and had long discussions with Sir Jack, who, of course freely passed on the fruits of his research and his thinking on the subject. The Minister's eventual Conference speech drew heavily on this material. That was scarcely surprising – but what *was* surprising was that it contained not the slightest reference to, much less an acknowledgement of, the work of his colleague in the European Parliament. Even allowing for individual egocentricity, that incident illustrates the fundamental embarrassment felt by many in the Party in relation to things European.

I am inclined to agree with those who trace this embarrassment back to the 'Ted Heath' problem. There is no doubt that Ted's place in history will be as the leader who took Britain into Europe, completing the hard preparatory work carried out by Macmillan. He led a party that was enthusiastic on the issue. Indeed, even after he had been voted out of office, the country as a whole still voted two-to-one to remain within the Community. However, the bitterness that his continuing feud with Margaret Thatcher generated led the new party leadership increasingly to damn 'Heath and all his works'. And Europe had been the *magnum opus* of those works.

As a party we are still suffering from the side-effects of that ill-judged exorcism.

The other political stimulus of the mid-1980s was the entry into the Community of both Spain and Portugal. A decade before, both countries had begun to shake off 40 years of isolation from the rest of Europe, following the end of the Franco and Salazar dictatorships. It is one of the triumphs of the Community that we were able, through the extension of membership to the two Iberian countries, to help them achieve the transition to sound and ever more prosperous democracies.

We in the EDG had a vested political interest in this enlargement. In 1982 we had attempted – rather naively and clumsily, it must be said in retrospect – to bring on board the Greek newcomers belonging to Nea Democratica, the only party that had a manifesto broadly compatible with our own. However, we soon found that in the matter of group recruitment at our end of the political spectrum the EPP (the European People's Party) had the game sewn up well in advance. This was thanks to their political foundations in several countries, especially Germany, which had at their disposal considerable resources, mostly financed from public funds, to promote political education and aid like-minded parties worldwide. This gave the EPP a power of attraction with which we in the British Conservative Party could not begin to compete.

I still have an open mind about whether some degree of public funding for political parties is a good thing, but I am increasingly inclined to believe it is. Democratic political action at party level does not come cheap. In an ideal world, the membership of each party would be so numerous that their flat-rate annual subscriptions would finance all the usual activities, including election campaigns and the salaries of permanent staff. Alas, we do not live in that ideal world, or even in a nearby galaxy.

In countries such as our own, which have traditionally eschewed subventions to political parties from the public purse, parties have been obliged to seek donations from other sources, above and beyond the annual subscriptions of members. This has very frequently led to controversial situations in which questions have been asked about the degree of influence secured by the donors. So a high price is paid, in terms of public esteem, for the purity of the 'no public funding' position. It is one of the quirks of history that at the end of World War II the victorious Allied powers, in order to foster democratic civil life in the new Germany, 'imposed' several measures such as sensible trade union structures and legislation, as well as the organisational structure and financing of political parties. These measures have been an outstanding success there – but it has taken us several decades to apply the same wisdom to the same problems in our own circumstances.

In the case of our recruitment drive in Portugal, we very quickly established that the like-minded parties were already as good as signed up for membership of the EPP, having been nurtured and supported by the Christian Democrats for several years beforehand. A nucleus of the EDG's Bureau nonetheless paid a reconnaissance visit to Portugal, and although it proved to be a wasted journey in terms of our immediate objective, the early friendly relations we established with some of the leading personalities – such as Lucas Pires of the Partido do Centro Democrático Social – were to stand us in good stead at a later stage.

Spain was a different case. There, the largest party of the centre right, the Alianza Popular, harboured serious doubts about joining the EPP, since in national Spanish politics it was keen to distance itself discreetly from any Church or confessional associations. Membership of the Christian Democratic EPP certainly would have involved it in such an association, and would therefore have been disastrous from a PR point of view. The reasons for avoiding such connections were complex.

At the death of General Franco in 1975, the remarkably smooth transition from dictatorship to democratic monarchy had been achieved largely thanks to the efforts of four men, who came from different backgrounds but who co-operated wisely – with many compromises – to hold the country together peacefully and to set up and operate new democratic institutions of governance.

The first of these was the young King Juan Carlos, who had been groomed by Franco to resume the throne vacated by his grandfather Alfonso XIII in 1931. He proved to be a unifying force for the nation, and his courageous defence of democracy during the attempted coup of 23 February 1982 mounted by reactionary elements within the armed forces confirmed Spain's political re-entry into modern Europe.

The second man was Adolfo Suarez, the centrist first Prime Minister of the new Spain, who had the unenviable task of redirecting the administrative machinery of state away from its lodestar of 40 years. The third was Felipe Gonzalez, the Socialist leader who had returned from exile, and who was later himself to dominate Spanish politics for fifteen years as a charismatic Prime Minister.

Finally, there was Manuel Fraga, the founder of the centre-right party, Alianza Popular. He had been a minister under Franco – indeed, at one time he was responsible for the application of censorship, a fact that was later to deprive him of the prize of the premiership. He was an important magnet for those who had sympathy with the *ancien régime* and for those who were simply against the Left. He energetically exploited this position in order progressively to build up the AP as the main opposition to the Socialists, mopping up smaller centre-right groupings as he went. But despite the fact that his supporters could defend his time as a Franco minister by claming that his role had been to soften and liberalise the closing stages of El Caudillo's reign, it gradually became plain that in a situation in which the young, especially, wished to turn their backs on the Franco past, the party would never come to power under Fraga's leadership. In due course he came to this conclusion himself, and stood down, skilfully moving not into oblivion but into the premiership of the regional government of his home territory of Galicia.

When I got to know him, Fraga was still the leader and father-figure of the Alianza Popular. I found him a fascinating character. He had an encyclopaedic knowledge of European history and a profound conviction that Spain must not miss her vocation as a member state of the new Europe. In his manner he was, however, not at all academic or studious, but extroverted and at times even rumbustious, particularly when on a party platform. He had been Ambassador in London in the early 1970s, and had taken away an admiration for British political moderation, as well as an abiding wet-weather preference for mackintoshes and bowler hats – which must initially have startled his neighbours in Galicia.

In the spring of 1984 I led a small delegation from the EDG on a prospecting trip to Spain, to meet the leadership of various political parties and to get a feel for the likely political priorities of the incoming Spanish MEPs. Our visit coincided with regional electoral campaigns, and the sheer enthusiasm for democratic politics was everywhere palpable. Membership of the European Community appeared to be a vastly popular prospect across most of the parties. Our visit was therefore the subject of considerable media interest. The visit also rated an audience with the King, who turned out to be delightfully indiscreet in his thumbnail sketches of the leading political personalities of the day, and also disarmingly frank about the abiding Anglo-Spanish problem – Gibraltar – and about its mirror-image, the Spanish enclaves of Ceuta and Melilla on the Moroccan coast.

Our talks with the political parties were fascinating but exhausting. I suffered considerable frustration at the propensity of some of our delegation members to spend a great deal of time in detailed discussion with the leaders of small splinter parties. Interesting and educational though this might be, I felt it was a waste of time not to concentrate on those who had a reasonable chance of eventually being elected to the European Parliament (the first Spanish and Portuguese MEPs were nominated for two years from their respective national parliaments).

For me, the Alianza Popular was the only serious prospect. Their manifesto sounded strangely familiar, with its emphasis on the free enterprise economy, rolling back the state, curtailing public expenditure, encouraging personal responsibility, and so on. I suspected that much of it was a Spanish adaptation of Smith Square publications. And we knew they had serious reservations about other possible coalitions within the European Parliament.

But some of our members had doubts. In particular, Lord Douro – who had extensive business interests in Spain and knew the country intimately – felt that the 'Fraga problem' would make our future relations with the EPP more difficult. Since I had inside information that the EPP were doing everything in their power to woo Alianza, I had very little sympathy with that argument.

My most vivid memory of that Spanish visit is of an evening spent at an AP election rally held in the bullring in Valencia. It was an electrifying experience: twenty thousand flag-waving supporters, a thirty-piece band, two soloists, eight warm-up speeches, and finally – at half-past midnight – the keynote address from Manuel Fraga himself, delivered with great gusto and humour, which sent the punters off home in high spirits, singing in the streets. Such democratic enthusiasm has, more's the pity, been largely lost in most countries in the TV era. And, unfortunately, it has faded too in Spain, as the novelty of free elections has gradually worn off. I feel privileged to have experienced it at its very peak.

A few weeks later, after the necessary reporting back to our respective memberships had duly taken place, the decision in principle was taken that the Alianza MEPs would join our group. As for the only real political problem between us – Gibraltar, again – we simply agreed to disagree and to 'put the issue into the fridge'. Perhaps inevitably, it was later to tumble out of the fridge and cause an uncomfortable mini-crisis.

The subsequent detailed negotiations about the share-out of posts of responsibility, budgetary allocations and staff numbers, went extremely smoothly. Fraga and his two negotiators, the Marquis of Perinat and Antonio Navarro, were hard-headed but straightforward in their dealings, and experience showed them to be men of their word.

Amusingly, the only trouble at this stage was with our Danish partners. They were now four in number since the elections of 1984, and they felt the pain of the transition from pampered minority to not-quite-so-pampered third national component of the group. The Danes were always useful members of the EDG and, particularly before the arrival of the Spaniards, showed great patience in putting up with occasional bouts of navel-gazing by the British.

There was one awkward passage – in 1983 – as a result of the UK's declaration of a twelve-mile fishing limit off our coasts. One of the

Danish Conservative MEPs was Kent Kirk, who happened to be a leading fisherman in his non-political life. He mounted a PR stunt, sailing into the forbidden zone with full media coverage, and rang me on his shipboard radio-telephone to 'send me greetings' at 5 a.m – and to counter an interview on one early news programme that morning, which had suggested that people in Britain would refuse to buy Danish products because he was breaking the law.

'Nonsense,' he said. 'They buy Danish butter, bacon and fish because of its fine quality.'

A clever way of turning a negative into a positive. There were no hard feelings, and the problem blew over – to the relief of all sides.

One of the new Danish MEPs in 1984 was Claus Toksvig, a TV personality in Denmark (as his daughter Sandy was to become on British TV). Apart from his many political talents, he was remarkable for the absolutely flawless and accentless English with which he spoke. Many Danes speak excellent English, but strangers could spend an evening in Claus's company without realising that he wasn't English. In group debates, he used to speak English exclusively, until he was criticised in certain Danish newspapers for this neglect of his native tongue. So he publicly undertook 'to speak Danish every day'.

What this amounted to was that after participating in debate for an hour or so, in English, he would suddenly say, in a Noël Coward voice: 'Okay, chaps, brace yourselves! Headphones – on!', before continuing in Danish for the next five minutes.

Life in the EDG certainly became more interesting after the Spaniards joined – and with the application of the Single European Act, political activity in Parliament generally moved into a higher gear.

9

THE EP PRESIDENCY:
A NEW CHALLENGE

> Who seeks for the truth shall be of no country.
> (Voltaire)

The office of President of the European Parliament is significantly different from that of the Speaker of the House of Commons, to which it is frequently compared for the sake of simplicity. It is true that the most publicly visible aspect of the two roles is more or less the same – that of presiding over the plenary session of the House. Even in that regard, the European Parliamentary President has, in practice, a more complex chamber to control, in that it is multinational and also contains a much greater variety of party political components.

Moreover, national parliaments of long standing have – over the decades, or even centuries – evolved not only tried and tested rules of procedure but also firm traditions which provide precedents for the orderly management of business in the House. The youthful European Parliament, on the other hand, although it had a initial set of Rules of Procedure, was finding its way and having to achieve within a few years a maturity that had taken long periods of time for national Parliaments to evolve.

The President of the European Parliament, in addition to his role as presiding officer (which he delegates for many debates to one of the fourteen Vice-Presidents), also chairs the meetings of the Bureau and the Conference of Group Chairmen, thus taking responsibility for guiding the decision-taking process for much of Parliament's work. Because the European Parliament has no Cabinet, no 'Government' as such, within its ranks in the manner of our national Parliament, it falls to the President to represent the Parliament (or to lead a delegation representing it) in relations with the other European institutions and also with the outside world. Some of this work is largely ceremonial, but it also frequently involves political initiative and reaction, which means the President must often walk a tightrope between his own instincts and the likely political positions (where these are not already established through adopted resolutions or other decisions) of the House as a whole.

A further difficulty is that the system of checks and balances ensures that the President is virtually always politically in a minority, in terms of the Right–Left divide, within the Bureau, since the overall balance is normally a fine one, and since the office of President counts as two Vice-Presidential posts in the overall weightings. A President from the centre-right thus usually chairs a Bureau with an overall left-of-centre majority, and *vice versa*. The post of President is therefore not one of intrinsic power but one of considerable responsibility – and, if used wisely, of influence.

After the two and half years' stint in office of Simone Veil, during which she did much to raise the profile of the European Parliament in France and many of the countries outside Europe with whom the EC had relations – but not, through no fault of her own, in the other member states – the Christian Democrats attempted to win the Presidency for their own candidate, Egon Klepsch. To do so they needed, crucially, the support of the EDG.

We had put forward our own Chairman, Sir James Scott-Hopkins, as a Presidential candidate, so negotiations had then to take place on the terms on which he might withdraw in favour of the EPP's man. I was not party to those negotiations, so I can't say precisely what took place. Evidently, however, there was at the very least a misunderstanding, and at worst – according to some of our representatives – a breach of faith. Conflicting stories circulated just before the final vote, with the result that the EDG vote did not hold up in favour of the EPP candidate. This let in Piet Dankert, a Dutch Socialist.

Before the next Presidential election, due in 1984, the leadership of the EDG had altered. Under our constitution there was an annual election of the Chairman and the eight other members of the Group's Bureau, its management committee. By 1982 there was a mood in favour of change, and I was asked by a number of members to stand for Chairman. It was something that had never been my intention. But after some hesitation, I agreed – and was duly elected. This caused some bad blood temporarily between Jim Scott-Hopkins and myself: a falling-out that I'm glad to say was happily resolved some time before his untimely death in 1994.

After the 1984 European elections – in which our British Conservative numbers were reduced from 63 to 32 – the EPP Chairman Egon Klepsch came to see me in order to avoid a repetition of the split of two and a half years before. The new Parliament was finely balanced between Left and Right, and the mathematics of the situation dictated that the EPP could only win if they had all our EDG votes. We had our own candidate, Lady Diana Elles, who had been a Vice-President and was a formidable Parliamentarian and lawyer, with excellent French and Italian – in short a first-rate candidate. The EPP's candidate was Pierre Pflimlin, who had been the last Prime Minister of the fourth Republic and one of the principal architects of the constitution of the Fifth Republic under de Gaulle. No one could doubt his abilities – but some had reservations about his age, which was then 77.

In the event, they need not have worried, for he was not only an energetic President but continued to pursue his political activities with undiminished vigour for considerably more than another decade. This time around, as the price for our support, we extracted a written assurance from Egon Klepsch that in 1987 the EPP would support an EDG candidate.

It was assumed, certainly by me, that that candidate would again be Diana Elles. However, in the autumn of 1986 I began to hear rumblings that the EPP, for undefined reasons, would not be happy to support Diana and believed they would be honouring their undertaking if they supported another EDG candidate. To this day I do not know who or what stood in the way of EPP support for Diana. I can only honestly say that I had no part in it, and nor do I know of any member of the EDG's having played a part in displacing her as our candidate.

Neither had I, until late 1986, ever contemplated the possibility of my becoming a Presidential candidate. I was forced to do so in a great hurry when, shortly before the Christmas break, a small group of colleagues from the EPP and my own group put it to me bluntly that with my candidature the EDG had a sporting chance – but only a sporting chance – of winning the Presidency. With any other candidate we were certain to lose. This calculation was based not only on sentiment within the EPP but on the likely willingness of members of the other centre-right groups – specifically the Liberals and the RDE (Gaullists and Fianna Fáil) – to vote for a British Tory. It was thought that my work within the loose co-ordination of the four leaderships might make me more acceptable (or less unacceptable!) than any other EDG candidate.

So I said Yes to the invitation to run – then swiftly set about campaigning as best I could in the short time available to me.

I knew that one of the other candidates would be Marco Pannella, the brilliant but erratic leader of the Italian Radical Party, whose votes, once he fell out of the race – as he surely would – would be crucial for the surviving 'big two' candidates, who would be the Spanish Socialist Enrique Baron Crespo and myself. Baron had a head start, being sure of the support of the largest group, plus the Communists. My only chance was to hold on to as many as possible of the centre-right votes and to challenge for a share of the smaller groups' support and of the non-attached members.

I had a difficult meeting with the Liberal group, some of whose members pressed me hard on what I could offer them in return for their support. I felt that my reply, which went no further than a commitment to be as effective a President as possible, was not much of an 'offer', but the leader of the Portuguese delegation surprised me, and probably saved the day, by saying, half in jest, that he would vote for me because he could believe my lack of promises!

The most delicate operation of all was my meeting with Jean-Marie Le Pen, leader of the French National Front, many of whose policy statements and attitudes, especially as regards race relations, were anathema to democrats of both Left and Right. Indeed, it was rumoured that moves were afoot to isolate his group within the Parliament to the utmost degree, amounting to outright ostracism of its members in the daily life and work of the institution. Le Pen privately blamed the centre-right for hatching this plot, and I was warned by one of his members – Jean Olivier d' Ormesson, who had defected to the National Front on having been dropped from the candidates list of his own EPP-affiliated party in 1984 – that as a result, his group were likely to vote *en bloc* for Enrique Baron.

It may seem strange to British eyes that the extreme Right would prefer the Left to the centre-right, but that has often been a feature of the French political landscape over the past thirty years. I knew that if Le Pen did throw his 16 votes behind my rival I had no chance of winning. I asked to see Le Pen, who insisted that the meeting take place in his office in the Palais Bourbon, seat of the National Assembly. D'Ormesson acted as broker, and I travelled to Paris accompanied only by Robert Ramsay, our Group Secretary General.

It was an awkward mission. News of the meeting could easily have leaked out. I was at Le Pen's mercy as regards its confidentiality and could in any case have been spotted in the precincts of the Assembly. (I drew the line at false whiskers or dark glasses.) Such news would almost certainly have driven away enough of my natural supporters to have sunk my boat – but it was my only chance.

Le Pen was uncharacteristically reserved and downbeat, and appeared to treat the meeting as a casual exchange of views about how Parliament was organised. My only theme was that, if elected, I would treat all groups according to the spirit and the letter of the rules. It was in fact my conviction, since strengthened by experience, that such an approach is the only sensible one for a President to employ; I have seen others get into a truly deep mire by trying to favour, or to do down, a particular group by the misuse of their position.

I have no idea what impressions Le Pen took away from the meeting – d'Ormesson volunteered no assessment afterwards – but news of it did not leak out, and the final electoral arithmetic would certainly suggest that the National Front MEPs either voted for me or abstained.

Some of my supporters expressed the view that the Irish Fianna Fáil members were unlikely to bring themselves to vote for a British Tory. I did not share that pessimism for I had had extremely good relations with many of them, even before my European Parliament days, based on a shared interest in matters agricultural. In the event I am sure that they all voted for me.

The day of the Presidential election, 20 February 1987, was a long and hectic one. All the other such elections, both before and since, have, on the day, been devoid of real drama, either because the two biggest groups – the EPP and the Socialists, who between them can nearly always muster an overall majority – have made a pact that one will provide a candidate in the first half of the legislative period and support the other's candidate in the second half, or, as in 1999, the candidate of one group has had so many 'natural' votes to begin with as to be a racing certainty.

In principle I am in favour of a genuine, open race – but I can't recommend that as being good for one's nerves.

There were four candidates. The pre-race favourite was the Spanish Socialist, Enrique Baron Crespo, and the interest in the final stages of the voting was clearly going to be focused on how the votes of the other two candidates – Marco Pannella, the Italian Radical, and Paul Staes, a Belgian ecologist – would transfer to the favourite or myself.

In the first ballot Baron polled 209; I received 199, Pannella 61, and Staes 14. In the second ballot, to my surprise, I moved ahead, with 233 votes to Baron's 219, but Pannella's 35 votes seemed much more likely destined to be in favour of my rival, given that his position on the overall political spectrum was definitely closer to the Socialists. However, in the third and final ballot, in an atmosphere of great tension, I scraped home 241–236.

A remark I made in the emotion of that moment was to stick with me forever afterwards: 'I was born an Englishman; I shall die a European.'

I meant it.

It had been a nail-biting finish that left me emotionally drained. But after a brief celebration with my closest advisers in the *Crocodile*, where we dined on *sandre au Riesling,* the next morning's meeting of the new Bureau under my chairmanship was the start of an intense thirty months activity during which practically every minute of every day was to be programmed in the context of the Presidency.

Thus from one day to the next, my life and my job were transformed. I had immediately to switch my thoughts from the problems associated with the running of the group to those of heading up the entire institution, both politically and administratively.

It was a daunting task, particularly at a time when that institution was clearly in a state of transition. There was a lot at stake, in that if the European Parliament was seen not to rise to the challenge of its new role under the Single European Act, its whole future could be called into question – particularly since it did not lack for critics in several national capitals who had never been in favour of a directly-elected representative forum at European level. I was determined not to become the captain of a sinking ship.

My experience as Chairman of the Agricultural Committee and of the European Democratic Group would, of course, stand me in good stead as regards a knowledge of the political landscape. But there would be a vast difference between taking part in the work of Parliament and being responsible for the overall running of the institution. It was like a lead violinist's becoming the conductor of the orchestra.

I remember travelling back from New York, and the man in the seat next to me asking me what I did. I said, 'I am a farmer, and a Member of the European Parliament – in fact, I'm the President of that.' I returned his question, and he said he was in similar business: he was a conductor of the Birmingham Symphony Orchestra. This tousled-haired youth was Simon Rattle, and in a fascinating discussion we both learned something about the art of controlling a diverse group of professionals.

On the other hand, he probably achieved much more harmony amongst his lot of professionals than I did amongst mine!

In my new role I was suddenly very grateful for the experience I had gained in the period 1975 to 1977 as President of COPA, the European organisation that brings together the farmers' unions from the various countries. It was to be invaluable in helping me perform one of the most difficult tasks of the European Parliament President – managing the multinational nature of the institution.

In practical terms, my weekly routine was also transformed overnight. I was going to have to spend even more time than hitherto away from my home base, for the demands of the Presidency would keep me on the Continent for most of my working week. Even the weekends would have serious inroads made into them by having to attend important political meetings in various member states.

My wife Marjorie was by now well used to my peripatetic lifestyle and to keeping the home fires burning, but this change would complicate both our lives even further. From time to time she was able to travel with me, but it is not generally appreciated just how difficult it can be for the wife of a politician, especially one involved at European level, to be alongside her husband in his work at all times. To travel to Brussels and Strasbourg sounds interesting, but as the politician vanishes into meetings for long hours of the day and even night, the novelty of those cities soon wears off, and the wife (or, one must say, *mutatis mutandis*, husband) of a politician has a lot of hanging about to do. Marjorie used to improve the hour by bringing her correspondence with her. She also managed to maintain a social life in our local community in Warwickshire – something that I could only dip into on an irregular basis.

My social life was about to shrink to even smaller proportions, but at least I had the certainty that the Presidency would last only two and a half years. I was determined to make the most of it.

My first and most urgent task was to select my personal staff, known in the Euro jargon by its French title of 'Cabinet'. This consisted of six administrators and fourteen support staff, drawn from two thirds of the member states represented in Parliament, thus providing a good spread of linguistic capabilities and national cultural awareness. The smooth and efficient functioning of the Cabinet is essential to the success of any presidency, since it not only gives him or her the personal support and organisational framework necessary to function day by day, but also provides the services of Parliament with detailed guidance for their activities. The general 'feel' of the overall administration of the institution is determined to a large extent by the success or otherwise of the Cabinet under its President.

Several Presidents have brought in administrators from national civil services, often with no direct experience of the workings of the European Parliament, to occupy the most senior posts in their Cabinet. The principal advantages of such a decision are to give the President a privileged link to his home capital, and to mark his own independence from the General Secretariat of Parliament. I always considered these advantages to be overrated in practice and to be far outweighed by the disadvantage of having the most senior members of the team floundering around in unfamiliar and sometimes shark-infested waters for the best part of a year. I believe that I made the right choice in combining outside independence with insider experience.

I persuaded Robert Ramsay to come with me from the EDG as my Director of the Cabinet. His number two, Emyr Jones Parry, came from the Foreign and Commonwealth Office, where his most recent posting had been as the Counsellor in the UK Permanent Representation in Brussels, with special responsibilities for liaison with the European Parliament. They and the rest of the team worked hard and harmoniously together for the next two and a half years. Staff problems, the bane of quite a few Presidencies I have known, never took up a minute of my time, and the atmosphere of a united family team was predominant.

The primordial duty of the President is, of course, to preside, and although I had had long years of experience in chairmanship at various levels, including European institutional bodies, chairing the plenary sessions of Parliament and Bureau was certainly new territory.

The former was naturally the riskier of the two, since it took place in public, with totally free access given to the news media, including the constant TV recording of proceedings. But in some ways I came to enjoy it more – with the exception of the voting sessions on important issues, such as the passage of the budget. These could go on for hours and were at times mind-numbingly boring. Yet total concentration was demanded at all times, since any slip-up – for example, in correctly putting to the House a complicated split vote on a crucial amendment – could cause enormous confusion, especially through interpretation, and take ages to unravel.

In a comparatively young institution such as the European Parliament, the President and his Table staff do not have at their disposal the benefit of the distilled procedural wisdom of the centuries – such as Erskine May in Westminster – to guide their rulings on points of order or other procedural conundrums. So there is always an element of adventurous improvisation on the part of the President and his administrative supporters who sit alongside him on the 'perch' whenever his intervention is called for in a difficult situation.

The Secretary General of Parliament, the immensely gifted Sicilian Enrico Vinci, was a genius at the creative use of the Rules of Procedure. One of my predecessors in office, Piet Dankert, once complained about the nightmare of being suddenly obliged to give off-the-cuff legal interpretations that were thenceforth to be applicable to parliamentary business. But, commented a colleague, surely it was a comfort to have Vinci at his elbow?

'Not really,' replied Dankert. 'You see, as a Calvinistic Dutchman, I wanted to know the appropriate rule before giving the answer. But when I turned to Vinci for advice, he would just whisper, "Tell me the answer you want Mr President, and I will find you a rule!" And he could!'

One of the innovations I surreptitiously introduced on an informal basis occurred at the start of business on the Monday afternoon of each plenary part-session in Strasbourg.

Members spend the morning and part of the afternoon travelling to that city, and begin by having group meetings to put the finishing touches to their political tactics for the week ahead. Then at five o'clock sharp the plenary begins, with a high level of attendance, because the first item of business is to finalise the arrangements relating to the business of the House for the next five days. This set-piece concentrates the political mind quite wonderfully, for there is much inter-group manoeuvring aimed at switching the debate slots for various reasons – to obtain some advantage, for example, in terms of likely media coverage, or to stymie one's opponents' procedural tricks. In short, it is the stuff of all democratic parliamentary rough-and-tumble. I had noticed that some skilful operators occasionally used this point on the agenda, under the guise of a question to the President or through some spurious link with a report down on the draft agenda for debate that week, to raise matters of public interest or concern.

My predecessors had all exercised a strict control on such non-pre-packaged interventions and cut the initiators off at an early stage in their speeches with the quite correct ruling that 'the matter being raised was not apposite to the fixing of the draft agenda'. I decided to be more lenient in the matter, and to let this unscheduled mini-debate on topical issues run for a little while each Strasbourg Monday. The result was that this slot in the programme came to be known as 'Henry's Happy Hour'. It was not at all popular with the movers and shakers of the House, who looked on this interlude as a diversion from their own more stage-managed business. Madame Veil, in particular, was often conspicuously fretful, demanding to know what point of the agenda we were on.

One irrefutable formal objection to my leniency was that every Thursday morning in Strasbourg there was an 'Urgent and Topical Debate' for three hours, so that there should have been no need for the informal opening debate I allowed to creep into the habits of the House. But the Thursday debate was really most unsatisfactory as a parliamentary occasion, in that the real political action surrounding it happened off-stage, in the offices of the groups. There, the motions for debate were drafted, and attempts made between group representatives to hammer out compromises in the form of joint texts. Group Chairmen, meeting in private early in the week would select five or six topics for debate, of which two were regular features: human rights issues, and natural disasters. (The latter, often cynically referred to as 'the bad weather item', sometimes had a very practical significance. For example, if it related to damage to property or crops in a Community region, a sympathetic resolution adopted by Parliament might greatly increase the chances of European monies being made available in compensation to the region concerned.)

In order to accommodate as many draft resolutions as possible, one of the tricks of the trade was to combine in a single resolution references to several (often only spuriously related) matters, which did nothing to enhance the overall coherence of the operation. Once all this wheeling and dealing had been completed behind the scenes, political interest in the debate itself waned. Moreover, by Thursday many MEPs were engaged in activities outside the Chamber – for example, looking after visitors' groups or attending sectoral meetings in their particular field of interest. So, apart from those waiting their turn to speak, the House tended to be sparsely populated, with only rarely a lively, well-attended debate.

By contrast, in 'Henry's Happy Hour' there was almost always genuine controversy, a full House and spontaneous expressions of opinions from the elected representatives of the peoples of Europe about the burning issues of the day. The tendency since – sadly – has been to swing back to controlled orthodoxy in this matter. I must say I believe the problem of ensuring the full expression of 'the voice of the people' has yet to be satisfactorily resolved.

Mind you, in all modern parliaments it is difficult to provide for a worthwhile contribution to a debate from the backbenchers, who, after all, are the direct representatives of grass-roots public opinion. The pressure on parliamentary time, largely due to the need to bring forward ever weightier programmes of legislation, means that the individual Member is forced more and more into the role of lobby-fodder for his party, and all too seldom succeeds in having his voice heard on the floor of the House. That problem is even more acute in the European Parliament, since the number of plenary days in the month varies between only four and six full days.

As for the allocation of speaking time, the European Parliament is at least fair. The total debating time available is divided in advance amongst the groups under our old favourite, the d'Hondt proportional system. Then within each group there is a further share-out according to the respective responsibilities in the field concerned, or the particular interests of national delegations. It is within each group that the fiercest horse-trading is done, and the result is usually to break the group's allocation into ever-smaller units of time in order to meet, however frugally, the many demands for speaking time.

The final details of this share-out are notified in advance to the President, who has the job of keeping each speaker on schedule – the duration of each intervention is shown on a large digital stopwatch that ticks away the seconds on the wall.

I sometimes had the feeling that I was impersonating a TV game-show host as I gave the floor to a Member with the ritual words, 'Mr Brown, for one minute, on peace in the Middle East'. Yet such sound-bite opportunities, ludicrous as they may seem in the context of the overall debate, do have the merit of permitting a large number of speakers to take part – certainly far more than in most national parliaments.

The technical infrastructure of the European Parliament gives the President an all-powerful disciplinary weapon. If a Member disregards a warning from the 'perch' that he is approaching the end of his time allocation, the President has only to press a 'disconnect' button on the desk in front of him to leave the speaker without amplification – and worse still, interpretation – so that he is not even a voice crying in the wilderness.

Seasoned parliamentarians frequently find ways round the rules – particularly round agreed speaking times – to achieve extra attention for their point of view. In the European Parliament one much-used loophole at that time was the 'Explanation of Vote', provided for in the Rules of Procedure. Evoking this right, a Member could, in explaining his vote, put over the guts of the speech he would have liked to make in the debate. Admittedly this *post facto* intervention could no longer, by definition, affect the vote, but it allowed the Member to place his views on record, and to publicise them to his home media as having been delivered in the European Parliament. Nowadays there is much encouragement for 'Explanations of Vote' to be submitted in writing, in the same way that opinions are frequently written into the record of the US Congress.

Another ruse I had to deal with was the 'point of order'. Members who rise in their place with their arms aloft and hands crossed can, in principle, expect to catch the President's eye and be allowed to raise a point of order. Sometimes the interruption was genuine and required a procedural ruling from the President. In the case of important and complex issues the fall-back position was available to refer the matter to the Parliamentary Committee responsible, *inter alia,* for Rules. But more often than not the 'point of order' was little more than a very brief political speech, cleverly advanced under the camouflage of a procedural argument. Invariably, in such cases, when I intervened to rule the alleged point of order inadmissible, the culprit would adopt that posture of outraged innocence common to penalised football players who have just scythed the feet from under the opposing striker.

On the whole I tried to be as liberal as possible and, above all, to ensure that the smaller groups got a fair crack of the whip, in the overall interests of democracy.

My fundamental belief in the need for a strong parliamentary institution at the heart of the European enterprise is coupled with my conviction that the European Parliament should come across to the ordinary citizen as something comprehensible, worthwhile and actively operating on his or her behalf. Certain practical problems, shared by all national parliaments, got in the way of that ideal.

Some of the problems had their origin in technological advances. I can think of many examples, but I'll cite just two.

The fact that Members can follow proceedings in the Chamber on TV sets in their offices, while simultaneously getting on with other aspects of their parliamentary business, means that during plenary sessions

MEPs actually in the House are often vastly outnumbered by visitors in the gallery, who are understandably disappointed by the deserted scene below them.

Secondly, electronic voting by smart card obviously makes voting much easier – but automatically increases the temptation to vote too often. There is a fine balance to be struck between taking occasional decisions on important matters of general principle and voting on every possible detail of the draft legislative texts (on the premise that 'the devil is in the detail'). In my view, the European Parliament still tilts too much towards the latter – and in my days of presiding over several hours of voting at a stretch, I probably held that view even more strongly than I do today.

Voting sessions apart, I quickly came to enjoy the challenges of presiding in plenary session, and I hope that I was able in some measure to lighten the tone of the formal proceedings and develop a more human rapport between the President on his perch and the individual Member on the floor of the House.

Presiding over the European Parliament Bureau was a different kind of experience, though equally challenging. The Bureau met twice monthly on average, and in a third meeting was joined by the eight political group Chairmen in an augmented assembly known accordingly and not unreasonably as the 'Enlarged Bureau' – which always struck me as an unfortunate appellation, all too suggestive of an unpleasant medical condition. Occasionally it felt like one, too, especially whenever there were clashes between a group Chairman and the Vice-President of the same group, each believing himself to be senior to the other in the political pecking order.

In reality there could be little doubt that the Chairmen of the largest three or four groups had more clout than most Vice-Presidents. But the problem was that there was no clear power structure, nor indeed clear guidelines as to who should do what. There were separate competences for the Bureau and Enlarged Bureau, written into an appendix to the Rules of Procedure, which largely reserved the more 'political' decisions to the larger entity. In practice, however, there were many grey areas – and if a Vice-President or a number of Vice-Presidents didn't like the way a particular discussion was developing in the Bureau, one oft-employed way to delay the decision was to contrive to have the matter referred to the Enlarged Bureau.

After my Presidency the group Chairmen succeeded in establishing the Conference of Group Presidents, as an entity quite separate from the Bureau. But even with a new set of guidelines, the issue of respective competence has not yet been entirely resolved. For what it's worth, my impression in recent years has been that the balance of power and influence has shifted towards the group Chairmen.

As the person responsible for chairing both the Bureau and the Enlarged Bureau, I was often caught in the middle of these turf wars. Fortunately, I became accepted as the honest broker – and the fact that I came from a group other than the two giants helped in that respect. The meetings of both entities were intimate and detailed, despite the need for interpretation facilities, while the work itself was carried out on the basis of high-quality position and option papers prepared by the services of the General Secretariat.

Being Chairman demanded great patience – for most issues had to be allowed at least one *tour de table* to give everyone their say – and also great concentration, in order to be able to spot the most potentially fruitful line to develop, for the Chairman's aim had to be that of achieving consensus. Decisions arrived at without a vote always had the best chance of being successful in practice, but there were inevitably issues that had to be put to the vote.

Within the Bureau, voting was more straightforward in the sense that the Vice-Presidents numerically reflected the strength of the political forces in the House. Amongst the group Chairmen, however, the forces represented by the leaders of the largest two groups could each be six or seven times greater than those represented by the leaders of the two smallest groups. There was no weighted voting system, but if a decision looked as though it was going to be distorted because of this factor, we had the fall-back option of referring the matter to the full House. That was very much a last resort, for group leaders were wary of putting the fate of important decision into the hands of the backbenchers 'who might not have had the opportunity to inform themselves fully about all the issues', as the Chairmen would have said.

It was fascinating to observe the differing debating and negotiating styles of the various nationalities. It seemed to me that in this regard there is a basic North-South culture divide, the South represented by the countries of Latinate cultural origins, the North by the rest. France, though linguistically in the Southern category, is something of a half-way house between the two, as befits a country stretching from the Straits of Dover to the Mediterranean. (The French believe this to be an important national advantage – but the downside is that they are frequently mistrusted by both categories. Yet they are admired by all for their powers of analysis).

The Northern and Southern European styles differ profoundly the one from the other; both have their advantages and disadvantages. The Northern approach is direct and simplified as much as possible, is more quickly understood, and takes much less time to put across. The Southern approach is more elliptical and subtle, and takes a monumental amount of time to put across. (Indeed, while everyone pays lip service to the virtues of brevity, I have the feeling that Southern Europeans, perhaps subconsciously, equate brevity of presentation with weakness of argument.) The biggest plus for the Northern style is clarity and speed. The Latins can often, however, find solutions where others have failed, using their genius for widening the angle through which a particular problem is viewed in order to identify acceptable compromises in a package of agreements that goes well beyond the original problem.

As a Northerner, I had to train myself to listen very attentively to interventions by Southerners, in order to be aware of messages being conveyed between the lines, in the sense either of a polite rejection of the ideas already advanced or of possible openings for eventual agreement beyond the speaker's first adopted position.

I did not attempt to modify my own style of chairmanship from that which I had evolved from my days as leader of the National Farmers Union and Chairman of COPA and the EDG. This was a conscious decision, for I believe that while within Europe it is important to understand and appreciate the distinctive cultural traditions and heritage of our various backgrounds, this very diversity is one of our greatest riches, and we should make no attempts whatever at homogenisation.

One of the peripheral administrative details of the Enlarged Bureau's organisation was that in the interests of inclusiveness, non-attached Members were invited to send, on the basis of a rota, an MEP to participate in the meetings, but without the right to vote. Normally this 'representative' – who in fact did not represent anything other than himself – would turn up, look confused by the debate, and leave early. There were two outstanding exceptions. The first was Marco Pannella of the Italian Radical Party, and the other was Eduardo Punset of the Centrist Spanish Party, the Centro Democrático y Social, who had been a minister in Adolfo Suarez's Government.

Both of these men had no trouble mastering their Enlarged Bureau file and were fully able to make trenchant contributions to any of its debates, often deliberately ruffling the feathers of the political Establishment if the chance presented itself. Both were natural 'participants', and I was therefore not surprised to hear that they were in the process of getting together a new group, the Technical Group for the Defence of Independent Members (TGDIM). This would bring them considerable advantages in terms of budgetary allocations, group staff and, of course, a permanent seat as of right on the Enlarged Bureau. In order to fulfil the requirements for the formation of a group they needed to attract a certain number of other MEPs, each additional nationality being a bonus.

There were several MEPs amongst the non-attached who were congenital loners – such as Ian Paisley – but word reached me that a number of others had pledged their support, and that the final effort was now focused on Leen van der Waal, a Dutch Calvinist who drew his support from a coalition of no fewer than three Church groupings in the Netherlands. He was a hard-working, sensible, right-of-centre MEP who had for several years been wooed by the recruiting sergeants of a number of groups. Indeed, the joke was that he had had more suitors than Princess Caroline of Monaco. On the cautious advice of his Church backers he had hitherto always said No – but to his surprise, on this occasion he had been told that if he decided to join the new group, that choice would be respected and supported.

The story goes that on the Friday afternoon he gave Punsett and Pannella his provisional agreement to their proposals, to be confirmed after the weekend. They dashed off to make last-minute arrangements for the launch of the new group. However, on the Saturday, Mr van der Waal tuned in to a weekly current-affairs programme on Dutch TV and began to watch an interview with Cicciolina, a former star of the Italian pornofilm industry, who was identified, much to his disquiet, as a member of Marco Pannella's Radical Party in Rome. His disquiet turned to dismay, however, when the actress-politician – on being asked about the imports of Italian melons – suddenly bared her ample bosom to the cameras.

At that moment the good ship TGDIM sank without trace, with the loss of all hands.

10

THE EP PRESIDENCY: PROFILE AND ROLE

> He himself is scared; nor does he know how
> to turn the reins entrusted to him, nor which
> way to take; nor if he did know, could he
> control those horses.
> (Ovid)

Once the initial flurry of activity was over, following my election as President, I set about the task of deciding on a number of goals and of attempting to organise my life in a way that would give me the best chance of attaining them, at least in some measure. Rigorous time management, set against clear objectives, is absolutely essential in the job, since there are so many external demands made on the President's time – and so many tempting invitations to visit interesting places – that without a game plan of one's own, a President would be carried hither and thither at the mercy of umpteen winds and currents.

All days were obviously going to be long and hard. Fortunately, my established office habits – based on my experiences from boyhood of rising early to milk cows and staying out in the fields to bring in the harvest, if necessary by arc-light – stood me in good stead.

The problem of the 'three workplaces' was inevitably a complicating factor. Unlike most MEPs, I now had to visit Luxembourg quite regularly, because I was formally in charge of the activities of the General Secretariat. The journey by road from Brussels takes only two hours, mostly through the pleasant landscape of the Ardennes, but it was the disruption to Private Office organisation that was the real penalty. My relations with the trade unions and the Staff Committee were, on the whole, cordial, mainly because I supported one of their fundamental tenets – an insistence on the maintenance and development of an independent European Civil Service with a truly European ethos drawn from the treaties, as opposed to an *ad hoc* administrative corps with some degree of national tutelage.

I think they also appreciated my willingness to look at the practical difficulties of their jobs. I recall once being particularly warmly received in the middle of the night when I made an unannounced visit to the print-shop, where the documents for the next day's parliamentary business were rolling off the presses. Even such a task as producing the verbatim report of the preceding day's plenary session – the European Parliament equivalent of *Hansard* – requires a much greater effort of co-ordination and management control because of the need to cover the working languages (nine in those days, now increased to eleven).

To the disappointment of some of my friends, I had as a presidential candidate foresworn my right to campaign in favour of a single seat for the European Parliament. I had done so not for calculated electoral purposes – there were as many votes to be lost as to be won on such an issue – but because I believed it was inappropriate for the President of the Parliament to campaign on a matter on which there were deep divisions within his own institution. It is one thing for the President to throw his personal weight behind a campaign if the matter has been the subject of debate, followed by a resolution adopted with an overwhelming majority in the House. It is quite another thing if the issue is one that is both sensitive and divisive.

Nor could I ever accept, on this or any other matter, that the President could retain total freedom of expression by making a distinction each time between a personal standpoint and one that had institutional backing. That way lies confusion, and a weakening of the representative authority of the office.

Grappling with the time problem, I made things more difficult for myself by simultaneously holding three UK-based non-executive directorships in the agro-chemical, food-processing and banking sectors. Preparing for, and attending, board meetings made the management of the diary all the more difficult – but I believe that it was beneficial to remain in constant touch with 'the real world', and not to become entirely absorbed by the necessarily esoteric world of Euro-politics and technocracy. The boards on which I served were generously flexible about the scheduling of meetings, and understanding of my need sometimes to cry off at short notice. I trust that I repaid them by my input, from a 'Brussels' point of view.

One saving in time I was able to make was that I no longer had the responsibility of chairing the EDG and its British Section meetings. A President's relationship with his own group can be a delicate one. If he distances himself too much from it, he is open to being accused of abandoning his roots. If he remains too close, he can appear to outsiders to be partisan and to his fellow group members to be denying his successor enough space to develop his own leadership. Fortunately, I enjoyed particularly good relations with Christopher Prout (now Lord Kingsland) who took over from me after a close contest with Lady Elles. Christopher, a brilliant lawyer, especially in constitutional matters, had been my Chief Whip, and we knew each other's personality and style of operation inside out, so there was no problem whatsoever between us.

A similar sort of balance has to be achieved in relation with one's own Party and Government. This was particularly important for me in terms of keeping abreast of what was happening, or about to happen, in the Council of Ministers and COREPER (the Council's technocratic preparatory body at Permanent Representative level). In this sphere I enjoyed a fruitful exchange with Geoffrey Howe as Foreign Secretary, Lynda Chalker as Minister of State at the FCO, with special responsibilities for Europe, and Sir David Hannay, the Permanent UK Representative to the European Communities in Brussels. I benefited greatly from their information and advice – but I am confident that, at the same time, I maintained within this dialogue the independence of my office on behalf of Parliament.

Having reviewed my responsibilities and assessed the opportunities available to me within the constraints imposed by time and the limits of my office, I decided on a limited number of objectives for the Presidency.

The first priority had to be the successful application of the Single European Act – then awaiting final ratification – and its coming into force as it affected Parliament. Linked to that goal was my ambition to improve the standing of the European Parliament in the overall set of institutional inter-relationships. That would, in its turn, serve my third purpose: the raising of the European Parliament's profile both within the member states, especially the UK, and in the outside world.

I have always believed that success in leadership depends largely on being able to concentrate the aims of one's forces on the minimum number of essentials, and on harnessing their energies to the tasks necessary for the achievement of those aims. In retrospect I can see that only my first priority was fully met. The others depended on that success, but there wasn't time enough to see them entirely achieved during my term of office. A start was made. Improvement of the European Parliament's profile and standing in public opinion nevertheless remains an on-going task, by no means nearing its end at the time of writing.

The successful putting into practice of the Single European Act – which included provision for a new role to be undertaken by the European Parliament: one in which I, as President, was inevitably heavily involved – was undoubtedly the most important European advance of the 1980s. In laying down the framework within which the single market might be created over the period up to the end of 1992, the Single European Act ensured through its application that the old 'Common Market' progressed so far along the road to a single economy that there could be no turning back.

As a Conservative, I was delighted that the sort of single market to be achieved was – according to the Act's insistence on genuinely free competition and a market liberated from former distortions like national restrictive practices (usually disguised behind such labels as 'precautionary health measures') – essentially one in tune with my party's economic philosophy. There would be irritations later on, over such Left-inspired items as the Social Chapter, but fundamentally there has never been any doubt that the single European market is rooted firmly in the concept of free market economic principles.

In respect of the European Parliament, the Single European Act introduced a new legislative procedure relating to a broad category of laws. This, I felt, had the potential to enable the institution to progress to another stage of development. Of course, such an advance was a far cry from the role of the European Parliament envisaged in Spinelli's draft Treaty of Union, but it was significant, nonetheless.

Over the range of legislation necessary to complete the single market and some new areas of Community policy – in particular, research – laws at European level would no longer be subject to the existing consultation procedure, involving one Reading in the European Parliament. In future they would attract a new 'co-decision' procedure, under which the European Parliament's opinion and textual amendments would be passed to the Council via the Commission; Parliament would then be re-consulted on the basis of new proposals, which would become the subject of renewed consideration in Committee, and a new opinion including textual amendments would then be passed back to Parliament for a Second Reading; thereafter, the further amended texts thus emanating from Parliament could be adopted by the Council in total or be dropped entirely or be amended yet again – but only on the basis of unanimity within the Council.

In that unanimity in the Council had historically been rather difficult to achieve, this last provision gave the European Parliament's Second Reading texts a vastly superior value, measured against Parliament's influence in the original consultative procedure (which continued to be applied to legislation in categories not covered by co-decision). And of course the very existence of Parliament's new powers meant that the other two institutions were *nolens volens* obliged to take us more seriously at every stage, and to try from the outset to present us with proposals that had – in the light of known priorities – a reasonable chance of being broadly acceptable. This increase in Parliament's influence was also extended, by means of similar procedures, to the adoption of agreements between the Community and outside countries, and to agreement on future enlargements of the Community.

I was convinced that the performance of the European Parliament in the early days of the new dispensation would be crucial to the reputation and future development of possibilities for our institution. Were we to fail the test, through a lack of organisation, irresponsible action or low quality of work, our chance of becoming a serious player in the legislative business of Europe would vanish, if not forever, then certainly for a very long time.

There were three aspects to the challenge:

· to co-ordinate the work of the Parliamentary Committees in such a way that they were geared up to operating a systematic legislative programme, and within tight timetables (Parliament's formal reaction to proposals in the new scheme of things was now normally required within three months);

· to organize the necessary administrative support for such action, in particular through the setting up of inter-institutional working groups to establish and monitor the critical path of each piece of draft legislation; and, most difficult of all,

· to change the whole ethos of the European Parliament at both political and administrative levels into that of a serious legislative assembly.

It was a tall order, and time was short.

Things could have been worse on the timing front, for the Single European Act had been expected to come into effect in January 1987,

185

coinciding almost exactly with the start of my Presidency. Providentially, however, there had been a delay in the ratification process. In the Republic of Ireland, a private citizen – Kieran Crotty – had challenged the process in the Supreme Court, on the grounds that the degree of 'surrender of national sovereignty' represented by the signing of the Single European Act was incompatible with the Irish constitution. Mr Crotty lost his case – but from my point of view the European Parliament had won a valuable breathing-space, in that the Single European Act, as a result of this delay, did not come into force until 1 July 1987.

The necessary changes were not easy to bring about – but they were effected, and in good time.

Hitherto, the European Parliament had certainly had a measure of routine legislative activity in partnership with the Commission and Council, but it had not been an essentially legislative House. Yet as an institution we had managed to make an impact on certain policies in a non-legislative way. For example, within the work of my own group there was the influence exerted on European thinking by the 'Freedom of the Skies' campaign waged by Lord Bethell against the airline cartels and their price-fixing activities. And the brilliant animal welfare PR exercise mounted by Stanley Johnston against the practice of culling seals in Canada.

But such sporadic successes would not, in the longer term, constitute a viable *raison d'être* of a European Parliamentary institution. Such 'own initiatives' would inevitably become rarer in the future, under the sheer pressure of the Parliamentary – and especially, legislative – timetable. The systematic participation of the European Parliament in a deeper way, over a wider range of competences, more than compensated for this partial loss of the liberty of individual action within Parliament. Youth had to give way to maturity.

The growing-up process involved a change in the status of Committee Chairmen. They now had to programme the agendas of their meetings to ensure that legislative work had priority, and that it was thoroughly organised in terms of both timing and technical content. This had the political side-effect of enhancing the relative status of the position of Committee Chairman. Similarly, the need for monthly co-ordination of the legislative work of the Committee Chairmen as a body brought increased importance to that grouping, which was to develop as a new power-centre within the House – at times rivalling the Bureau and the Enlarged Bureau – on the grounds that the work of the Committees was the key activity of Parliament.

The changes had implications for inter-group relations, too. One of the 'checks' imposed by the Single European Act on Parliament's new powers was that votes on legislation that came before the House under the new co-decision procedure required, in order to pass, a majority of the total number of the Members of Parliament (not a simple majority of those voting). To muster the magic number of positive votes – 260 – was to become a routine challenge. The basic arithmetic of the House was that the two biggest groups – the Socialists and the EPP, with 165 and 116 Members respectively – could, between them, on an average turnout of votes, garner the necessary 'SEA majority'. But of course they were ideological rivals for the leadership of European political opinion.

While I am generally in favour of the various political families setting out their stalls and carrying on their business in total transparency, I am nevertheless grateful – in the institutional interests of the European Parliament – that there was a fair amount of abnormal consultation and covert co-operation between those two groups, particularly in the early days of the Single European Act's application.

That co-operation was facilitated by the chance factor that the two group leaders Rudi Arndt (Socialist) and Egon Klepsch (EPP) were able, when necessary, to work together. Together they were known as 'the two big Germans', a nickname that held several layers of meaning. The duo were certainly big, physically (knuckles of pork, sauerkraut and beer leave their mark). They were big in terms of political clout, both within their respective groups and within Parliament. And they proved to be big in spirit, in that they had the vision to realise that the success of Parliament's role vis-à-vis the Single European Act depended to a significant degree on *ad hoc* understandings between them.

Changes caused by the Single European Act also had immediate and longer-term effects on the backbench membership of Parliament – particularly in respect of the numbers who attended and the seriousness with which Parliamentary duties were performed.

I am not being in the least chauvinistic when I record that British MEPs, regardless of party, by and large always did carry out their duties in a conscientious way. Those who held dual mandates – being Westminster MPs as well – were particularly industrious (although it gradually came to be accepted that the burden of a dual mandate was too great for one individual, and the practice afterwards died out). The same could not be said for some other nationalities: the French and the Italians were the worst offenders. Things have changed radically in both France

187

and Italy since – there are, for example, legal limitations on the number of public offices a citizen can occupy simultaneously. But at that time both the desultory attendance numbers and the unimpressive work-rate of quite a large proportion of Members were undoubtedly contributing in a serious way to the all too well-known caricature of the lazy, junketing, snout-in-the-trough MEP.

Such caricatures are much more swiftly created than dismantled, and even today hard-working MEPs suffer from the lingering negative aspects of the image transmitted in the early days of the European Parliament. In reality, the profound change came in 1987, when groups had to insist on proper attendance, serious work and serious voting, on pain of various sanctions. Political group meetings, hitherto often held in one of the twelve national capitals, were thereafter largely concentrated, for the sake of convenience, in Brussels – thus adding to that city's role as the *de facto* centre of Community operations.

The only exception to the Brussels location for group meetings – since enshrined in the administrative Rules – is the additional week of 'Study days' which each group is entitled to take anywhere within the member states.

These 'Study days' have always been the bane of the British political parties' lives, for despite our own national tradition of holding annual Party Conferences at seaside venues – which have, I suppose, the merit of being windy and wet, and therefore not at all decadent – the holding of group meetings in, say, a sun-kissed Taormina or Marbella has always been awkward because of the feverish embarrassment of British Members who then find themselves portrayed in the press in a frivolous light. The Sunday papers used regularly to send snoop photographers to such events in the hope of catching Members in – or, better still, only half in – their beach attire.

I was generally pleased with the speed and efficiency with which the organs of Parliament, thanks in large part to the enthusiastic support of the staff, made the necessary changes to adapt to Parliament's new role under the Single European Act. There was one minor hiccup – not of Parliament's own making – when for the first time a co-decision Second Reading vote was used deliberately to reject a line of action proposed by the Commission and Council.

It was in relation to a protocol involving financial support within the framework of a trading agreement with Israel. Controversy had arisen not over the terms of the protocol itself, but because of political realities on the ground. A majority in Parliament were sympathetic to Palestinian complaints that their agricultural producers were being prevented from organising a proper export trade because of bureaucratic harassment by the Israelis at the border crossing points. There had been considerable diplomatic activity over this, but by the time the vote was due to be taken the situation had not been resolved.

The position adopted in Parliament in March 1988 was that we should vote down the Financial Protocol as a way of registering our dissatisfaction with the Israeli action, in the hope that this would act as a catalyst in accelerating a solution – after which a new vote could be taken, this time with a positive outcome.

The difficulty arose over the last part of this scenario. The Commission and Council were obliged to accept Parliament's rejection of the Protocol, but representatives of the Council – with their eyes more on the precedent the case would set than on the intrinsic importance of the Protocol *per se* – let it be known that they could not see, following the actual text of the Single European Act, how the procedure would be re-launched at the request of Parliament, for Parliament did not have the right to make any such request. As far as the Council was concerned, the procedure in this specific case had been completed and was over and done with.

In fact, of course, the real reason was that they did not wish to yield anything that might be interpreted as giving the European Parliament the right to demand the re-submission of a measure.

Fortunately, at that precise moment in the first half of 1988, the Presidency of the Council was held by the Germans, who were much less hostile towards Parliament on this point than was the Council as a whole.

Over a working lunch with Mrs Irmgard Adam-Schwaetzer, the German Minister for European Affairs, it was agreed that the solution should be for me, as President, in conveying the result of Parliament's vote, to express in a covering letter the hope that 'in due course the situation on the ground could be improved', in which case I would 'formally request' the Council to re-submit the Protocol to Parliament. 'Formally' could be understood by Parliament as being of significance within the co-decision procedure in a juridical sense, and by member states as being merely an appropriate adverb for the President to use in *any* communication to the Council.

Ignatius Loyola might have been happier with the solution than I was – but it worked. And in October that year, the Palestinian exports assured, the Protocol was duly adopted.

There had always been informal meetings between the heads of the three main institutions, but as part of my drive to improve Parliament's position especially in relation to the workings of the Single European Act, I managed to put these contacts on a more regular and business-like basis. The monthly 'summit' for such meetings was still a lunch on the Tuesday of the Strasbourg week, when the President of the Commission, the President-in-Office of the Council and I had in any case had to be there for the plenary session. Our respective staffs were in almost daily touch, and they prepared for us a menu of points for discussion and decisions to be taken.

This did nothing for the Presidential digestion, but greatly eased the business management of the three institutions. Gradually, the inter-institutional staff meetings used to power this particular summit expanded into a whole network of co-operation.

Of the three Presidents, Jacques Delors led the Commission throughout my time, and there were nine national ministers on duty according to rota.

The more I saw of Delors, the more I liked him. His cerebral powers were respected and admired by all, even though his professional style of delivery could be off-putting. Sometimes in a meeting he would be asked a question which appeared to require a one-sentence answer. Before replying he would pause for several seconds, as if utterly uncertain of the answer. Then he would begin, in a totally matter-of-fact way, with 'I think there are six aspects to this, . . .' and proceed with the delivery of a perfectly constructed, coherent, multi-faceted analysis that could have been printed verbatim and without correction in the next day's *Le Monde Diplomatique*. But he was not all macro-economic forecasts and inter-institutional relationships. He found equal stimulus in jazz, football, or the Tour de France – for which meetings in his office might be interrupted for a clandestine TV viewing, when he would display all the guilty delight of a truant schoolboy.

What I particularly liked about him was his readiness to admit that he did not know things. For example, I recall his asking a German minister about details of the background to the setting up of the Federal Republic in 1948. He did so without any embarrassment at this perhaps surprising gap in his knowledge, at the same time displaying a modesty with which few French intellectuals are blessed. Looking further ahead, it has remained a mystery to many why Delors did not, at the last minute, run for the Presidency of France against Jacques Chirac in 1995. I believe that in the final analysis, the crucial difference between these two highly gifted and ambitious men was that Chirac's political appetite for power was the keener. A fear of failure in such a tight situation must have been common to both. In Chirac's case his appetite was stronger than his fear – with Delors, it was the reverse.

As for the national ministers I met, both during the Council Presidency held by their particular member states and in other contexts, I was struck above all by how few of them were fully tuned in to the European theme of which their own activities were part. British Foreign Office Ministers were notable exceptions to this pattern . . . although I had the impression that in London they felt constrained to hide their light under a bushel because 'Europeans' were never going to be flavour of the month.

Reflecting on which ministers left the greatest impression on me from my dealings with them in the 'three Presidents' context, I realise that the most memorable were not necessarily those from the most influential member states, nor those who had the most outstanding achievements to their name.

I think, in particular, of Theodoros Pangalos, of Greece – a man whose politics I would certainly not share. Nor was he renowned for wise judgement – he was later to get into very hot water for expressing his criticism of Bonn's policy on Yugoslavia in the statement 'Germany has the body of a giant and the brain of a child.' Hmm. Yet he stands out in my memory because of his intellectual energy, grasp of detail, enthusiasm for his job, and his interesting and humorous off-duty conversation.

Mrs Irmgard Adam-Schwaetzer was particularly helpful, and very protective of the European Parliament's interests. Her boss, the legendary Hans-Dietrich Genscher, would occasionally show up at important set-piece events, but he was always clearly 'in transit', which was his style. Indeed, the wags had it that if two jumbo jets were to collide head-on over the Atlantic, Genscher would probably be found to have been a passenger on both of them.

In my efforts to raise the profile of the European Parliament I had an early and unexpected success. A European Council meeting – one of the 'summits' held three or four times a year between the heads of state and government – was on the horizon, to be held in Copenhagen in December 1987. It had been customary for the President of the European Parliament to prepare a position paper, conveying Parliament's views on the principal issues of the day, and to have a brief meeting with the Chairman of the summit to hand this over.

While my staff were working on the preparation of the paper, drawing together the Resolutions of Parliament concerning the major themes of the Council meeting, I said, 'Why shouldn't I attend the summit – after all, the President of the Commission does – and present our views in person?' More in hope than in confident expectation the advisers sounded out the Danes, and at the political level I did my best to canvass support amongst other nationalities. The initial response on the Council's side was extremely cautious. But I can only assume that in the last minute 'tour of the capitals' that the summit hosts traditionally carry out just before the meeting in order to gauge member states' feelings in top-level bilateral conversations, the Danes found more support for, than objections to, my proposal. So for the first time ever, a President of the European Parliament attended a European summit meeting.

In my maiden speech delivered to the House of Lords on 9 November 1987, I felt privileged, and welcomed the opportunity, to speak in the debate on the 4th Report of the European Communities Committee on Financing the Community (1978–88). To put fifteen years of development into perspective – and also in the light of current debate – some of the points I mentioned at the time make interesting reading.

I started by referring to the (then) forthcoming Copenhagen summit, emphasising that it must resolve at least the majority of the problems if the European Community itself was not to slide backwards with detrimental effect for every one of our (then) 321 million citizens.

First, there is the achievement of the internal market in Europe and the closer identification of our economies. That is not just a vaguely desirable objective but a commercial and economic necessity. It is indeed the motor of economic growth, especially in these uncertain times, and it sits squarely with the priorities of Her Majesty's Government. It seeks to liberate the European market from the unnecessary constraints often imposed by nationalist objectives. All of this protectionism (for that is what it is) within Europe as well as anywhere else is, in the long run, self-defeating, illusory, and negative. However, an extension of free trade, on the contrary, holds out the glittering prospects of more prosperity and more jobs.

Secondly, and at the heart of the many problems we face in the Community, is the overwhelming need to modernise the Common Agricultural Policy. Our surpluses damage the Community's reputation while paradoxically failing to give sufficient benefit to many of its farmers. The present situation damages our trading systems and we must therefore take resolute action to correct the many imbalances. When 50 per cent of the money spent in supporting the Common Agricultural Policy goes towards the cost of storing or disposing of surplus stocks, it is of no benefit to the farmer or the consumer, and is a useless burden on the taxpayer.

The central element in all this, therefore, is a managed market, particularly in the cereal sector, where we need an effective set-aside scheme to reduce the volume of production. This is not just a British problem, and not just a European problem, but a problem of worldwide proportions. That is why I have initiated a World Food Conference to be held next April in Brussels – a conference hopefully drawing together the experts from every continent and every link in the food chain, to search for a coherent set of proposals, and to help to bring the food equation into a better balance. This is a matter of high degree and high importance on the agenda of GATT, and I hope we are in a position to make a substantial input into those deliberations.

We in the European Parliament have proposed a clear shift in agricultural expenditure towards structural support. We must therefore think not only of technology but of the very life of rural people, which depends not only on an economically healthy farming community but on employment in rural areas. However, we must do so in cost-effective ways. We must obviously operate under budgetary control and budgetary discipline.

Thirdly, and against this background, the Community will need to finance its existing commitments and new obligations it has taken on with the Single European Act. Additional resources will be necessary. The Community simply must be put on a sound financial footing – one that is sensible, adequate and fair. It is indeed longer-term proposals we are looking for. We cannot afford *ad hoc* annual budgets. Each failure to agree adds to uncertainty and frustration – and it certainly adds to confusion. In all this, it is the ordinary people in member states who end up suffering: those who are involved in small organisations, the beneficiaries of the social and regional funds.

Lastly, we must concentrate on the positive aspects of building the Community. It is time to put aside the deplorable waste of time and energy that Europe has for so long suffered over budgetary questions. There are many other tasks to consume our energy, not least the building of a politically united Europe. Yesterday we remember; today we must concentrate on the peace and security of our people. These, then, are the main items of immediate concern.

In my other institutional incarnation, we are energetically coming to grips with our co-legislative role under the Single European Act. I shall be privileged on behalf of the European Parliament to put its views forward to the European Council when it takes place in Copenhagen.

I cannot pretend that I took the Council citadel by storm. I was listened to in a polite silence. There were no questions or comments. The chairman thanked me for conveying Parliament's message ... And the business moved on – impatiently. However, a start had been made – and at subsequent Council meetings the degree of my participation dramatically increased. My successors have been able to build on this advance in the intervening years.

One of the standard duties of the President of the European Parliament, within a few months of taking office, is to make an official visit to each of the capitals of the member states. Typically, such a visit includes an audience with the head of state, a courtesy call on the Speaker of the national parliament, and meetings with ministers who have departmental interests closely involved with Community affairs, as well as with Opposition party leaders and leaders of organisations such as employers and trade unions. Although the overall content of every one of those visits was very similar, true to the theme of European diversity each had its own particular flavour.

The distinctive characteristic, I came to believe, was established from the moment the Presidential limousine set off from the end of the red carpet at the airport with its accompanying escort of motorcycle outriders.

In Bonn, for example, the car was preceded by a V-shaped formation of ten outriders who moved at moderate speed but with the utmost grace – and within centimetres of one another. I had the impression of watching a display of precision riding at a military tattoo. In Rome, on the other hand, at that point of the visit I had the impression that I was not only a spectator at, but a participant in, a cross between a bank raid get-away and a 500cc TT race, as the motorcade and motorbikes roared through the traffic at breakneck speed, outriders dashing ahead to secure a clear passage, and forcing vehicles coming from the sides to screech to a resentfully smouldering halt. Restful it was not – but characteristic it was.

On the second day of the official visit to Italy, my party arrived at the office of the Prime Minister – only to find that no one was expecting us. After a ten-minute wait, feverish telephoning and a security frisking, I was finally shown in to see the head of Government, Bettino Craxi. He had just received a severe mauling in the Camara di Deputati and at that moment was the glummest politician I had ever met. Perhaps the problems – later to take him into exile in Tunisia as a fugitive from justice – were already casting their shadow. Usually Italian politicians are extremely upbeat about Europe. Cynics used to say that was because they welcomed the prospect of a supra-national rescue from the chaos of their national politics. But not even the topic of Europe could shake Craxi from his gloom. When he saw how the political parties and the press behaved, he confided, he simply despaired of democracy. Fortunately, this was not a mood widespread among my other Italian hosts.

A courtesy call on the Pope was arranged as an addendum to this official visit to Italy. Protocol was, as I had expected, superficially complicated, with much toing and froing beforehand between my office, the Parliament's Information Office in Rome, and the bureaucracy of the Holy See. And on the arrival of my party in the Vatican itself the stiffness continued. The system for the reception of VIP visitors granted a private audience with the Pope involved filtering the visitor through a series of antichambers, in each of which a few minutes were spent talking to an ever more senior clerical official, who then scurried away, presumably to update the briefing notes for the Pope on what points were likely to arise outside the agreed agenda. All this struck me as a trifle excessive for a courtesy call, but it was no doubt standard procedure.

Yet when I finally reached the private study of the Pope, the bureaucratic trappings fell away: my audience with John Paul II was extremely relaxed, and ranged far and wide – well beyond the prearranged parameters of the discussion.

I had been told that my audience was one-to-one, with no interpreter, and that I would have to stand throughout our meeting. When I entered, I received a very friendly greeting. The Pope smiled warmly at me.

'I understand you are a countryman. So am I. I like talking to country people. Do sit down'.

I said carefully, 'I prefer to stand, Your Holiness.'

He looked ever so slightly chagrined. 'I know what they told you outside. *Do* relax and sit down.'

During our discussion, he had on his desk a pile of papers he said were speeches in different languages in preparation for his visit to South America. I said how impressed I was with the worldwide support for his global travels – but weren't the young leaving his Church, as they were my Anglican Church? And why *was* that? I refered to my son's returning from Argentina and joining the Born Again Christians. We had a fascinating discussion, before exploring various issues relating to Europe.

The Pope's main 'official' interest was in the relationship between the European Community institutions and the Council of Europe, and how the two could best jointly influence developments in the Soviet Union and its satellites. I was surprised at the vagueness of his knowledge about the constitutional differences between the two European entities – he had apparently not fully taken on board the degree to which the EC's legislative and policy action had already been integrated. But his deep knowledge of Central and Eastern Europe shone through in his insights into what was fermenting there.

Even he, though – while optimistic that in the long run Communism could not hold sway over so many people who in their hearts rejected it – had no idea how swiftly and fundamentally things were to change throughout the Soviet bloc. I asked him whether he thought that Gorbachev's reforms would continue successfully. He paid tribute to what the Soviet leader was trying to achieve within the existing system, but sadly expressed his opinion that these efforts would end in failure and in the short term, at least, be reversed.

'His own associates will simply not allow him to go on down the path of reform,' he said.

I asked him whether that was the opinion of a Pole or of a Pope.

He smiled at the impertinence of my question, then reflected long and hard before replying, 'Probably both.'

After the exchange of official gifts, the Pope prolonged the meeting for another fifteen minutes to receive my staff and to talk more generally about his concerns for Western Europe. He was particularly exercised about the lack of idealism among young people in general, and the failure of all the Churches to engage their attention. 'Europe' as a concept would have to offer more than the prospect of material improvement, and the Churches would have to strive harder to communicate with the young if a spiritual vacuum was to be avoided.

At the end of the audience I officially conveyed an invitation to the Pope to address a plenary session of the European Parliament in Strasbourg.

The Pope's return visit duly took place in October 1988, and provided one moment of awkward drama on the floor of the House, involving – almost inevitably – the Revd Ian Paisley. The man from Northern Ireland was not without supporters in opposing the Pope's visit, for the largest political group in Parliament, the Socialists, had agreed to the invitation only on the condition that in protocol terms it was related to the Pope as head of state of the Vatican, and not as Church leader. But given his known views and past record, we had a fairly clear notion that Dr Paisley would scarcely pass up such a golden opportunity not only to protest about the visit but to engineer a confrontation with the Arch-Enemy that would be a worldwide media spectacle.

The first part of his demonstration passed off perhaps unexpectedly smoothly. On the eve of the visit, when the business of the next day was routinely and briefly debated, Dr Paisley took the floor and began to deliver his protest. To the surprise of many in the House and, increasingly, of the Member himself, I allowed him to elaborate on his reasons for objection. He clearly expected me to cut him off at any moment and therefore raced through his speech at an ever-faster gallop. But I had decided to let him have his democratic say – better the day before than on the day itself.

Meanwhile I had scrutinised the Rules of Procedure carefully (they were by no means my usual bedtime reading!) and concluded with key members of staff that on the day, if Dr Paisley attempted to interrupt the Pope's address, I would issue two clear formal warnings, with reference to the appropriate Rule, then call upon the ushers physically to remove him from the Chamber.

The papal entourage, alerted to what might happen, were understandably nervous, but the Pope himself remained relaxed. I told him that should an interruption occur, he should simply stop delivering his speech and let me handle the disturbance. He then delivered himself of a phrase that was to pass into European Parliament folklore – and was something I shall never forget – 'Okay, my friend, Henry. You're the boss.'

There was a last-minute scare when one of the ushers reported that Dr Paisley was in his place very early, and that a clinking noise (assuredly not from bottles) had been heard emanating from his briefcase. Could this be a chain, with which he would attach himself to the furniture in the Chamber? A messenger was dispatched to the maintenance department to fetch wire-cutters, and the tension mounted.

In the event, everything went according to plan. The Pope was two minutes into his address when the Ulsterman rose and began shouting his opposition at a volume that completely obscured his actual words. While I was rapidly going through the procedural warnings, he also produced a protest banner from the recesses of his vast jacket. This was snatched from him by an outraged Otto van Hapsburg – but Dr Paisley had several more of them hidden in his capacious poacher-style pockets. The ushers, on cue, came for him, and out he went –

peacefully, but scarcely quietly – and the doors of the Chamber closed on him, to the relief of all, including, I would guess, himself.

The Pope thereupon continued his address, to the appreciation of all who heard it.

It was a strange feeling to carry out my official visit to the United Kingdom in November 1987 and to be treated as a VIP visitor from somewhere else. Of course I had known for years most of the people I was to meet, but my Presidential role provided an opportunity to discuss developments at European level in a new way.

One topic of national debate at that moment was the possibility of the UK's joining the Exchange Rate Mechanism. The Government mantra on the subject was 'When the time is right' – and I must say that in the light of what they have both since written on the subject, neither Geoffrey Howe the Foreign Secretary, nor Nigel Lawson the Chancellor of the Exchequer, gave anything away in their respective analyses of the situation. They were both scrupulously loyal to Mrs Thatcher's line, even though – as we now know – they were increasingly at war with her over the policy on this issue.

My audience with Her Majesty the Queen was a very agreeable occasion, and sowed the seeds for a future royal visit to Strasbourg.

Five years earlier, Piet Dankert – my predecessor-but-one in office – had had a bit of a spat with Buckingham Palace about the dress code for royal occasions. The invitation to the occasion to which he had been invited stipulated 'morning dress or national costume'. He lightheartedly chose to interpret 'national costume' as extending to a lounge suit, which he claimed had become the national dress of the Netherlands. Such an assertion can only have reinforced the reservations of Palace officials about the European Parliament as an institution.

In my private talk with the Queen in her study, I gently pointed out that she was the only head of a member state who had not so far addressed a plenary session of the European Parliament. I also expressed the view that such a visit would do more to influence British public opinion in a favourable way than any information campaign we as an institution could possibly mount. I would naturally be even more gratified if she would accept an invitation during my own term of office.

Not altogether unexpectedly, the Queen was guarded in her reply. I knew from various sources, after all, that she had been receiving contrary advice from influential quarters on the other side of St James's

Park. It remains a disappointment to me that the Queen did not visit Strasbourg during my Presidency – but I was delighted when she eventually did go, some three years later, and was warmly received by Egon Klepsch, as President, and by the whole House.

Before my audience with her ended, the Queen asked me for what she described as 'a piece of professional advice'. Was this going to be a question about the Common Agricultural Policy and its implications for the royal estates?

No.

'What on earth can one do with Canada geese? They simply eat up the lawns,' said Her Majesty, pointing down at an offending flock dabbling around the edges of the pond in the garden below.

'If you will import them from Packington Park, Ma'am, this is how they multiply.'

'Please tell Ian [the Earl of Aylesford] from me that he can come and take them back,' she said.

The Earl did not believe me when I gave him the message.

11

PRESIDENTIAL VISITS

From whatever place I write, you will expect that part of
my 'Travels' will consist of excursions in my own mind.
(Samuel Coleridge)

The period during which I was President of the European Parliament,
1987 to 1989, was one of transformational importance for the European
Community. The consequences of the Single European Act and of the
obvious progress towards the completion of the Single Market by 1992
were that the member states were committed to a much closer
relationship than ever before. 'Europe', in the EC sense of the word,
was taking on a new meaning – indeed, a more closely-defined identity.
It was important that this development be understood within our own
member states – a goal that (for reasons I will come to later) was,
sadly, far from achieved – and that this new identity be projected outside
Western Europe.

It was at this time that the rest of the world began to realize that the
Treaty-of-Rome-Europe was not just another international trading
association but an integrating economic and political unit of an entirely
unprecedented type, and one to which they would have to relate in a
completely new way.

I was keen to contribute to the projection of this new European identity
– for several reasons. Firstly, it was important that the outside world
should begin to think of the member states not just in bilateral terms
but as a unit; in turn, that perspective would help the constituent parts
of the Community to develop a more unified self-image. Secondly, I
wanted to take the opportunity of promoting the image of the European
Parliament as a major institution of the new Europe. As a directly-elected
forum we had only been on the scene for eight years and thus had a
twenty-year handicap to make up vis-à-vis the other EC institutions.

And thirdly, it gave me the chance to campaign for 'parliamentarianism' in general, on virtually a worldwide basis.

The parliamentary dimension is, of course, an essential aspect of democracy. But in many countries – despite apparent advances such as the introduction of Select Committees – Parliamentary influence in political life has been diminished while the power of executive Government has correspondingly increased, usually under the cloak of 'efficiency'. I am in favour of strengthening the Parliamentary aspect of democracy at every opportunity, and I am equally in favour of inter-parliamentary contacts across national boundaries. This latter aspect is often undervalued because, unlike inter-governmental contacts, it is never seen to produce immediate, tangible results. But inter-'parliamentarianism' can do a great deal to increase broader inter-national understanding over a longer period, and to help nudge public opinion on important supra-national issues.

The European Parliament is, of course, a special case in this respect, since it is in itself a multinational representative body from within which the views of the electorate from every corner of the EC/EU are put forward. In the context of 'the new Europe looking out on the world', I was determined to focus attention on this unique institution and its role within the evolving European scheme of things – it was the unifying theme of all the official visits I made and of all the official visits I formally received – although looking back on that programme, I am struck by how different each one of them was in their character, in the events that happened in connection with them, and in the impressions they made upon me.

Israel and Jordan

One of the most interesting, yet frustrating, visits of my Presidency was in January 1989 to Israel and Jordan. No visitor to that region can fail to be moved by a sense of the immediacy of history and the feeling that one is in touch with important sources of our Western civilisation. At the same time, one is at almost every turn brutally confronted with the sad fact that deepseated animosities are preventing the peoples of the region from developing their full potential in peaceful co-existence.

But the outsider must realise that for the peoples concerned there is no luxury of a *tabula rasa* on which they can write a new and rational life history. All sides are the prisoners of their own and their rivals' past. All sides are to some extent hostages to their own extremists. All leaders are vulnerable to the accusation of betrayal whenever they attempt to make the sort of concessions necessary for a lasting solution. Parallels with the Irish situation spring instantly to mind.

For me there was an additional layer of frustration, in that it was clear to me that the Israeli political class had not yet come to grips with the significance of the European Community or of the European Parliament. Whereas they attached importance to Europe in trading terms, politically they focused almost exclusively on the United States as their extra-regional interlocutor. In so far as Europe impinged upon them, their strong preference – as both Prime Minister Shamir and the Labour Party leader Rabin made clear to me – was for bilateral relations with individual member states.

This seemed to me to be both shallow and shortsighted as a policy background assumption, and in my formal address to the Knesset I tried to encourage at least Parliamentary consideration of the potential for a more worthwhile interaction with Europe. I sincerely felt such a development would be in Israeli's national interest.

Firstly, there was, in their looking solely to America as protector and Middle East power-broker, the risk of all monopoly situations – a dependence that could at some point become extremely costly, should the 'supplier' wish to change the ground rules of the relationship for any reason. The Israelis clearly had confidence in the fundamental benevolence of the United States, but could they really be sure that under all sorts of pressure from various Arab states, as well as the Palestinians, that support would *always* hold up in *all* circumstances? There was no need to be congenitally pessimistic to envisage, for example, another world oil crisis in which it would be in America's national interests to seek the co-operation of key Arab producers, perhaps at the cost of an adjustment in US foreign policy with a 'tilt' away from Israel. In such a scenario, the cultivation of a second 'protector' would seem to be a sensible precaution.

Secondly, the basic Israeli reasons for wishing to keep the EU as such out of the game were, in my opinion, misguided. Israelis evidently felt that the game was complicated enough as it was, and that the EU was not as pro-Israel as the United States (which had such a built in *préjugé favorable* thanks to the profound influence exercised on public life by the Jewish population in America). I could not deny that the Middle East peace talks had been complicated, and that to be realistic, the involvement of another key player would probably slow the pace of progress. On the other hand, I believed that an eventual agreement underwritten by the EU as well as the USA would have a better chance of sticking in the years ahead, which would be the most important aspect of the process.

I did not fully accept the Israelis' underlying assumption that an EU influence would shift the balance of settlement in the Arabs' favour. This Israeli notion appeared to be based on their reaction to what they perceived as unfair criticism of their actions by European political opinion.

For example, Israeli police or army operations against terrorist activity frequently sparked European objections on the grounds that such operations – summary arrest and detention, the destruction of premises used by terrorists, and so on – constituted an infringement of human rights. The Israelis, who considered themselves permanently in danger of extermination, felt strongly that such criticisms – which they saw as not being balanced by condemnation of the terrorist activities that had made the security forces' operations necessary in the first place – represented a judgement involving prejudice.

I made little headway with my reply that this apparent disparity in the criteria of judgement sprang from the fact that Europeans had taken on board a fundamental tenet of Israel's case – that the country is the only genuine democracy in the entire region, and *should* therefore be open to judgement on the same criteria as are other democracies. It might appear harsh in the circumstances, but it did point to a basic identification with the Israeli position that should be seen as an element to be built on, not as a cause of alienation.

An important background factor at the time of my visit was the first real escalation in the Palestinian *intifada*, the policy of civil unrest in the form of street violence waged by disaffected Arab youths, which was beginning to complement the traditional terrorist activities of bomb attacks and assassinations.

I expressed to my hosts some apprehension about the public relations dangers the *intifada* could pose for them, and was surprised at their reaction, which seemed to me to be complacent, especially on the part of people normally alert to every sort of danger. They were confident – as, indeed, I was – that in terms of warfare they could contain it, and that it did not pose a serious threat in military terms. But when I raised the hypothetical spectre of the impact on the outside world of the TV footage of such unrest, and more importantly, the unavoidable Israeli response to it, which would inevitably be robust in the extreme, the reply came that they would limit foreign media coverage. 'We won't repeat Britain's mistakes in Northern Ireland,' I was told by both Government and Labour politicians.

I had my doubts.

I found the Knesset to be a fascinating Parliamentary building, at once striking in its modernity yet recalling the ancient roots of the Israeli people. The building itself and its furnishings and equipment had been financed by Jewish groups overseas, among whom British business families were by far the most prominent. Its architecture placed the Knesset congruously in the Jerusalem cityscape and provided Parliament with all the facilities necessary for the efficient running of a modern democratic legislature.

In meeting the political group leaders I was struck by the overriding characteristic of Israel parliamentary politics: its excessive fragmentation, the result of proportional representation coupled with a low 'threshold' figure. That is certainly democratic, as far as the composition of the House is concerned, but in the arithmetically inevitable horse-trading that takes place in order to cobble together Government coalitions, the system in practice gives disproportionate influence, and even power, to the small parties at the fringes of the political spectrum.

I was the guest of the Speaker of the Knesset, Dov Shilansky, a gentle and witty man who had survived the horrors of the Nazi occupation of Poland. He expertly guided me through the sitting of the plenary session during which I delivered my formal address to the House. In the evening he then hosted a dinner for me in the splendid hall hung with the magnificent Marc Chagal tapestries depicting the history of the people of Israel. I reflected on this remarkable continuum – a small nation with more than 5,000 years of history, which has had such a profound influence on Western civilisation and whose destiny is once more at the focal point of world politics.

Unsurprisingly, Israel, through the political reconverging of the Jewish diaspora, has the reputation of being the most polyglot country in the world. It has been a remarkable feat simultaneously to allow this diversity and to impose a modernised Hebrew as the official *lingua franca*. I was initially shocked to learn that Speaker Shilansky would not tolerate German to be spoken in his presence. It was, of course, at one level highly understandable, but, like the ban on the music of Wagner observed by Israeli orchestras, irrational.

When I put that point of view to a parliamentary journalist, he replied, 'Everyone in this country will agree with you – rationally. But where would Israel be without emotion?'

I was to experience the depth of that emotion on the following day, when I went to Yad Vashem, the memorial museum to the victims of the Holocaust, to lay a wreath on behalf of the European Parliament. It is at once a place of horror and of family tenderness, depicting the enormity of the cruel tragedy inflicted on the Jewish communities in Europe and keeping alive the memory of the 6 million individuals who perished. No one could fail to be moved by such details as the reconstructed pile of children's tiny shoes found outside the gas chamber of an extermination camp, or the flickering flame of remembrance in the gloom of the inner sanctuary of the memorial.

Looked at objectively, this emotional focus on something so devastatingly negative could be psychologically unhealthy. It seemed to me, however, that the Israelis resisted the temptation to dwell morbidly on the tragedies of the past. Instead, Yad Vashem is used as a cathartic instrument, and its most potent message is that *this must never be allowed to happen again*. The national reflex that corresponds to that message explains to some extent the Israeli policy of unfailing and immediate retaliation to any attack, whether military or political. An essential element in Israeli policy generally, it has served the state well in military terms – but I would suspect it has also made it more difficult to fashion the right approach to finding an accommodation with the Palestinians.

One of my most interesting, yet depressing, meetings was a breakfast with the Arab mayors of Bethlehem, Nablus and Ramallah. They were men of dignity and responsibility, trying to do their best for their people. I could see that they were faced at every turn by the problems that confront all moderates in a polarised situation. They were only half-heartedly assisted by those in power, yet to be helped further would have reduced them to the status of Israeli puppets. They demanded more rights for their population but tried to keep protest within peaceful bounds. This meant that they were gradually being outbid by more radical elements in their own community, who could make a much more emotional, if irresponsible, appeal to Arab sentiment.

I sensed that they were particularly sensitive on the subject of Yasser Arafat and the PLO. Their distaste for the strain of terrorist-backed action these names implied was barely concealed – but they were powerless to speak out against it and could not compete with the PLO's attractions as ultimate champions of the Palestinian cause.

I had the distinct impression that their days of influence were numbered and that they knew it.

Conversely, I spent a stimulating afternoon at the Hebrew University of Jerusalem, where the faculty and students of several departments had been invited to meet me. If I had been disappointed at how feebly the European Union featured on the politicians' radar screens, I was now overwhelmed by the Euromania of the academics. They were not only well informed about the EU and all its works, their principal interest was in the possibility of Israel's being able to join it as a member state. Morocco's overtures had, of course, been politely rejected by the EU, on the grounds that geographically the country was not part of Europe. But many at the university agreed that the fact that Turkey's candidature had not been ruled out was a hopeful sign. They went on to assert that the cultural, religious, historical and democratic links between Israel and Europe were more important than the decreasingly significant factor of physical distance.

Before I left Israel I had lunch with President Chaim Herzog. He had been born in Belfast – where his father was a rabbi – grew up in Dublin, and had been a British Army officer in World War II. His speech carried the mark of all three of these layers of his past, and he was a most entertaining and informative host. Freed from the constraints of party political disciplines, he could take an overview of the evolving situation in the Middle East.

Knowing that I was on the point of leaving for Jordan, he asked me to convey his best wishes to 'my good friend, King Hussein'. I was not sure how serious he was being, but it transpired that the two did meet frequently. Each had a modest official yacht, moored respectively in Eilat and Aqaba at the north-eastern apex of the Red Sea, which facilitated private lunch meetings on board in neutral waters, at which views could be exchanged on the region's affairs and on matters of mutual interest, without the glare of publicity. Herzog certainly saw Hussein as an Arab leader with a vested interest in an overall peaceful and permanent settlement, and therefore as a useful intermediary vis-à-vis the other neighbouring states.

After lunch, our motorcade threaded its way down from Jerusalem to the floor of the Jordan Valley in order to cross the river and border by way of the historic Allenby bridge. As we drove through that desolate and inhospitable landscape I reflected that even today a traveller suffering a breakdown on the road towards Jericho would be in great need of a Good Samaritan. The River Jordan at that point was now little more than a trickle because its waters were being siphoned off upstream to irrigate a narrow but fantastically fertile strip on both sides of the border. There followed a dusty drive, accompanied by Jordanian military police, through a windswept desert region until, suddenly, the white city of Amman rose before us.

I had told our hosts that it was my first visit to the city, so I was taken on a tour as soon as we had been installed in our hotel. The centre of Amman was most impressive in its cleanliness and orderly layout and the splendour of its mosques and official buildings. At least three royal palaces were pointed out to me, but I discovered that my meeting with the King was to take place in the depths of a fortified army camp, which was his headquarters and, indeed, where he spent most of his days and nights.

As my party went through the rigorous security checks that surrounded and protected the King, I realised what a precarious and burdensome life was led by such a leader in the Middle East. But I was amused to find that the last line of defence in the royal ante-chamber was not a crack team of SAS-type commandos but an aged, toothless Bedouin tribesman, swathed in a copious ammunition belt and with a curved sword dangling from his waistband. I assumed that the King valued loyalty above technology.

King Hussein came across exactly as his appearances in television interviews had led me to expect – friendly, unpretentious, intelligent and persuasive. He was frank about the limits on his ability to help achieve a regional settlement. Without directly criticising them, he indicated that Syria, Iraq and Iran had less of an immediate interest in peace than he had. 'The Hashemites may well be the best people in the region – but we are few in number,' he said, smiling broadly. He also spoke openly of the threat to the future of his kingdom posed by the 40 per cent (and rising) of the population who were Palestinian refugees and therefore prey to those advocating radical and non-peaceful solutions to their problems. Nevertheless, he remained optimistic about the prospects for a political settlement.

Surprisingly, he seemed more anxious about a future problem he saw on the horizon – water. This was clearly a subject that had taken up a great deal of his time and energies, for he launched into a mini-seminar on resources, growing regional needs, a cost-benefit analysis of desalination, and the national rivalries that shortages would be sure to engender. It is a topic I have watched with interest, and not a little apprehension, ever since. And I recall the King's summing up – that there were solutions to be found for problems of political boundaries, but no solutions if the water ran out.

Ironically, the following day, when I was due to visit Petra, the heavens opened and the road was washed out for the first time in years. I was disappointed not to see the 'rose-red city, half as old as time', but my reputation within our family as 'the rain-maker' – guaranteed to produce precipitation anywhere in the world during my trips abroad – was further enhanced.

Cyprus

Before visiting Cyprus I had already had meetings with the governments in Athens and Ankara. The prospect of a Cypriot application to join the Community was already being talked about, and, of course, Turkey's own candidature was already a factor. Nothing I heard in either capital, or later in Cyprus, gave me much cause for optimism about Greco-Turkish relations, about Turkey's position in respect of Europe, or about the internal conflict in Cyprus. I felt rather like a West End theatre-goer watching the five-hundredth performance of a well-worn play's run with the same cast – everyone knew their lines perfectly, but the performance of the actors was a trifle somnambulistic.

Virtually all the major parties in the Turkish Grand National Assembly took the same line as that Prime Minister Özal had put very forcibly to me. Europe, they said, had dealt – and continued to deal – unfairly with both Turkey and the Turkish Cypriots. When it had suited us to have a staunch ally securing the south-eastern flank of NATO, we had been glad to embrace Turkey. But on the subject of Community membership we were raising one obstacle after another, exaggeratedly criticising the country's human rights record, exercising stringent economic criteria, and stimulating fears about the sheer size of the Turkish population and the supposedly consequent dangers of Islamic fundamentalism. As for Cyprus, Turkey had only intervened in 1974, as she was entitled to do as a 'guarantor power' under the 1960 settlement, to protect the Turkish Cypriot population from their Greek Cypriot neighbours who were being led towards '*Enosis*' (unity with Greece) – and towards a policy of genocide by the coup leaders sponsored by the mainland Greek military junta.

Needless to say, the view from Athens was very different. While Greece had thrown out the colonels and become a fully democratic member of the Community, Turkey – according to the Greeks – was still far from a peace-minded democracy, as was shown in her belligerent stance over bilateral territorial issues in the Aegean region. How could the Community accept into its membership a country that still occupied part of a neighbouring state by force of arms and suppressed the Kurdish minority within its own borders?

Both sides claimed for themselves the best of goodwill and a readiness to see all the points of irritation resolved, but nevertheless expressed grave reservations about the willingness of the other side to compromise.

On the island itself I found these attitudes mirrored by the protégé communities. Both could make out a persuasive case of self-justification, but on each side there was a major blind spot, which appeared to me to make reconciliation unlikely for the foreseeable future, even though there was undoubtedly a generalised 'wish' to see a solution to the underlying problem.

Only the Greek Cypriot Government and administration in the southern half of the island were internationally recognised, but, with some diplomatic difficulty, I had managed to have a brief visit to the North included in my programme. (The protocol compromise reached on this point was that I would meet Mr Rauf Denktash, the Turkish Cypriot leader, not in his official office but in the residence of a senior United Nations representative. Far from being thanked by Mr Denktash for having made a special effort to find this way round the 'non-recognition' problem, I was berated by him for the first five minutes of our meeting for this 'insult' to his people!)

The blind spot I detected in the outlook of the Greek Cypriot community was the state of denial in which they lived as regards the realities of history, not only about the events of 1974 but in relation to the whole period 1960–1974. They simply did not face up to the responsibility their leaders and they themselves carried for that tragedy. The 1960 Constitution was an extremely complicated one, full of all sorts of checks and balances between the Greek and Turkish communities. The irony was that a system so complex would only have worked in practice if applied in good faith and with goodwill on both sides. But it had been the lack of those commodities that had justified the veto-riddled constitutional arrangements in the first place.

The pushing of the Turkish Cypriots into a number of cramped enclaves; the constant threat of 'Enosis' with Greece (even though Archbishop-President Makarios had gradually cooled to the idea as he warmed to the role of undisputed ethnarch, thus actually provoking the intervention of the colonels in Athens); the attempt at Hellenization of the entire island; and finally the coup d'état by Nicos Sampson, the colonels' puppet – all these things contributed to the disaster of 1974. A recognition of these facts by the Greek Cypriots, it seemed to me, was a psychological prerequisite for a compromise settlement.

On the Turkish side, the blind spot was over their constant denial of their minority status and their claim for parity with their Greek Cypriot neighbours. Thanks to the force of arms deployed by their protectors from mainland Turkey, the Turkish Cypriots – who had constituted 18 per cent of the pre-1974 population – now occupied almost half of the land. Furthermore, they had from that year embarked on a demographic offensive, bringing in Anatolian settlers to work the newly-occupied zones in a bid to justify their demands for the future settlement to take the form of a loose confederation between two equal, quasi-sovereign states.

I came to believe that without an acceptance by the Turkish Cypriots of their minority role, a durable future settlement would remain a pipe-dream. A minority may well need to be protected, or even privileged, but if it does not accept the basic fact of life that it *is* a minority, then even if its demands for parity were to be conceded in negotiations by the leadership of the other side, the artificiality of any settlement based on such a concession would in the long run bring down the edifice because of resentment on the part of the majority.

Peace talks, under various auspices – mostly the United Nations – had been going on intermittently for some fifteen years, with no sign of a breakthrough. I sensed that despite many declarations to the contrary, both sets of ruling political classes had become very used to the *status quo* and would be in no hurry to exchange the cosiness of the current situation, despite all its drawbacks, for an uncertain future within the inevitably novel framework of a new constitution.

The question of accession to the European Community had now been inserted into the Cyprus situation as a potent catalyst for change. Leaving aside, for the moment, the factor of inter-communal conflict, the island as a whole could certainly put forward a good case for membership. 'The situation' of course clouded the democratic criteria, but at least there existed, on both sides – albeit regrettably in isolation the one from the other – basically democratic, parliamentary institutions, freedom of speech, of the press, and so on. These were certainly factors that might readily be developed, in a post-settlement Cyprus, in ways to meet the membership criteria. As for economic development, in both parts of the island – and particularly on the Greek Cypriot side – the potential was good: agriculture and tourism were flourishing, and the possibilities for the development of light, hi-tech industries were excellent, especially in view of the high educational level of the population, which boasted proportionately the greatest concentration of graduates in the world.

Another factor in favour of a Cyprus candidature was its small scale. The territory could be absorbed into the European system without posing major problems for the other member states. But what of the fundamental problem of the island's *de facto* partition and its two administrations?

The Greek side, led by President Georgios Vassiliou, an international businessman by background, was adept at exploiting its trump card – namely, its recognition at UN level as the only legitimate government of Cyprus. They spoke grandly, but vaguely, of being able to assure the representation of the Turkish Cypriot community in the negotiations that would precede accession.

President Denktash, on the other hand, was adamant that only after an overall internal settlement had been agreed upon could Cyprus be admitted to the Community. He obviously hoped that if this premise were generally accepted, the Greek Cypriot enthusiasm for membership – which was certainly much stronger than his own – would encourage them genuinely to seek an accommodation with him. It was clear that, in any event, he would agree to nothing that had not been approved by Turkey, whose vassal he was in every respect.

I found it difficult to assess the extent to which the Community membership issue was accelerating or retarding the process of inter-communal negotiation. But I freely confess I was astonished when in 1998 the European Union accepted the Greek Cypriot Government as our interlocutor for pre-accession negotiations, albeit with special provisos in respect of Turkish Cypriot interests. While I would hope that the two issues – internal settlement and EU membership – can be made to interact positively and in parallel, I firmly believe it would be absolute folly to accept the island of Cyprus into the European Union with only a unilateral assurance of an overall settlement.

The insights my visits gave me into the Middle Eastern and Cyprus situations also gave me cause to reflect on the nature of what has come to be known as 'the peace process', as applied to several intractable situations in the world. There is a general assumption that a peace process must, by definition, be a Good Thing, and I must say that I am by temperament and through experience favourably disposed towards an approach that relies on rational negotiation rather than confrontation. However, it is important to recognise that a 'peace process', in the sense it has come to be understood, has serious limitations and may even pose dangers.

To deal first of all with the advantages. If a peace process is set in motion by benevolent promoters, such as the United Nations, the conflict situation concerned is immediately placed in a broader context, which helps to blunt the sharpness of the internal antagonisms. Indeed, in many cases it would be difficult to imagine the opposing sides being able to *start* serious negotiations in a one-to-one format. Even to their own constituencies, the protagonists generally find it easier to present their initial peace moves as a response to an outside body rather than as a willingness to sup with the devilish opposition. And as negotiations get under way, the peacemakers can help to organise the agenda and to identify to each side where its respective positions should be modified if they are to stand any chance of being accepted.

All that is positive and useful. But there is a downside.

On the part of the peacemakers themselves there is a tendency to become so committed to the process – especially when its sponsorship is bringing political kudos – that the temptation is there to force the pace with the protagonists, who meanwhile have taken on the status of clients. This forcing of the pace, often to coincide with an electoral or reappointment calendar, can manifest itself at an inopportune moment from the point of view of the real participants, whose interests seem abruptly to have become secondary to those of the peacemakers.

From the point of view of the principal parties in conflict the main drawback of the typical 'peace process' is that negotiation tends to take place between each party and the peacemakers, rather than between protagonist and protagonist. This means that the peacemakers sooner or later attempt to *impose* certain elements of a package, in the name of the final goal, the peace settlement. In such a scenario a package may indeed be cobbled together when unlikely otherwise to have come into existence – but when the peacemakers have gone and the parties on the ground are left to implement the settlement, such forced issues remain to constitute time-bombs for the future.

To take but one concrete example of this. Does anyone seriously imagine that in Northern Ireland the inclusion of Sinn Fein in regional government would have been a factor in the Good Friday Agreement had it not been imposed from 'outside' – specifically, by the sponsoring peacemakers, the British and Irish Governments? It can be argued that the Agreement would never have come about without a peace process, yet this imposed element, unwelcome to a majority in both communities, will almost certainly maim the settlement in the long run.

I can see great benefits in a peace process which *facilitates* negotiations between parties in conflict, but I am wary of a process in which the sponsors attempt to become *brokers*. I believe India has well understood this point in the position the nation has adopted vis-à-vis Pakistan over the Kashmir question.

Argentina

Before an official visit abroad as President of the European Parliament, I was briefed not only by the Parliament's own diplomatic services but by the ambassador of the countries concerned, who would come and see me in Brussels. Without a doubt the most detailed, and nervous, briefing I received in this context was that of the Argentinian Ambassador, who was, in the time-honoured Latin American tradition, a brother of the President, Raul Alfonsin.

The reason for his nervousness was clear. I was to be the first British politician received at the highest degree of protocol in Buenos Aires since the Falklands War. The fact that I could be invited not *qua* Briton but as an elected European made it less of a problem for Argentinian public opinion, and provided a useful testing of the waters for future visits and for the eventual resumption of diplomatic relations. The Ambassador impressed upon me the delicacy of the situation on their side. He would have liked, I felt, to have gone as far as to give me a list of imperative do's and don'ts to keep me – or, more to the point, himself – out of trouble. It took him three meetings of elaborate diplomatic circumlocution to put his message across to me to his own satisfaction.

In fact I had no hidden 'British' agenda – it was the main intention of the European Parliament to develop further the existing parliamentary links through the South American delegation. The Latin American countries were at that time endeavouring to strengthen parliamentary democracy within individual states and to achieve greater co-operation between democratic states. In both of these domains they were increasingly looking to Europe not only for models but for 'partners of encouragement'.

Democracy had returned to Argentina in the aftermath of the Falklands War, but was not yet completely consolidated. Just a few weeks before my arrival in Buenos Aires an attempt was made by some army units stationed at a military base on the city's outskirts, not far from the airport, to mount a *coup*. It had not been supported by the army at large, to the general relief of the population. Nevertheless, there was still a certain uneasiness in the political climate during my visit.

Argentinian attitudes to Britain have frequently been ambivalent. On the one hand, the significant role of the British in building up the country's original infrastructure is acknowledged: things British, whether fashion articles, educational systems, or sporting traditions such as polo or rugby, enjoy a certain social cachet. Warm and genuine friendliness is displayed towards individual British visitors. But of course, the issue of the Falklands and the War inevitably hangs over the relationship.

Yet the War itself is not such a bone of contention as might be imagined. It is true that it is a source of great sadness, and specific controversies – principally the sinking of the *Belgrano* – still provoke some anti-British feeling. But the War as such and the suffering of the Argentinian soldiers are blamed squarely on the military junta who led the country into such an ill-advised adventure. And the politicians make no secret of the fact that the military failure was the crucial factor in the collapse of the dictatorship and the restoration of democracy.

That does not mean, however, that 'possession' of the Falklands has ceased to be an issue of the greatest sensitivity. It may seem strange to people in Britain that a democratic Argentina – which has never in history occupied those small, far-flung islands, and which has a truly vast landmass at its own disposal – is not content to respect the wishes of the people who actually inhabit the islands to remain British in their culture and constitutional affiliation. But that is to overlook the fact that the annexation of *Las Malvinas* has featured for generations as a quasi-mystical cultural goal in Argentinian consciousness, reinforced by the schools and by an endless series of politicians who have played the nationalist card. To grow up in Argentina is to be convinced that the *Malvinas* are sacred, but occupied, national territory. To talk of relinquishing the Argentinian claim to sovereignty over the islands would be tantamount to treason.

Unsurprisingly, those attending the press conference organised for my first day in Buenos Aires were really only interested in putting Falklands-related questions to me, in the hope that they could detect some new nuance in 'the British position'. In vain I tried to convince them that I came as President of the European Parliament and did *not* represent the British Government.

At one point a reporter began to harangue me rather aggressively about the Argentinian position. 'Look!', I said, interrupting him. 'Don't go over all that ground with *me*. There's no need. I have an Argentinian daughter-in-law, and I fully understand the Argentine position regarding the Falklands-*Malvinas*.' I rarely feel aggrieved by my treatment at the hands of the news media, but I must admit that I was a good deal less than ecstatic when several TV stations and newspapers reported my remarks in a selectively abbreviated and distorted form. 'Lord Plumb has understanding for Argentinian policy on the Malvinas', they trumpeted.

When I met President Alfonsin the next morning, there was a press photo-call for our exchange of official medals. I had mentioned my discomfiture to him, for I could imagine how the story could be reported, at second-hand, in Europe. He merely smiled and shrugged. But his hospitality rose to new heights in my eyes when he was asked by the journalists to comment on my remarks. 'Lord Plumb understands the Argentinian position, just as I understand the British position. Neither of us *shares* the other's position.' Well done, that man. Diplomatic incident averted!

I had been told that a British Foreign Office official, working out of the Swiss embassy, had been expected at my meeting with the President. He didn't show up, and there was a vague message that his car had broken down. I never did discover whether his breakdown was the mechanical equivalent of what in certain circles used once to be called 'Adenauer flu'– a convenient excuse.

In a round of meetings with Parliamentarians I found the main topic of interest was the forthcoming Presidential election. The predictions were – rightly, as it turned out – that Carlos Menem would be the winner. This forecast was accompanied by certain foreboding, for Menem was considered such an unconventional, even exotic, figure that his Presidency might just pose a threat to the stability that the post-Galtieri democracy had struggled to establish. Menem certainly lit up the 1990s by his personal style – not to say, antics – but thankfully for the people of Argentina, the prophecies of doom were not fulfilled.

Knowing of my interest in farming, my hosts invited me to spend a day on the *estancia* of the Minister of Agriculture, Ernesto Figueras, near Bragado, some 120 miles (190 kilometres) west-south-west of Buenos Aires. This involved a drive across the rolling pampas, which gave me the opportunity to savour once again the near-perfect conditions enjoyed by Argentinian cattle-breeders.

Apart from the technical interest the visit provided, the hospitality of the Minister was nothing short of magnificent, in the local style. After a swim, our party were treated to a traditional *parilla,* prepared by a team of *gauchos* at the poolside. The world of files and committee meetings suddenly seemed to belong to a different planet altogether.

But on the long drive back to the capital I was given an unpleasant insight into the not-totally-reconstructed military mentality of our 'minders'. One of the five cars in our motorcade blew a gasket, so its occupants – less the driver – were redistributed among the remaining four. As we set off again, I pointed out to *my* driver that his colleague had simply been left by the roadside. 'That is his problem,' was the terse reply.

It was at least 6 miles (10 kilometres) to the nearest village – through which we roared, with never a backward glance, much less a phone call for assistance.

The United States

In September 1987 I paid an official visit to the United States, including a meeting in the White House with President Reagan. The meeting took place in the famous Oval Room, where he was relaxed but apologetic for the 30 minutes' delay before our meeting. When I left him, saying as I did so that it would probably make no difference that I was now missing my flight back from Washington to Boston, he said, 'I'll think you will find it's waiting for you.' It was – even though we technically had only five minutes to get from the White House to the airport!

I had first met the President at the opening of the American Farm Bureau in Dallas, in 1984, when he announced the PIK ('Payment In Kind') Program. This was a programme to reduce the overall volume of grain on the market, which in that year was selling at a price of $2 a bushel – way below the cost of production. The programme was designed to encourage wheat farmers to store grain on a voluntary basis, and to take out of production the equivalent amount of land to the tonnage they stored. President Reagan told the 10,000 farmers present on that day in Dallas that the best estimate of his experts on Capitol Hill was that, on this voluntary basis, 23 million acres (9.3 million hectares) of land would be taken out of production, thereby doubling the price of wheat the following year. He received a standing ovation.

When I talked to farmers afterwards, I asked if he'd got it right. The answer was, 'Hell, no. It'll be double that amount!'

I came back from that visit amazed at what I saw as a truly incredible situation. Forty-six million acres of land – almost exactly the amount we have producing food in the UK – left derelict, and at a time when children and adults were starving in countries like Ethiopia! In the event, 84 million acres (34 million hectares) of land came out of production

217

in the USA that year. And of course it had the desired effect of doubling the price of wheat and encouraging wheat-growers to replant for the following harvest – an excellent example of a stop-go policy.

Only on a European scale could we on our side of the Atlantic talk to the Americans on anything approaching a basis of equality. On a national scale, as the UK by ourselves, we would simply be dwarfed.

That was, and is, certainly true in respect of agriculture – but I believe it to be valid right across the board. You see, I believe that relations between the USA and the European Union are one of the most important factors in world geopolitics in the 21st century. I have frequently, and particularly in the UK, encountered the naïve view that because these two democratic free-enterprise entities make up most of what is comprehended as 'the West', there is really nothing of significance to be said or thought about the relationship – we are both on the same side.

The reality is, in some respects at least, quite different.

It is true, of course, that it is in the 'West versus East', Communism versus Democracy, Cold War context that the relationship was primarily understood in the period 1945–1990. But even then the picture was not without distinct shades. NATO provided a long-lasting and successful alliance in the defence and geopolitical sphere. Not all of the current EU states were, however, members of it – Austria and Finland were neutral out of necessity, Ireland by choice. And when the Cold War was in its crucial phase, during the battle of wills over the deployment of cruise missiles in Europe in the 1980s, some of the European allies were less than rock solid. In the European Parliament I often felt the tremors of this shakiness, as debates on defence and arms issues revealed considerable underlying anti-American feeling.

Britons have always tended to underestimate the influence of the Communists and their allies in Continental Europe. Partly because of the role they played in combating Fascism, both the French and Italian Communist parties were extremely important forces – and had it not been for the political damage caused by Soviet activities in Hungary in 1956 and Czechoslovakia in 1968, their strength would undoubtedly have been greater still. It has always been true, nevertheless, that a large majority of the EU states had an internal majority ideologically in favour of the United States.

If I may sidetrack a little on a national theme here: the subject of the 'special relationship' between the USA and Britain has always fascinated me. I have no doubt that it is a great deal more 'special' to the British than it is to the American side. And I have often noticed that when French or German television programmes show a visit by the French or German President or Prime Minister/Chancellor to the White House, there seems to be exactly the same bilateral complicity to depict the relationship with the United States as 'special'. In the case of the Germans, the emphasis is on Germany as the leading European economic power. The French like to think of themselves as seen by the Americans as the leaders of culture and fashion.

My impression is that the Americans view this sort of partnership with quiet amusement. It is in their interests to keep the individual EU member states as sweet as possible, while recognising – evidently at times more clearly than some European political leaders – that it is Europe as an integrated entity that is ultimately the more useful, the 'special', partner.

There is a school of thought in Britain, led influentially through his media outlets by Mr Conrad Black, which holds that Britain's relationship with the United States is so special, because of history, language and commercial culture, that the UK should be a 'bridge' between the North American Free Trade Area and the European Union (with which the British relationship should be not one of full membership – certainly as far as the Single Currency is concerned – but one of a vaguely defined association). Quite apart from the fact that such a nonsense flies in the face of the basic principle that a country cannot be in *and* out of an integrated body such as the EU, the Americans would much prefer, and have explicitly said so, that the countries of Europe progress together along the path of ever closer union.

There are several reasons for this preference.

Firstly, a Europe of totally independent sovereign states is in American eyes 'fragmented', and therefore potentially vulnerable and volatile. And of course, much more difficult to do business with, in every sense of the phrase. 'What is Europe's telephone number?' may be less of a pertinent question today than it was a few decades ago, now that foreign defence and trade policies are much more harmonised within the European Union, but it was once a question that encapsulated US frustration over bilateral relations with individual European countries.

At the time of my visit to Washington, the break-up of the Soviet Union was on the horizon. Although the upheavals that would result from that break-up were not yet discernible, there was already a consciousness that the existence of the Community would provide an invaluable zone of stability alongside the countries in which profound political, social and economic changes were about to take place. The fact that in the years since then a large number of those countries have become strong candidates for early membership of the European Union itself demonstrates just how useful – from an American as well as a European point of view – the existence and vocation of the EU has been.

Contrary to the arguments advanced by many British Eurosceptics, the Americans do not look askance at moves within the European Union to develop a common foreign and defence policy. They are only too happy to see the European 'pillar' taking on a burden commensurate with its means and one with unified policy goals. On the world stage, the American role as the only current Superpower can be a lonely and thankless one. Having a powerful democratic partner is a potentially attractive proposition, not least in the context of managing an internal isolationist 'opposition' within the USA.

Furthermore, since the main thrust of America's economic policy is to foster free trade on a worldwide basis, it is advantageous to have another major trading bloc dedicated to the same fundamental aims.

All that is the positive, and most visible, side of US-EU relations. There is, however, a negative side as well, which shows through from time to time and is, in fact, always there as a latent source of trouble.

The most important aspect of this is in the context of trade, and within that context it is agriculture that is the crux of sensitivity at which nerves begin to stretch to breaking-point. For while both the USA and the European Union proclaim their total devotion to a free-trade philosophy, it is obvious that even under ideal circumstances – that is, whenever both parties are agreed that the market is completely free, with no artificial distortions – the two sides are in competition within that market. And in the case of agricultural exports and imports the Americans and Europeans have been in dispute for decades over the question in principle, and the calculations in detail, of the degree to which each side distorts the market through subsidisation.

The American view, as I have heard it expressed a score of times, tends to be black-and-white in its simplicity. It starts from the position that because of the fundamental factors in favour of US agriculture – vast land resources, economies of scale thanks to the streamlined ownership structure, advanced mechanisation, the application of pioneering science and technologies, and the efficiency of transport services – US products are bound to come on to the world market at unbeatable prices. On the other side of the equation, they see the European

Common Agricultural Policy as a huge and market-distorting series of subsidies aimed at propping up a relatively inefficient out-dated agriculture for socio-political reasons – principally the need to keep small, old-fashioned producers on the land.

From a European standpoint there are two major objections to that picture. Firstly, as regards efficiency, the realities of the situation have been changing rapidly over the past three decades. The best of the European producers in many sectors compare favourably with their US counterparts, whether they are grain producers in the Parisian Basin or East Anglia, olive oil producers in Tuscany or viniculturalists in Spain. Moreover, climatic statistics show that over the longer term, the weather is kinder to European producers, with fewer years of heavy losses in their harvests. Scientific support for EU agriculture has gradually closed the gap with the USA, and the modern European emphasis on value-added quality means that former assumptions about the invincibility of US agricultural exports are no longer valid.

So when, for example, the EU wins a contract to supply Egypt with a vast amount of wheat, the US reflex judgement that this loss of a traditional American market must be the result of a market distortion, is no longer a sound one.

And on the subsidisation side of the equation, I believe impartial observers must conclude that the US case is by no means as clear-cut as Americans would have us believe. It is true that there is no American equivalent of a CAP-type agricultural support structure. US support has tended to be 'stop-go' in nature, with sporadic bouts of *ad hoc*, and generous, payments, usually to rescue a particular sector experiencing a slump, or as a judiciously-dosed pre-election sweetener. In this respect we have already seen that in the early 1980s the US Government poured in billions of dollars, under the Payment-in-Kind scheme, to subsidise the putting into store of a monumentally huge tonnage of wheat in order to support the market price of grain. The volume involved was in fact double the tonnage of the entire UK grain production at that time.

So the Americans cannot realistically present the world scene as one of subsidised European agriculture on the one hand, and a completely unsubsidised US agriculture on the other. On both sides of the Atlantic there has been, for a considerable time, a recognition that agricultural subsidies will sooner or later be phased out and the finances of the sector placed on a reality-based footing, in the interests not only of the relevant budgets but of agriculture itself.

Whether this is actually being achieved and over what time-scale has itself remained a matter of dispute between the USA and the European Union. It was an issue that proved to be insoluble in the final GATT negotiations, and was finally put on one side, to be carried over as a problem for the new World Trade Organisation.

Interestingly, the last round of the GATT negotiations in the 1990s demonstrated very clearly the benefits to European Union member states of membership of the wider Union. Individual countries would have been in a very weak position vis-à-vis the USA, but together, in a single negotiating team, their clout was at least a match for the Americans'.

Agricultural trade is undoubtedly the most difficult of the world trading issues, but it must be assumed that there will be others in which the USA and the European Union will find themselves in competition and even in dispute. From Washington's point of view, then, the downside of having a major trading partner is that that partner can become, as the European Union has become, an even more powerful trading bloc and a rival on the world trading stage.

At the time of my visit to Washington, the European Single Currency was merely a talking-point as a future possibility, but since then it has become an important reality. The American view of the Euro has, from the beginning, been benevolent, on the grounds that it will help cement a certain degree of European 'unity', which in their political terms is regarded as a desirable development because of the stability it represents. I found – and still find – the Americans to be relaxed about the prospects of the Euro's potential to become a major reserve currency. Many felt that was unlikely to happen; others believed that it could be a good thing, in terms of the overall world monetary scene, to have a new reserve currency available.

I am glad that is the Washington view, although personally I am surprised that there is no US anxiety that the Euro, once it truly reflects the strength of the integrated European Union single economy, could outshine the dollar. So far, it must be said, this subject has cast no shadow on US-EU relations, and it may well be a number of years before it does so.

One other negative aspect of US-EU relations – although not one that seriously threatens the fundamentals of the partnership – is the occasional edginess between the only remaining Superpower and the embryonic Superpower that is Europe. Happily, this rivalry is not a 19th-century one over territory or conquest, but one instead of spheres of influence, with, of course, trading overtones.

Within the European Union it is France that is unquestionably the most vociferous critic of 'US hegemony' and 'cultural imperialism'. This refers, for example, to the dumping of American entertainment products on the European market, and the perceived lowering of quality standards in fast-food franchises. There is also resentment at the pervasiveness of American English as the international language of business, information technology and popular music and films. This factor may seem trivial to the British, but its psychological importance to the other European nationalities, especially the French, should not be underestimated.

On a more serious level, it is inevitable that the rivalry in trade terms will become increasingly mirrored in geopolitical terms generally, as the European Union develops its common and defence policies, intensifies its own integration, and expands to the east. By and large, the USA has been content to see the European Union exert a powerful influence on the former Soviet states in Central and Eastern Europe, viewing that as a natural development and one that fills a potentially dangerous vacuum caused by the collapse of the USSR.

However, Washington has been less sanguine about the renewed interest taken by the European Union in Latin America – historically considered to be their own back yard – following the accession of Spain and Portugal in the mid-1980s. How to prepare Cuba for a successful transition from Communism to democracy is a particularly thorny issue, and the Helms-Bruton legislation has occasionally caused discomfort between the allies, raising, as it does, the question of how far the USA would wish to push its self-appointed (but *de facto*) role of world policeman.

These negative, or potentially negative, factors give certain nuances to the picture of EU-US relations, but they are far outweighed, and are likely to remain far outweighed, by the many positive elements in the overall relationship. What has always struck me forcibly in Washington is that so many of the American leaders have a clear and benevolent understanding of the European Union's potential and probable development path – often displaying, in my view, a greater lucidity in this respect than some leading European politicians and commentators. I believe this is because the Americans are used to 'continental thinking': to the concept of federal subsidiarity, to the advantages of a single market and a single currency, and to the need for state 'equalisation' (by which rich states such as California and New York pay in, and poorer states such as Alabama and Mississippi benefit).

My exchange of views with President Reagan had to a great extent been pre-packaged by our respective staffs in the form of a draft press release. The meeting began late, for the President's meetings that day were running behind schedule, as I gathered they usually did. In a very professional way, he ran through the points of the press release with me at a rapid rate of knots, 'making an honest woman of the document,' as he put it. Then, handing the release to his Press Secretary, he turned in a most relaxed way to the specific points that really interested him.

These were the likely outcome of the reforms in the Soviet Union, and the US-EU agricultural dispute. He was optimistic on all fronts, even though, while superbly briefed on the details, he was noticeably vague in his own opinions. But I felt his great personal charm and his mastery of the presentational arts, and I sensed that his success was built on the way in which he could bring these advantages of optimism, courage and charisma to bear on the 'personal' relationship he had been able to forge with the American people. What they had needed was not new national policies, but this kind of man to lead and reassure them.

Whatever revisionist historians may now write about that period, there is no doubt that the Reagan Presidency represented an American Restoration, particularly in terms of national pride and self-confidence.

Equally, there is no doubt that the emergence of an integrated Europe is a development that the United States has both welcomed and facilitated.

USSR

I had been to Moscow several times before, but my official visit in September 1988 was certainly special, not only because of the entrée my role as President of the European Parliament gave me to the power-centre of the Soviet Union but also because it came at that particular moment in history.

No one could have foreseen at that time how swiftly the end of the Soviet system and of the USSR itself would come, or how profound the changes would be to the whole political, economic and social structures of its component countries. But change was certainly in the air – *glasnost* and *perestroika* were the buzz-words. In my talks with almost everyone I met I could sense anticipation that improvements were on the way in terms of civil liberties, the extension of free enterprise, and even moves forward to a pluralist political system. My principal meetings were with the leadership of the Supreme Soviet, the parliamentary body that had hitherto been a rubber-stamp assembly for the decisions of the Politburo, but which at the time of my visit was beginning to have some stirrings of democracy in it, and hopes for a more worthwhile future.

Its President, Mr Augusts Eduardovich Voss, an old party hack from Latvia, was clearly in fear of losing his position in a future change. I also had meetings with the President of the COMECON, the Communist common market, who clearly saw the writing on the wall and predicted that the entire system would change, economically, within five years. He did not, however, believe that political change would follow.

The most interesting meetings at official level was with President Gromyko, the infamous 'Grim Grom', whose career stretched back to being Soviet Ambassador to Britain in the 1940s. I found on the part of all my hosts an acute awareness, not matched in many Western capitals, of the significance of what had been taking place in Western Europe, with the coming into force of the Single European Act the previous year, which was aimed at completing the internal market of the European Community.

To my surprise, they did not see this as an increased capitalist threat. Instead, they saw two advantages in it from their point of view. First, they felt that the Community would eventually be an additional counterbalance to the United States as a Superpower. And, more importantly, they welcomed the fact that the Germans, about whom they were quite obsessive, would now be anchored even more firmly into a European framework and less likely to be a loose cannon in the future.

One of the changes in the air in Moscow related to civil liberties, a fact symbolised just a few months previously by the return from 'internal exile' and the professional reinstatement of Professor Andrei Sakharov. Some weeks before my visit, I had asked, through the Soviet Ambassador in Brussels, if I could meet Professor Sakharov, who had been the subject of many human rights resolutions in the European Parliament. There had been much diplomatic to-ing and fro-ing about my request, and several contradictory signals from Moscow. It was only on the second day of my visit that our Foreign Affairs hosts told me that it had been arranged for me to meet Sakharov at his scientific Academy the following day.

The Academy was housed in a run-down, seemingly antiquated building several miles from the city centre. There, under the watchful eye of his devoted wife Yelena Bonner, Sakharov received our party in his small, drab office which in Britain might have housed a sociology lecturer in a 1960s polytechnic. He was well acquainted with the efforts Western governments and the European Parliament had made on his behalf, and he expressed his gratitude for this sustained support. He had been particularly encouraged over the years by the unrelenting campaign mounted by my colleague (Lord) Nick Bethell, the Conservative MEP who had been a thorn in the flesh of the Soviet Government – and indeed of Western governments whenever they appeared to him to be going soft – on human rights issues.

Sakharov was visibly a sick man, broken by his many years of imprisonment and by the condemnation heaped upon him by the authorities. He saw himself as a Russian patriot and, I believe, as a good Communist who had been betrayed by the system. I sensed no great joy on his part at his rehabilitation. Perhaps he was just too exhausted; perhaps he saw the difficulties ahead more clearly than the others. When I asked him if he thought Gorbachev's reforms would succeed, he had no hesitation in expressing his pessimism:

> Gorbachev has done much and genuinely wants to change the economic structure of the country. But he has three great forces working against him. The *nomenklatura* simply do not wish to change, since any change is bound to be, for them, a loss of privilege. Then, a whole class of middle-to-top managers are afraid of change because they are not confident of being up to the mark in delivering the goods. And finally, and most significantly, the little ordinary man of Soviet life, who spends hours every day waiting in queues and complaining about the inadequacies of the system, will also turn against change because, despite his grumbles, he knows how to survive in the present system and he feels in his bones that profound change would, with his luck, never be to his benefit.

It cannot be said that Sakharov foresaw exactly how things would pan out in the Soviet Union, but much of his pessimistic musings have turned out to be justified. Before I left, his wife insisted on making us coffee on a small stove in the corner. Her husband was by now wilting with the effort of talking and as she busied herself at the stove she took over the conversation, expressing all her frustration at the Soviet authorities' lack of vision and their basic *stupidity* (she spat out the word).

She was one of those women in the mould of Golda Meir, who could run a family, a business or a country with equal efficiency and in the same style. I sensed that in all her dealings with officialdom she was utterly fearless.

The Sakharovs came with us to the front door of the Academy to see us off. At the foot of the steps a dozen or more drivers, bodyguards and Foreign Service officials were waiting. At the appearance of Sakharov they spontaneously broke into applause. A real sign of the times.

My call on President Gromyko the next day was in a very different setting – although it too was marked by the reflections of a man at the end of his career, indeed of his life, for he was to die some nine months later. The long corridors in the Kremlin leading to the Presidential suite of offices were thickly carpeted and ornately furnished. At every corridor junction stood a tall, uniformed guard, long leather boots gleaming, machine pistol clasped across his chest. Each wore the glazed parade-ground stare of the soldier who has put himself into a trance in order to see out his watch without flinching.

Gromyko greeted me with stiff formality but when we sat down at his work table I was taken aback by his informal friendliness, which chimed not at all with what I knew of his habitual performance as 'Mr Niet' at the United Nations and similar arenas. His opening theme was the then current Soviet policy line about 'the European House' and its various inter-locking apartments. Respect for the USSR and its interests was a prerequisite for peace.

He quickly moved on to what, I was astonished to learn, was his personal hobbyhorse: the environment. That was to be the big European issue for the next century. We would all have to cooperate to put right the terrible things we had done to Mother Nature in the name of industrial progress.

'We in the Soviet Union have been the worst offenders – but we were forced by circumstances to do what we did, in order to modernise our state,' he declared.

He struck me as an unlikely eco-warrior, yet I felt he was sincere about much of what he had to say about environmental restitution – most of all when he insisted that the West would have to help pay for Soviet action – in their own interests, of course.

At one point in the conversation he paused to ask me if there was anything he could do to make my stay in Moscow more enjoyable. This was a traditional set-piece that I had been tipped off about weeks in advance. I had also fed in my 'request' long before leaving Brussels. It related to a Jewish refusenik, George Samoilovitch, who was gravely ill with cancer and who had been offered specialised treatment in the United States. Medieval as it sounds, the Soviets would often grant an exit visa, or a release from prison, for someone on whose behalf such a request was made by an official VIP visitor.

So I trotted out my request on behalf of Samoilovitch. Gromyko feigned ignorance about the case but said he would look into it – which was par for the course. When I tried to press him on the matter, he replied that such exit visas were frequently a problem. 'We can't let someone go if he has had access to state secrets, or is a criminal, or would leave dependants to be a charge on the state.'

As drinks were being served at the end of the two-hour interview, Gromyko began to reminisce about his days in London, as Soviet Ambassador during the war – a time during which he claimed to have developed a warm relationship with Churchill.

He had another confession to make: he loved Royal Days at the horse races, and was a great admirer of the Queen Mother. I saw his interpreter's eyebrows arch noticeably as he translated this information from the President's Russian. Gromyko then recalled one particularly exciting day when Her Majesty's horse almost won an important steeplechase, 'but at the very last fence', said the interpreter, 'the horse falled.' Gromyko tapped a cold hand against the interpreter's elbow. 'The horse *fell*,' he corrected, without allowing himself the slightest sign of satisfaction, annoyance, or any other emotion.

As we parted at the door of his office, Gromyko profusely wished me a pleasant stay during the rest of my visit. Pushing my luck, I again mentioned the Samoilovitch request. Gromyko's bonhomie vanished at once. 'Are you still on about your little Jew?' he snapped in English, then adding, 'What is it to you or me if he lives or dies?'

I felt the chill of the Gulag suddenly sweep over me.

Some weeks later George Samoilovitch was, without explanation, allowed to travel to the United States.

The Russians were keen to show me one of the jewels of Soviet agriculture: a collective farm some 50 miles (80 kilometres) south-east of Moscow. It was a mixed operation, incorporating an allegedly prize-winning dairy herd, a market garden, some wheat-growing, and a fruit and vegetable bottling plant. It covered only a few thousand acres/hectares but 'employed' an amazing 200 people.

Undoubtedly the best-equipped section of the farm was the library — well stocked with works on the application of Marxist-Leninism to various aspects of food production. Elsewhere, machinery was of a decidedly 1950-ish vintage, and the animals looked as though they had survived a long winter on half rations — and I was there in early autumn. The workers certainly gave every sign of being busy, but I wondered about the overall economics of the operation. The manager left most of the talking to the 'political director', but although he was clearly a well-versed theoretician, he could not advance even an approximate estimate of the total value of the inputs of the farm, or of its outputs. 'We consistently meet our production targets,' was as far as he could go.

The bottling plant was perhaps the saddest section of all. The production line involved rows of admittedly cheerful women cramming pickled gherkins into crude, three-litre glass jars. I could not escape the fantasy that this had been the source of British Airways in-flight cocktail nibbles in the days of nationalised airlines! If this farm was a showcase of efficiency, as my Soviet hosts believed, then clearly their whole economic structure must be in a truly deplorable state.

Arafat in Strasbourg

Despite my attempts to keep control of my schedule and to prepare for the items on it thoroughly and in good time, occasionally my best-laid plans would suddenly go uncomfortably 'agley'. One such unwelcome upheaval was the visit of Yasser Arafat to Strasbourg in September 1988. He had been invited by the Socialist group, with the support of the other left-of-centre groups, and was to speak to several meetings within the precincts of the Parliament. That in itself posed problems for me, in that his large team of bodyguards wanted to retain their sidearms within the European Parliament building. As the Palais de l'Europe had extra-territorial status, the responsibility for security matters rested with the institution: the College of Quaestors made it clear that they were handing the decision to me, as President. After an often heated meeting between Arafat's advance team, the local French police authorities and Parliament's internal security service, a compromise was found. The French and EP security men took responsibility for Arafat's personal safety on the approaches to the building, and during his time within it; his bodyguards would accompany him at all times — but they would deposit their arms with the EP services before entering our building. I was told that the weapons thus temporarily surrendered would have armed a medium-sized revolution.

A more delicate problem was posed at the political level. The Socialist group and their allies who together could usually muster a slight overall majority in the House on most matters, formally requested that I receive Mr Arafat. At the time he was still a very controversial figure, and the idea that this leader of the PLO should be afforded that degree of protocol recognition provoked an angry reaction on the centre-right, not least amongst my fellow Conservatives.

I received a welter of contradictory political and legal advice from across the political spectrum and from my advisers. The best course seemed for me to follow my own instincts. So I agreed to receive Mr Arafat – and immediately the opening diplomatic niceties had been observed I launched into a frank harangue on the theme 'Get out of violence and get into negotiations!' He was taken aback at this onslaught, but soon began a self-justificatory analysis of the plight of the Palestinian people. Their only possible way forward had been 'direct action', but now, as their leader, he was moving to the stage of seeking a peace deal with the Israelis, provided they could be persuaded to face up to the realities of their situation. He hoped Europe could influence Israel in that direction.

At the end of the meeting I told Arafat what I would be putting in the press release, including my message about violence. 'Thank you, Mr President,' he said with a low bow. 'Ours will say that I have understood your message. I hope you understand mine.'

My two lasting impressions of the encounter were of Arafat's wiliness and of his apparent ill health. The world has since seen much evidence of the former; the latter may only have been part of his trademark, like the *keffiyeh* headdress.

Sir Joshua Hassan in Strasbourg

Another visit to Strasbourg that ruffled a few feathers was that of Sir Joshua Hassan, the Chief Minister of Gibraltar. The constitutional position of the colony vis-à-vis the European Community/Union has always been a strange one. For many purposes it is treated as part of the United Kingdom, but has never been allowed democratic representation at European level. Within the European Parliament there was a cross-party group of British MEPs who informally held a brief for Gibraltar's interests; six of my Conservative colleagues were members of it. This activity was regarded with a jaundiced eye by our Spanish group, members from the Alianza Popular party – and although we had a gentlemen's agreement to keep the problem permanently on ice, from time to time it threatened to fall out of the fridge.

So I was less than thrilled to learn, very late in the day, that Sir Joshua would be in Strasbourg the following day, and that the Gibraltar inter-group were requesting a meeting with me, to introduce their visitor. I checked with the UK Permanent Representation who, metaphorically speaking, took six paces back from the issue, claiming that they were merely providing Sir Joshua with logistical support and appropriate hospitality; the political context of his visit was not their business.

Before long, my Spanish colleagues were knocking on my door, very upset and feeling 'bounced'. If I received the Chief Minister, the resulting headlines in Madrid would force them to withdraw from the group. On the other hand, if I did not receive Sir Joshua there would be all hell to pay on the British side. Such dilemmas depressed me, not because they were insoluble but because behind the fuss there was no real practical issue, merely posturing on both sides. To break up a useful political coalition in Parliament over a matter so trivial as a courtesy call by a Gibraltarian politician seemed to me to be too crazy for words.

I eventually persuaded the Spaniards to accept that I would meet Sir Joshua, who of course was not an official guest of the Parliament, at the residence of the British Consul General. They were unhappy with this compromise, as were my British colleagues. But this balance of unhappiness at least prevented political nuclear action by either side.

The evening ended in farce. I went off to the Consul General's nearby residence, but Sir Joshua – who later claimed not to have been told of the new venue – turned up in my offices, where he loudly proclaimed to all and sundry that that he had been snubbed. A member of my staff smoothed things over with the circling pressmen, and arranged transport to the referred meeting. Sir Joshua had very little of substance to say, but complained bitterly and at extraordinary length about his treatment. The Consul General kindly invited him to stay for dinner, but he declined, citing a prior engagement in town.

I later learned that this engagement was a dinner appointment with a Spanish business associate!

China and Hong Kong

One of the most fascinating missions abroad that I had to carry out was to China and Hong Kong in July 1988. One of my daughters, Elizabeth, her husband Anthony and their two sons, Charles and Thomas, had lived in Hong Kong for several years where Anthony was engaged in the international shipping business, so we had visited that part of the world a few times on family holidays. But of course, nothing could prepare anyone for seeing mainland China from the inside – and especially from the ultra-privileged position of a VIP visitor.

The 13th Party Congress of the Chinese Communist Party had in April that year confirmed the need for reform and modernisation, with a distinct focus on economic liberalisation already well under way. As part of that policy, the leadership was intent on modifying the image of the country abroad, and in developing more open relationships and trading links with the rest of the world. They were clearly focused on the emergence of the European Community as an economic and even political force – a fact that had manifested itself in the close attention paid to Community affairs and personalities by the energetic Ambassador in Brussels, who had been an increasingly frequent caller upon me there.

I personally benefited from the Chinese view of the European Parliament's dove-ish positions (in their eyes) on Tibet and the Dalai Lama as 'helpful', even though my own opinions were known to be less favourable. So the reddest of red carpets was rolled out for our party, which included my wife Marjorie, Elizabeth and Anthony.

The reception committee at Beijing airport comprised a truly vast number of senior officials from the Chinese Foreign Office supplemented by the ambassadors from the individual European member states and the European representation office. Once the multiple greetings were over, we set off, at speed, in a long cortège of limousines through streets that had been cleared of traffic to make way for us. I noticed a Chinese variation on the motorcycle escort ploy. Just in case side-traffic should seep through and across our route, the vehicle leading our convoy was a motorbike-and-sidecar unit, the sidecar containing a diminutive policeman equipped with coloured flags, which he waved with crisp vigour as he stood up before every major street junction.

Our accommodation, in a state guesthouse in a park reserved exclusively for a whole complex of six houses, was symptomatic of the entire organisation of the visit: elaborate, formal, and controlled. Our party – including Chinese Foreign Office liaison officers, interpreters, bodyguards and drivers – was housed under one roof. We were a 'packaged' visit, and obviously not going to see or hear anything the Chinese did not wish to include in that package.

In all the official meetings, after-dinner speeches and even informal table-talk, our various hosts stuck rigidly, but with great charm, to the briefing lines that had clearly been established for the Chinese input into the visit. At one such occasion – a banquet with some 1,000 Chinese – the Chairman asked me if I would respond to the toast to the guest. I stopped fiddling with my chopsticks, aghast.

'But I speak no Chinese!' I said.

'That's no problem. You stand, and bow. That is all that is necessary.'

I did as I was asked – and received a standing ovation!

I was so embarrassed – and so gratified at how easy it was – that almost automatically I stood again, bowed to the centre, bowed to the left, bowed to the right, and back to the centre.

This time there was polite silence. There might even have been a little hissing.

'What have I done wrong?' I said in urgent undertone to my host.

'They don't like long speeches!' was the reply.

A good Chinese lesson!

At all these functions, a recurring theme was the importance that Beijing attached to the European Community, and its shared role with China as a political and economic counterweight to Superpowers. Economic liberalisation was inevitably emphasised as being the guiding domestic policy. But political reform, democratisation and human rights were decidedly off-limits, and any reference to them on my part was politely but firmly deflected. Small talk in more relaxed moments during the mammoth dinner-parties tended to be essentially a padding-out of the set-piece speech the speaker had delivered only minutes before. Not that the Chinese tried to pretend that we were visiting Utopia – it was simply that there were areas too taboo to be trodden on.

On the other hand, our hosts were frank about the problems they faced within policy areas regarded as open to discussion. For example, the relaxation of price controls – an indispensable facet of economic liberalisation – was, they acknowledged, going to be a major political difficulty. Some products, such as cotton, cereals and vegetables, had already increased in price by 50 per cent that year, which might very well produce hardship for many ordinary families, together with the risk of social unrest.

Similarly, the Chinese were open about the difficulties surrounding regional disparities in their vast country. There were only limited resources available to develop a modern infrastructure, so the coastal provinces – best placed geographically to take advantage of the new economic policies – had been favoured as priority areas. I saw this for myself in the contrast between the city Guangzhou and the province of Shanxi. The former was a dynamic and prosperous regional capital that had already attracted significant financial investment and had more the feel of an enterprise economy than of a Communist state. In Shanxi province, however, most peasants, we discovered, earned the equivalent of about $60 per year, and even the potentially valuable coal deposits in the region could not be exploited because of the inadequate infrastructure

My programme was hectic, interesting, and impeccably organised. It kept precisely to timetable, which was of course facilitated by the 'clear-the-roads' policy applied to our overland journeys. Internal flights were the only cause of slippage – a hitch by no means unfamiliar to me in my European *déplacements*. The lunches and dinners given in our honour were elaborate and, cumulatively, a threat to the digestive system in their sheer volume. One of the things the Chinese believe foreigners expect in their country is to eat duck. That delightful bird therefore made its appearance a little too often and in too many guises during the week. On one occasion, *every* course contained some element of duck. Appropriately enough, this was in The Duck Restaurant.

We did manage two tourist-style sidesteps from official meetings. The first was on the intended obligatory visit to the Great Hall, where I almost gave my bodyguard/minder a heart attack by slipping on some wet paving-stones and coming a cropper. Fortunately – for both him and me – no serious injury was sustained.

The second outing was entirely unscheduled. When visiting the magnificent sports stadium in Canton, I learned that there was to be a football match that evening between China and Hong Kong, starting at 9 p.m. 'What a pity –' I sighed, 'we have an official dinner that evening.'

Much muttering amongst the Mandarins who were accompanying us.

'Football match postponed until 10 p.m.,' said the leader.

And when we arrived, just before the kick-off, the 50,000-crowd stood and applauded our party. I reflected that in Europe we would have been lynched – and with due cause!

The next morning we had our last breakfast in mainland China – fifteen courses, including the inevitable duck. I also managed to transact a final piece of European Parliament business. The Parliament had for some time been lobbying for membership of the International Parliamentary Union (IPU), in the face of some continuous blackballing by the representatives of one or two national parliaments in Europe, who were not keen on the Strasbourg upstart. I sought the support of the Chinese, in the light of the next IPU meeting to be held in Sofia, Bulgaria, two months later. It did seem strange to be seeking backing from Beijing against the wiles of Parliamentarians I had known for decades.

The Chinese solemnly took due note of my representations, without any sign of amusement at the situation. And the European Parliament's application was thereafter successful. Perhaps I did not regard membership of the IPU as particularly important in terms of the overall impact of the organisation, but acceptance in it of the European Parliament was symbolically significant, marking another phase in the EP's evolution as an internationally-recognized parliament.

The few days we spent in Hong Kong following the visit to China served to highlight for me the fundamental difference between a totalitarian and a free society. The two places had many things in common, not least the ethnic and cultural backgrounds of their inhabitants. But the whole atmosphere was completely different. It reminded me of the contrast between East and West Berlin. In Hong Kong you could feel the assurance of an economy that prided itself on the absence of government intervention.

I had wondered about how the hand-over to China, then only nine years ahead, was viewed by the Hong Kong people themselves. I found them to be looking at '1997' pragmatically. They believed China to have a vested interest in a successful transition, and seemed reasonably happy that the policy of 'one country, two systems' would be maintained. There were some contradictory signals – a significant number of mostly wealthy Chinese in Hong Kong were seeking citizenship abroad – but they were far outnumbered by Hong Kong graduates returning, with confidence, following study elsewhere in the world. Overall, I found the prevailing atmosphere much less apprehensive than I would have expected before my visit.

On my return to Brussels I was once more targeted by the Chinese Ambassador, now more enthusiastic than ever to promote relations with the European institutions, including the Parliament. He had high hopes for a dramatic improvement in trading, cultural, and even political contacts, so convinced was he of the rate of positive change in Beijing.

In June the following year, the drama was, alas, of a different kind: the Tienanmen Square massacre. The Ambassador vanished from the Brussels scene – his good intentions, hard work and ambitious plans swept away, overnight, by events.

12

FARMING TODAY

He that counts all costs will never put plough in the earth.
(Rural saying)

The closing years of the twentieth century were among the most difficult for agriculture in Europe, particularly in the United Kingdom. For not only had the sector to deal with the myriad structural challenges in a period of profound changes, there was also the totally unforeseen catastrophe of BSE ('mad cow disease'), followed by swine fever and the disastrous outbreak of foot-and-mouth disease – *and*, a drama at perhaps a lower level but nevertheless a grave problem for the industry, there was the deteriorating relationship with the public over such issues as genetically modified (GM) products.

BSE (bovine spongiform encephalopathy) turned a deeply unfavourable spotlight on farming for several years, and as the drama unfolded I saw its political impact in both Westminster and Brussels. It was a sorry tale, right from the beginning. The Philips Report, published in 2000, comprehensively chronicled the various stages of the problem, and it is certainly not my intention to refute any of its findings. But what I can add to the story, from my vantage-point as a member of the European Parliament's Committee of Inquiry on the subject, is the observation that the political and administrative problems at European Union level were undoubtedly exacerbated by the way in which the crisis was handled by ministers, officials and scientists at the British national level.

If ever there was a moment when we needed friends in Brussels, this was it. Yet it seemed to me that the lack of openness and co-operation displayed by those most prominently responsible turned the other member states against us with what amounted to revulsion.

On the Committee of Inquiry I fought as hard as I could to bring a sense of proportion and fairness into its considerations – I went so far as to register a minority Report – but I was conscious throughout that shortsighted nationalistic behaviour, particularly of the politicians in London, had removed an important element of goodwill and co-operation we could otherwise have hoped to enjoy. For example, the refusal of British ministers to appear before the democratically-elected representatives of the peoples of Europe, to discuss a matter of such deep concern to the European public that it could only be solved at European level, was political folly.

The outbreak of foot-and-mouth disease in February 2001 very soon turned into a national emergency and for three months was the primary focus of media coverage, with daily stories – and images – of slaughtered livestock and blazing funeral pyres. The damage done to agriculture, tourism and our national reputation was swift and immense. That the epidemic was brought under control by May was a tribute to the Herculean efforts of the country's veterinary officials, slaughtermen, soldiers, and all the others involved on the ground, including, of course, the farmers who had to suffer so much and without whose co-operation and vigilance the disease could never have been contained. The overall cost to the national economy has still to be calculated, but those outside the farming world can scarcely begin to appreciate the cost to farmers, farmworkers and their families in terms of trauma and anxiety.

The Labour Government claimed credit for bringing the outbreak under control – in my opinion, quite unjustifiably. For an administration popularly renowned for slick communication and central control, their performance throughout was a weak one. They made a disastrously slow start to the campaign to combat the disease, which quickly spread and was discovered in several different locations. Ring vaccination to contain the infection within these areas might well have been a viable option at that stage, but it was not even seriously considered. Furthermore, communication with the public and co-ordination of effort were sadly inadequate. The Government failed to alert the public to the full picture of what was at stake, in order to win their vital co-operation, then overreacted in ways that strongly suggested the entire countryside was being closed, with all the damage that inflicted on the tourist industry. It then had to swing back, at vast expense, to a message that Britain was 'open for business'.

The co-ordination of the drive to eradicate the disease through a policy of slaughter of affected and 'suspect' (i.e. neighbouring) herds floundered for several crucial weeks, and was only secured by bringing in the army and their 'command and control' expertise.

Perhaps the most inglorious aspect of all in the Government's performance was their vacillation in approach. Having originally ruled out ring vaccination at a time when it should have been seriously considered, they then, in the last week of April – under pressure from ill-informed public opinion, horrified by the scenes of mass slaughter – were openly prepared to switch to an emergency vaccination policy.

Fortunately, Ben Gill and his colleagues in the NFU showed more courage and resolution than did ministers, and by sticking with the slaughter policy secured the ultimate benefits of that painful course. By contrast, Government ministers sometimes appeared to be less interested in taking the right, scientifically-based, decisions than in pandering to populist anthropomorphism, exemplified by their media-hyped concern about the fate of an orphaned calf, inevitably dubbed 'Phoenix', which had survived the cull of its herd and was found beneath the body of its dead mother.

It is, of course, too soon to draw detailed and definitive conclusions regarding the 2001 foot-and-mouth outbreak. Considerable scientific analysis, vital to such an evaluation, remains to be done. But I'd like to feel it might be useful to set out some preliminary reflections.

I am convinced that foot-and-mouth is such a scourge that the Government should constantly update an administrative War Book in all the appropriate departments and agencies, so that at the very first sign of an outbreak, those concerned with containing and eradicating it can at once spring into action, and in a coordinated way. I was horrified to hear ministers saying, in February 2001, that they had no blueprint for dealing with the outbreak. They *should* have had. I was equally disturbed to discover that many young vets (who nevertheless did a magnificent job) had not been taught about foot-and-mouth in any useful detail during their studies. It is a *must* for their curriculum.

Secondly, veterinarian surgeons – obviously – play a key role in animal health. In recent years, more and more of them have been leaving large animal practices for economic reasons, and as a result, effective disease treatment and containment have been suffering. During the mid-1960s, Alistair Steele-Bodger and I produced a scheme for 'prevention rather than cure', involving, among other things, a veterinary visit to each farm in the country every month. It would be costly but, we believed, a good investment in the long term. Unfortunately, our recommendation was not acted upon. I believe the time has come to review that recommendation.

Thirdly, communication must be swift and comprehensive, so that the public at large know at once what is at stake, and what to expect, as the authorities grapple with the problem. First reactions must be immediate and, if necessary, draconian. It would appear that by reacting in this way in 2001, the French, Dutch and Belgian authorities succeeded in curtailing the spread of the virus at the outset.

Fourthly, we must be more vigilant over the importation of products, and over the clear labelling of the imports' country of origin. We already have all sorts of red tape and rigorous enforcement in relation to relatively unimportant matters – we now need more stringent controls, transparently and vigorously imposed, to deal with *this* matter. I am totally in favour of free trade in agricultural as well as other products, and totally against the use of the WTO's arguments for 'ensuring plant health' ('phyto-sanitation', would you believe!) as a disguised method of discriminating against imports. But I am convinced that we in the UK and the European Union do need to be strict in applying genuine regulations framed to monitor the health aspects of imported agricultural products.

You might well say – as I already have, once earlier – that it is comparable with speed limits on our roads: without the perception of police control and enforcement, there would never be any respect for limits.

Fifthly, there must be an urgent and specific examination of the role of swill in such outbreaks. It cannot be coincidental that in the period 1954 to 1965, for example, 110 cases out of a total of 200 in the UK were traced to premises on which animals were fed on the left-overs, scraps and wastes ordinarily called swill. I believe that we should legislate to ensure that such food fed to pigs is cooked at a registered centre where the material is processed under supervision, or is totally banned and incinerated under equally close monitoring.

Sixthly, research for the production of vaccines must continue and increase. Scientists may ultimately produce a vaccine that will be effective without the need to slaughter so many wonderful herds and flocks. Living in a world where people can travel to the moon, surely we should have the knowledge and ability to control the mobility of a virus.

Those are specific recommendations. But the problems of the 2001 outbreak also raise questions in a wider context relating to the very nature of farming as it has evolved in the UK in recent years.

Perhaps the public will come to realise that the general 'cheap food' policy coupled with the stranglehold held by supermarkets have forced farmers to cut corners to a dangerous degree. Efficiency is one thing, but there comes a point at which risks are taken, and sooner or later one of those risks leads to disaster – to the detriment of both the public and agriculture.

The damage to agriculture and its image caused by the scares over genetic modification has not, of course, so far been of the same order, but I believe it has added to a certain alienation between the farming world and its public that had already begun to creep in over the previous decade. As in the BSE context, scientific fact has all too readily been ignored in favour of half-baked emotive propaganda. This is a trend all those engaged in agriculture must strive to reverse.

These two extraordinary blows to British agriculture simply extended the more general scene of gloom and difficulty for our farmers.

In the past few years, exacerbated by the BSE fiasco, we have seen a hiatus in all livestock production. Farmers who started in the mid-1990s had to borrow more money in order to keep their heads above water. They had to dispense with hired help, work with machinery well past its use-by date, and they consequently worked longer hours with no respite. Some farmers also found other work and encouraged their wives to find employment away from the farm. To a degree, of course, there is nothing new in this – but now the numbers are higher, the hours are longer, and the interminable filling-out of bureaucratic documentation has become an indispensable part of modern farming.

The growing red-tape phenomenon of the post-BSE era means that paperwork within the context of the ominously-named Integrated Administrative Control systems has greater priority than ever. When the farm work is done, instead of going out for a relaxing drink or spending some time with the family and watching television, it is only then that the average farmer can plunge into his 'office work' – for there is often more money coming to the farm through the DEFRA cheque than from the market.

At the same time we see great stretches of British farmland becoming derelict – and that despite the great interest in conservation and environmental issues. It should be understood that a great deal of this 'green' concern is in reality a desire to conserve landscape that was put in place by previous generations of farmers at a time when people spent three times as much of their earnings on food, and when there were five times as many people working on the land. To provide cheaper food, the farm holdings were intensified and farmers were encouraged to work larger units for less money. The word used to describe the development was 'rationalised', and the concern currently being expressed by the conservationists and environmental groups (said to total some 5.5 million people in the UK alone) is that this rationalisation – which has resulted in fewer farms, all better equipped to deal with larger herds, flocks and modern machinery – has resulted in a loss of bio-diversity of unacceptable proportions.

The point should be made that the farmer is not the villain of this piece. He is, if anything, the victim.

What is not generally understood is that rationalisation has been driven by economics – the political imperative for ample food to be made available to a growing population for less money: i.e. the 'cheap food policy' of successive UK Governments since the 1947 Act. To a large extent, the primary producer has been reduced to the equivalent of a factory worker. Gone are the days when a farmer specialised in possibly three or four products, producing a consequent broad range of bio-diverse products. Instead, we have created a specialised monoculture that obliges each farmer to rely on one product.

This could be seen as justifiable in economic terms – except when the one product the farmer has been encouraged to rely on is either not required or in surplus. Then the price goes through the floor. And with it goes the farmer's income.

In unit production terms, the concept might have been acceptable. But in real terms and with the advantage of hindsight, we can now see that we have created a catastrophic situation in which farming is driven by immediate economics and not by the time-honoured yardstick of working in a holistic way, which allowed the farm to be handed over either to younger family members or to another farmer in a better state than when it was first received.

Not only is it shortsighted in ecological and environmental terms, but it is disastrous in human terms. Sons and daughters of farmers are disillusioned as they witness their parents working their entire lives for little return, and without sufficient funds to retire in any comfort. Moreover, working on the family farm allows a youngster little time to associate with other young people – and even if there was more time, the youngster wouldn't have any money to spend. Young people are increasingly choosing a future away from farming, which they see as a life of penury. The percentage of them now studying agriculture is at an all-time low. Most of the fun and challenge has been taken out of the industry – and the consequence of this could well be a calamitous shortage of people able and willing to carry on farming, and especially livestock farming.

In economic terms, British farming has had a roller-coaster ride over the past 30 years. When the UK joined the European Union in 1973, British agriculture became controlled by the Common Agricultural Policy, which greatly stimulated agricultural trade between member states. Since 1973, therefore, the main factor that has influenced food prices in the UK – and hence UK farm incomes – has been the exchange rate of the pound against the continental European currencies – now the Euro. As the pound weakened over the period 1992–93 to 1996–97, following its delopement from the Exchange Rate Mechanism, UK farming incomes rose to a fully acceptable level. Farmers reduced their debts and could afford proper levels of maintenance and capital expenditure on plant and equipment. After 1996–97, however, UK farmgate prices and profits fell dramatically as the Ecu/Euro plunged in value against the pound. By 2000 they hit their lowest levels since the 1970s. The result was a crisis that affected every sector of agriculture.

Not for centuries – certainly not since the end of the 19th century – has so much of agriculture been in such a desperate state.

The competitive position of UK farmers is made more serious still by the higher level of fuel taxes they pay, compared with their continental counterparts. The threat in the UK remains of a pesticide tax and a climate-change levy. Meanwhile, the general burden of red tape has been deliberately exacerbated by Whitehall, which has all too often 'gold-plated' European Union requirements by adding further complications of its own.

In recent years, too, UK farmers have suffered, compared with their continental competitors, because they have not received the full amount of agrimonetary compensation available to compensate for adverse currency movements. This compensation has to be partly funded by the member state Government – and in this Britain has been noticeably less generous than, for example, France or Germany.

In response to the losses they have been making, farmers have cut back drastically on new investment in plant and machinery, and reduced hired labour. Sadly, they have been forced also to curtail some of the excellent environmental conservation work they were doing in the mid 1990s. When a farmer is trading at a loss, he is unlikely to spend money on the renovation of dry stone walls and hedgerows, or on new buildings or on planting trees.

For many the pressure was overwhelmingly great and either they sold up or they retained their farm and house but handed the farming operation over to a professional contract farming company or a neighbour. This process continues. Modern machinery and farming techniques offer great economies of scale, and whereas a 1,000-acre (405-hectare) arable farm was considered large – and was viable – ten years ago, now it is often not, and 2,000 acres (810 hectares) can be farmed more economically using the same labour, but with bigger machines. The farmer who gives up farming in this way effectively liquidates his working capital and machinery – and can reduce his borrowings while still deriving some income from the contract arrangement.

From a cold economic perspective, it would be hard to argue that this trend is detrimental to UK agriculture, since it is forcing the kind of rationalisation that may become essential in the longer term if our agriculture is to compete with that of a developing Eastern Europe and to trade more freely with Oceania and South America. In some sectors, however, the pain has gone too far. In pig production, and increasingly in the poultry sector, UK production has severely diminished and may well never recover. The UK now has to import more pig meat and poultry products than ever before, and the sad fact is that these imports often come from countries outside Europe where animal welfare and production standards are nothing like as high as our own.

Beyond the purely economic perspective, however, the picture is much worse. Many farming families have owned their houses and land for generations. They have worked for long, hard, antisocial hours to milk the cows and crop the land. Their level of pride is often a joy to see – but they may have few skills and little training for any other work. When financial circumstances conspire against them – and this has happened for a high proportion of them in the last few years – the personal pain is huge. They may well appreciate that other industries, like mining and shipbuilding, have also gone through massively painful adjustments. The thousands of farmers involved could perhaps be forgiven for pointing out, however, that they most often happen to be the owners of their farms as well as the labourers, and that they generally have created an attractive asset, which appeals to a huge proportion of the population – the British countryside.

Furthermore, in literally thousands of British villages life is being dramatically changed by lower employment on farms, fewer farmers and fewer rural-based ancillary businesses supplying farming inputs.

The extreme impact of the pressures involved is starkly evident in the increasing numbers of suicides: farmers are now among the most vulnerable of all professions.

My periods as Chairman of the Agricultural Mortgage Corporation and as a director of a British bank brought home to me some of the unique features of farming businesses. A farmer's home is an integral and central part of his business. It is often right in the middle of his 'factory', and almost always it is inseparable, as a piece of real estate, from it. Almost always the deeds of the farm include the house – and almost always a bank will require a mortgage over the whole property to secure its lending. More than 80 per cent of farmers are in debt to banks. Yet the value of agricultural land normally bears little relation to farming profits. Land values reflect a whole range of inherent factors, including potential development uses and amenity values. The result is that for the 90 per cent of farmers who own at least a part of the land they farm, the return on capital is poor even when the agricultural economy is fairly sound. In 2001, after three or four debilitating years, most farmers are losing money.

These unique aspects of land – which for most farmers is their biggest asset – are compounded by the emotional element of its inheritance. Still less than 2 per cent of land is traded every year. Most farms, including the farmhouse, pass from father to one or more children. The heir thus inherits not only a capital asset but also an emotional tie that is hard to break. This is a fact not well understood by those outside agriculture.

The anomaly of the value of land as one of the assets used by farmers also partly explains the unique relationship between farmers and their banks. Compared with more typical businessmen, farmers may have a strong asset base, but they have always had a very poor return on capital. Any lending is therefore inevitably long-term – and the banks generally accept this – but is well secured. The asset base also means that farmers making losses in difficult times can survive longer than most other businesses – either by liquidating some of their asset (e.g. by selling some land) or by increasing the debt. As a result, the banks have regularly observed that there is quite a lag between a period of low incomes in agriculture and the demise of farming business. Then, when farmers are finally forced to give up, they often do so while the assets still exceed the liabilities. Either the farmer or his banker sees the writing on the wall in good time.

The application of milk quotas is another anomaly in UK agriculture. The volume of milk that any European Union dairy farmer can produce is determined by the quota available to him. When quotas were first introduced in 1984, UK dairy farmers were in the process of expanding production quite rapidly. The UK was, however, still not self-sufficient in milk and milk products – largely because of the concession to New Zealand butter imports the Government secured during our EEC entry negotiations. Soon after quotas were introduced, the total level was cut across the whole EEC.

The impact of this was particularly severe in the UK, where milk production was increasing and where the climate is especially suited to the growth of grass, which is a very economic source of feed for dairy cows (only Ireland and north-western France have a comparable climatic advantage). The UK Government, quickly and sensibly, made UK quotas tradable between farms, so at least the efficient could expand while those wishing to retire had a new capital asset to encourage them to do so. The cost of acquiring quota for those who remain, however, is an added burden that reduces their international competitiveness. It is estimated that this cost – involving leasing, interest charges on quota purchase, and the management of annual milk production to be within quota – is equal to an average of over 2 pence per litre *extra* in a total milk production cost of around 20 pence per litre.

It is a fact that milk quotas have, by constraining production, given European Union dairy farmers a higher milk price than they would otherwise have achieved. But an increasing number of UK dairy farmers are now sceptical of the overall benefit, and would prefer the freedom to produce as much milk as they wish.

The recent history of agriculture in general and the dairy sector in particular in the UK might have been a happier one had there been a better degree of co-operation between producers. Alas, the history of co-operation in UK agriculture is dismal. In the UK the turnover handled by farmer-controlled businesses (FCBs) as a proportion of total agricultural output (at farmgate) is lower than in the USA, and lower than in all countries in the European Union except Portugal, Spain and Greece.

Perhaps more significant than overall turnover is the proportion of the product that is *processed* by farmer-controlled businesses. FCBs clearly become far stronger if they can *successfully* finance and manage a processing operation because:

  · it adds value to the product for the producer – in effect it is an additional source of income for him;
  · it increases the bargaining power of the FCB if it still has to sell some of its commodity solely as a broker; and
  · it slightly reduces the volatility of price of the end-product.

However, the proportion of UK farmers' produce processed by businesses they control is particularly low compared with the proportion in most other countries of the world.

Continental European Union farmers have had the huge advantage that they have been willing to work together and co-operate. It can be argued that they have also had strong Government support. They have. But that has only come *because* their governments saw that farmers there are *willing* to co-operate, and saw too that the support of enthusiastic agricultural co-operatives is a very good way of supporting the whole rural community.

The problem is particularly acute in the case of milk, in which producers owned more than 30 per cent of the UK milk-processing capacity prior to deregulation of the market in 1994. Now they own only around 5 to 10 per cent. The result has almost certainly been harmful for producers. Their weak negotiating position probably explains the fact that farmgate prices fell by around 35 per cent during the period 1995 to 2000, while the Ecu/Euro only fell 25 per cent against the pound. And UK producers saw no real benefit from the substantial hardening in world milk product prices and the reduction of intervention stocks during the first nine months of the year 2000.

Farmers have formed themselves into milk groups – but with a few highly successful exceptions who have gone in for processing, the majority have failed to achieve any market strength at all. They are far too small to be able to derive any benefit from reduced transport costs, match specification demand with supply, or carry any marketing muscle.

Fewer stronger groups can never enable farmers to get money from the market if the fundamentals of supply (UK, European Union and world) and demand will not allow it. (That fundamental fact can only be bypassed if farmers reduced themselves to so few groups that they were again in a monopoly position – and the Government would clearly not allow that.) But a smaller number of groups would at least be able to fund a secretariat and market analysis, and thus be better prepared with good-quality facts about the market place – just as the buyers are – and so also be better prepared when it came to price negotiations.

Should we expect the Government to help in the situation which milk groups now find themselves in?

Frankly, it is hard to see why the Government should – except in one way. That way has to do with schemes such as the Rural Enterprise

Scheme and the Processing and Marketing Grant Scheme, which are part-funded by the European Union.

These schemes have some interesting features for groups of farmers who wish to invest. The sums allocated sounded good at the first time of hearing – a total of £196 milllion. But this is over the period until the year 2007.

It is interesting that at the same time these UK schemes were announced, the US Government announced a new $130 million Venture Capital Fund for co-operatives investing in processing, and reconfirmed its commitment to its Loan Guarantee Programs, which give guarantees to banks for loans at the rate (currently) of $1,000 million per year. The USDA (United States Development Agency) describes these schemes as necessary and 'in the public interest because of the disparity of market strength between producers and processors/retailers'. That disparity is far greater in the UK than it is in the USA, and it will become more so as we see increasing globalisation of food retailing: Walmart and Aldi are examples of large businesses coming into the UK; Tesco, on the other hand, is an example of a UK company looking outward.

For those farmers who survive the current crisis I'd like to feel that the pressures will provide a major new stimulus to co-operation, despite the disappointments of the past.

During the 1990s, reflecting upon the sorry state of British agriculture and considering its inevitable place within the European framework and against the equally inevitable backdrop of world trade, I came increasingly to the view that it was necessary to re-think the very concept of 'farming' as traditionally understood. The production of food would, of course, have to remain the core of any definition of farming – but it had to be placed in a wider context, not least in order to be better understood and appreciated by the 98 per cent of the population outside farming, and in order that it should find its proper place in the modern world in which the inter-linking of sectors of activity previously regarded as 'compartmentalised' has become the norm.

It was a theme I repeatedly developed on the various platforms available to me – in the European Parliament, in the House of Lords, and at numerous conferences and seminars. Perhaps I bent the ear of the European Commissioner for Agriculture, Franz Fischler, so many times on this subject that he could stand it no longer. In the autumn of 1996 he invited me to chair a conference of experts in the agricultural, environmental and social fields to focus on the theme of 'rural development' and to advise the Commission on the elaboration of policies at European Union level to give practical support to this concept.

The Conference was held in Cork, southern Ireland, in November that year and resulted in a Declaration I believe points the way forward to what we called 'the Living Countryside'.

In the consensus of thought stimulated by the conference there was much that was painful to the traditional farmer who wanted simply to be left to produce food in return for a fair income. We had to recognise that agriculture and forestry were no longer predominant in Europe's economies, and that their relative economic weight would continue to decline. Furthermore, it had to be accepted that the Common Agricultural Policy would adapt to new realities and challenges in terms of consumer demand and preferences, international trade developments such as the GATT and WTO framework, the future enlargement of the European Union, and the continuing shift away from price support mechanisms.

On the other hand – and this is where the consensus widened the framework within which the agriculture of the future could be understood – we started from the principle that agriculture would remain a major interface between people and the environment, and that farmers had a vital role as stewards of many of the natural resources of the countryside – a role through which they must be enabled to derive adequate remuneration from society at large.

A key factor was rising standards of living. People had become more and more interested in the overall quality of life, particularly in health and in leisure activities. This trend constituted a new opportunity for the European farmer because rural areas are by definition in a unique position to be exploited within the new concept of quality of life, and with special reference to the development of tourism.

I remember going down to Dorset, where I stayed with a great friend of mine, Simon Chick, who farmed quite extensively. As we passed through the village that Sunday morning, the church bells were ringing and we saw a vast number of people turning out of their cottages and walking up to church.

'You must have a good vicar here,' I said, impressed, but half-questioningly.

'The vicar's not all *that* brilliant,' he replied. 'You see, all these cottages belong to *us*, for we've amalgamated the farms. Well, it may surprise you but I never sell, or let, any cottage to people from the city who want just to recharge their batteries at weekends only. Actually, I don't sell or let a cottage at all unless the incoming people promise me that at least one member of their family will go to church on Sunday when they are here.'

That he had managed to have a clause to that effect written into a contract sounded positively medieval – I was astounded. But he explained, 'It may seem feudal, but it works. We have created a community! During the week, the village used to be like a morgue. At weekends, people from the city were coming and going, but keeping themselves strictly to themselves. Now they get together through the church, and many of them enjoy staying the whole week – particularly the womenfolk. They've formed their own groups to further their different interests, and have altogether revived village life that used to be pretty dead!'

Simon was ahead of his time. It was an early example of a personal initiative through which it was possible to create 'a living countryside' in a given context. Against the background of ever-increasing crises in farming, such a way of thinking had gradually developed into an organised approach, and subsequently into a formulated policy that might then be put into practice.

We saw it as a most positive token that the concept of public financial support for rural development, harmonised with the appropriate management of natural resources and the maintenance and enhancement of bio-diversity and cultural landscapes, appeared to be gaining increasing acceptance.

Our conference in Cork therefore urged upon the Commission a ten-point programme for rural development throughout the European Union – although we insisted that this should be done, in accordance with subsidiarity, on a 'bottom-up' basis – harnessing the creativity and solidarity of rural communities – rather than be an approach imposed uniformly from and by Brussels.

We recommended that there should be a coherent European Union policy focused on financial support for the development of tourism and small-to-medium enterprises in rural areas, and we made a number of technical suggestions on how EU programmes could be simplified, refined and financed.

Not enough of this thinking found its way into Agenda 2000, in my view, but I am satisfied nonetheless that the fundamental conceptual change from 'farming', understood in isolation, to 'rural development' has been achieved, and that this can be built on in the future. On many farms, 70 per cent of family income comes from alternative sources of rural development, and since the demise of MAFF – replaced by RDS (the Rural Development Service) within DEFRA (the Department of the Environment, Food and Rural Affairs) – farmers will have to adapt to change from their subsidised industry.

Whether such change should include the production and promotion of genetically modified (GM) food, for instance, is an issue as complicated as deciding on joining the Euro. The debate arouses strong emotions, and the outcome will eventually affect farming methods and consumer sales. Sensational headlines about 'Frankenstein' foods, suspect animal welfare, and the use of baneful chemicals for production or pest control, totally ignore the objective analysis of the risks and benefits that scientific experts have produced. The Select Committees of the House of Commons, the House of Lords and the European Parliament, for example, who receive and require evidence from so many experts, are totally disregarded and have little impact on public opinion.

Some time ago I went to see my dentist. There was a lady sitting in the waiting-room reading the daily paper. The headline was 'GENETICALLY MODIFIED FOOD CAN CAUSE MENINGITIS!'

She asked me what I thought.

'More importantly, what do *you* think?', I said.

'Oh, we wouldn't touch it. We only buy organic food. In fact, we don't buy cows' milk, even pasteurised. We only buy organically-produced soya milk!'

'Where does that come from?' I asked.

'Oh, it's British,' she said, airily.

I frowned.

'You may like to know that we do not grow soya in Britain. It is probably American, and 70 per cent of American soya is from GM seed!'

When I arrived at the dentist's chair, he asked me what I had done to so upset his previous patient.

I believe in making sure that all food marketed is as safe for consumption after processing and packaging as it can be. Justice and healthy democracy require national debate, just as they require the testing of evidence – and the disregarding of rumour and hearsay. I regard the public's growing distrust of scientists and research workers, and its indifference to scientific evidence in the debate about genetically modified plants or BSE, as a trend with potentially very dangerous consequences.

To stop all experiments designed to establish the safety of products – and to prevent the determining of the effect production may have on the environment – is folly. The organisations that suggest such limitations are apparently abandoning all concern for the law, life and property, but also quite unwarrantedly making out to a credulous general public that they have advance knowledge of the outcome of such research.

As John Beringer, former Government adviser on GM foods, once observed, it was that kind of 'advance knowledge' which used to get witches burned. There is no such thing as 'advance knowledge' when dealing with living and growing products, even with ever better technology. Food scares can set the market awry within hours – but that only emphasises something we should already be sure of: farmers are becoming increasingly answerable to the customer, both directly and indirectly, for the product is constantly under public scrutiny.

Under the banner of accountability, the customer is demanding safe, high-quality food produced with care and consideration for the environment all the way down the food chain. The demand for verification of the source of produce and the method of production has long been illustrated by quality assurance systems, which are contracts between the farmer and the first-hand buyer.

Agriculture has not been so quick to follow this systems approach, partly because we have not readily been competing in a free market situation, and partly due to lack of pressure.

Recent food scares have illustrated that if such situations are to be avoided in the future, it is essential to look at our own methods of production. In the years to come there will be more pressure on farmers to show what they are doing. The marketplace will demand it, but there may be some advantages such as cost saving, increased staff motivation, and better management and quality performance. This should all lead to enhanced environmental sensitivity, leading in turn to a securer market and happier customers.

More and more farmers are turning towards what is called 'integrated crop management', which is a well-balanced and commonsense approach. It combines the best traditional methods with appropriate modern technology, balancing economic production with positive environmental management.

LEAF (Linking Environment and Farming) is part of a pan-European project set up in 1991 to promote farming practices which, as well as being profitable and productive, minimise environmental damage while conserving the countryside. Similar projects exist in Germany, France, Sweden, Luxembourg and Spain.

Growing crops or producing milk or meat is a risky business, and never more so than now. There is a growing interest in organic farming, with a price incentive that begins to look attractive as incomes fall. The Government has increased payments to support organic production five times since 2000, and yet they still represent only 1 per cent of the total financial assistance to UK farming. The budget of £6 million for 1999 was spent long before the year 2000 began – a fact that gives a clear indication of the number of applicants who wish to switch to organic farming.

In the meantime, around 70 per cent of organic produce sold off the supermarket shelves in the UK is imported. Can we be satisfied that all of this is truly organically produced? If organic farming in the UK is to go on growing over the next few years,

- demand will have to remain strong;
- financial support for organic farming within European Union countries should be set at similar levels to prevent artificial disparities between production costs in individual member states;
- growers should capitalise on the increase in overall production, to access more customers and use economies of scale to reduce production and distribution costs;
- the availability of different organic seeds must be ensured;
- the pressure from organic cereals grown in countries such as Australia, Canada and Argentina – where organic cereals can be produced at a cost low enough to undermine European producers – has to be recognised.

In summary, to balance the need to protect the health of consumers against the need to champion the interest of producers and maintain stability in such a volatile world is a tall order.

What *are* the demands of consumers?

On the one hand, Friends of the Earth might claim that it is immoral to interfere with plants by inserting new genes, or might make out that we are acting 'against nature'. On the other hand, scientists and practical farmers could argue that it is hard to see what principle is involved that was not breached centuries ago. It is certainly possible to make a good case for saying that *all* food production is, in a sense, unnatural. God told his people to be fruitful and multiply – which is exactly what farmers have done throughout the ages by breeding more crops, including hybrid crops in which genes have been transferred from one plant to another by traditional means. Animals have been transformed by selective breeding.

Why should that be seen as unnatural when such methods are used in a laboratory, but natural if used on a farm?

Public debate often revolves around its preoccupations and prejudices. From a recent poll it became apparent that the general public now regards scientists as only little more trustworthy than politicians – which shows that the general public now prefers to believe the sensational headlines so delighted in by the media. But in considering the validity of scientific research and the justification for its applicability, we should not ignore the decisions and attitudes presented in other parts of the world where public health and food safety are equally important.

Americans, for example, seem to have no fear about the use of hormones as growth promoters in beef cattle. They think nothing of boosting milk production by injecting dairy cows with the hormone bovine somatotropin (BST). More than 70 per cent of their soya bean crop is grown from genetically modified seed, much of which is imported into the UK.

In other words, they *trust* their Food and Drugs Administration, which has expressed no reservations about declaring their products safe to eat.

But consumer demands vary. In the UK, we ate £2.4 billion of fast food in 1998–99, which is more than the French, Danish and Italians managed between them. In other words, we consumed 50 sizzlers a second. Indeed, 14 per cent of the population in Scotland say that they *never* eat fruit or vegetables. Our country is now officially the fattest nation in Europe; 40 per cent of us describe ourselves as overweight, and it is suggested that 20 per cent are in fact 'clinically obese'.

So we eat what we like. Despite the incredible Government-led panic over BSE and Professor Lacey's telling us that no fewer than 500,000 of us may be walking about with latent Creutzfeldt-Jakob disease (CJD, the human form of spongiform encephalopathy) through eating beef, we are actually eating more junk food now than we did in 1994. If a task force on obesity imagines that it can reform this cholesterol-proud nation of ours, its chances are slim.

The European experience has shown that Governments quake and multinational companies cave in. The main initiatives of our Government should therefore be (a) to stand firm behind the Food Agency with the responsibility for safety; (b) to support labelling of products, including the country of origin and ingredients; and (c) to encourage the reshaping of the UK's failing farming sector through diversification, the development of new markets and new outlets, and imaginative marketing.

Without a much greater commitment to the funding of green farming schemes, the minister's laudable aims for the future of British farming will remain a pipe-dream, to the cost of the farmers, consumers and the countryside, together with our national economy.

13

THE DEVELOPMENT DILEMMA

There is a good deal of difference between travelling
to see countries and travelling to see peoples.
(Rousseau)

When I was re-elected to the European Parliament in 1994, I decided to devote myself to my other major interest outside agriculture – the development of the poor countries of the Third World. In fact, in many ways my two great interests are closely interrelated. Farming is about producing food and maintaining the land through good husbandry and careful management of the soil and its resources – animals and crops. It is about maximising yields in an economic, and, at the same time, a sustainable, manner. Development shares the same basic principles. If a poor country can make optimal use of its resources – *all* its resources – then it will prosper.

The question is how to make best use of these often scarce resources. What makes the difference is not so much the absolute value of the basic resources as the way they are used.

For example, Angola with its oil and diamond reserves, the Democratic Republic of Congo with its mineral wealth, and Nigeria with its oil, should logically be among the richest countries of Africa. Yet their peoples – the ordinary citizens of these countries, the man or woman in the village street – are among the poorest in the continent.

It always strikes me as significant that in 1997 Nigeria had a real per capita gross domestic product (GDP) of only $920, while its relatively resource-barren near-neighbour Ghana had a per-capita gross domestic product (GDP) of $1,640. In the same way Swaziland, with reasonably fertile land but little else, had a per-capita GDP of $3,350, while Sierra Leone, rich in diamonds, could attain only $410. I was impressed by the way that Angola, blessed with diamonds and oil, could achieve a per-capita GDP of $1,430, while its neighbour to the south, Botswana, equally rich in diamonds but lacking oil, had a per-capita GDP of $7,690 – five times higher than Angola's.

Why? What makes the difference?

It is clear that the difference lies in how the countries are managed. It is not just a question of 'human resources'. I am invariably impressed by the intelligence and ability of Ethiopians and Nigerians, yet their countries are among the poorest in Africa. The difference must lie in 'human resources' of another nature – management skills in the widest sense of the term. The sort of skills that a successful farmer needs. The skills that combine financial management, technical efficiency and personnel management, with special emphasis on the latter. A farm cannot work efficiently if its labour force, large or small, is fundamentally dissatisfied. I do not refer to the odd grouse, which is inevitable, human, and even healthy. I mean a fundamental dissatisfaction.

Unless staff at all levels believe in their managers and have a degree of confidence, tempered by scepticism, in the leaders, the operation, whether a farm or a country, will not function properly. This trust in leaders requires a high degree of integrity and honesty on the part of the leaders, and a determination to stamp out malpractices and dishonesty from the start. Experience has led me to conclude that those countries that have succeeded, and in which citizens can live in peace, security and with increasing levels of material comfort, are those in which leaders apply the management principles that succeed in agriculture and elsewhere.

The 'quick buck' approach, the bullying approach, and the 'fingers in the till' approach give the same negative results everywhere.

This may appear to be a digression, but it lay behind my thinking as I embarked on my stint as European Co-President of the ACP-EU Joint Assembly in June 1994. My concept of the European ideal involves a Europe *looking out to the rest of the world*. I have always believed in maintaining and further advancing human rights and fundamental freedom, in Europe's responsibility to the other, starving, half of the globe – not by playing the role of 'food donor' but by finding a way to help such peoples to help themselves, to bring relief to the world's poorest countries still enslaved by debt, and to argue the case for fair trading.

When visiting the poorer countries during my Presidency of the European Parliament, I often reminded myself of William

Wilberforce's speech in the House of Commons in May 1789, when he said:

> Let not Parliament be the only body that is insensible to the principles of natural justice. Let us make reparation to Africa, as far as we can, by establishing trade upon true commercial principles, and we shall soon find the rectitude of our conduct rewarded by the benefits of a regular and growing commerce.

I still wonder how far we have moved in more than two hundred years.

A few days before my election, the Joint Council of the Assembly had approved a special programme of assistance to traditional banana-growers, many of them former British Commonwealth countries like the Windward Islands, who were threatened by the much cheaper 'dollar banana', an issue aggressively defended in Strasbourg by Mrs Eugenia Charles, Prime Minister of Dominica.

Thumping her brown fist on the table, she said, 'All right, if you don't want my bananas, you'll have to take my cannabis!'

This time without being thrown in, I jumped in at the deep end – and not for the first time, I may say. Development aid was increasingly linked to progress towards democracy and respect for human rights. Aid to Sudan, Togo and Zaïre among others had been suspended on that basis. In addition, many of the poorer countries in Africa were careful to limit imports of products like beef, which might threaten their traditional farming.

I was very much aware of the choppy water ahead, not least because the existing financial relationship under the Lomé Convention (IV, Part II) was to come to an end in February 2000 and there remained a great deal of controversy unresolved about changes to certain clauses.

As a born optimist, I felt that we could overcome these problems, because the point of the ACP was, and still is, not to hand over 'conscience money' from rich countries but to work in partnership and to help our neighbours to help themselves. In my view, it would have been entirely wrong to see all this as a means for the developed world to push the Third World around and to infringe their principles, as some critics suggested. To me, what was involved was a gradual but intractable move towards democracy and the rule of law *everywhere* in the world – and I saw no point in pretending otherwise.

From a European point of view – that of a 'British' European, in fact – I saw my new role as one of ensuring that the work of the Joint Assembly would also underline the growing need to show that the European Union should not be seen as 'Fortress Europe under construction'. I was convinced that Europe could act in unison to trade and aid on behalf of the poorer countries, in which food and agriculture are the keys to successful co-operation.

At the same time, I was fully aware of the increasing number of anti-European myth-makers in my constituency, my own country, marching along the political roads and knocking down any signpost leading to a meeting-place of common sense. This observation made me feel even more determined to improve the European Union's image and reaffirm its role as the world's largest provider of development funding. And I wanted to play my own part in ensuring that taxpayers' money would be used wisely in the interests of development and humanity.

The ACP–EU Joint Assembly – created specifically because of this common desire to establish a cooperative body that goes beyond just economic considerations – embraces the fundamental objectives of humankind and the establishment of peaceful relations between the nations of the world. It is a democratic parliamentary institution that aims to promote and defend democratic processes in order to guarantee the right of each individual country to choose its own development objectives and how to attain them.

Yet it is undeniably a strange animal. It is the parliamentary organ of the Lomé Convention, the agreement that brought together 71 countries of Africa, the Caribbean and the Pacific region, with the 15 European Union member states, in a formal international treaty based on mutual respect.

The first Lomé Convention was signed in 1975, and the fourth Convention expired in February 2000. Two of the most significant aspects of the Lomé Conventions are the fact that Lomé Countries can export some 99 per cent of their products to the European Union without import duties – the 1 per cent exception being some sensitive agricultural products – and the provision of very substantial financial aid (for example, some £1600 million in 1999), mostly in the form of grants, for projects in areas such as agricultural development, food security, rural development, industrial development, environmental protection, education and health. The sums involved are considerable, but the Lomé Conventions are much more than mere conduits for money. They deal with issues that affect men and women directly, including respect for human rights and the promotion of democratic values, and are highly political in nature.

The Joint Assembly consists of a member from each of the 71 ACP (African, Caribbean and Pacific) countries, and an equivalent number of MEPs. It meets in plenary session twice a year, once in an ACP country and once in Europe in one of the European Parliament's 'workplaces', Brussels, Strasbourg or Luxembourg. In between, there are meetings of the Assembly's 'bureau' (its board of governors – 12 European and 12 ACP members), as well as meetings of working groups set up to study particular subjects, such as refugees or climate change or the future of ACP–EU relations.

It may appear to be rather peripheral, but in fact many of the matters dealt with are of direct relevance to the lives of ordinary men and women in Africa, the Caribbean, and the Pacific Islands.

For example, a water pump installed in a remote village may mean that a woman no longer has to spend two or three hours every day carrying a bucket of water on her head for 4 or 5 miles (up to 8 kilometres) from the nearest water source to her hut. Moreover, borehole water is usually cleaner than river or waterhole water, and so improves her health and that of her children, as well as making her daily life much less onerous. Similarly, a road through the bush can enable a farmer to sell his crops on the market rather than just in the village, thereby increasing his prosperity, giving him some reserves for times of hardship or crop failure, and opening up whole new areas to economic development. The benefit of a health centre or rural clinic where none existed before is evident.

I found the work often taxing, but most stimulating.

Rwanda and Zaïre

The Co-Presidency involved constant travel. Just after my election as Co-President of the Assembly I went on an emergency fact-finding visit to Rwanda and Zaïre with Bernard Kouchner, the newly-elected Chairman of the Committee on Development and Co-operation, and other MEPs including Glenys Kinnock, Jan-Willem Bertens, a Dutch Liberal former Ambassador, and Leonie van Bladel, a Dutch member of the 'Union for Europe' political group.

It was a harrowing 'mission' (to use the European Parliament term). The massacres in which nearly a million Rwandan Tutsis and moderate Hutus had been hacked to death by their neighbours had just taken place. The Rwanda Patriotic Front, the Tutsi-led rebel power-group, based largely in Uganda, had recently taken over and driven out the Hutu Government and army. Most of the former leaders, the gendarmerie and the Hutu-led army, who had effectively been responsible for the atrocities, were in camps, mainly in Zaïre (as the Democratic Republic of Congo was still called in 1994).

We visited a broken, suffering, traumatised (literally and metaphorically) Rwanda, where the smell of dead bodies was a constant reminder of the immediate past. We met a Minister of Justice and a Foreign Minister in ministries without windows, typewriters or even telephones in most offices. The physical desolation was omnipresent. The psychological desolation was the worst I have ever seen. Kigali, the shattered capital, will forever remain in my memory.

Travelling around Rwanda was not for the faint-hearted. Young boys with Kalashnikovs manned roadblocks on all the main roads. Any time our car stopped, we knew a trigger-happy teenager could at any moment fire at our vehicle, for after such horrific events life had become cheap.

We visited camps for refugees in Zaïre – camps with almost no food or medical supplies. The chaos and fear among people who were wandering helplessly on the roads created a massive distribution problem.

The International Red Cross were magnificent in a terrifying situation. My colleague, David Lowe and I visited one camp in the south of Rwanda that was run by a small team of Irish nuns. As we arrived one of then came running to meet us, threw her arms round my neck and said, 'You are the answer to my prayers. I know you. I used to listen to you on the farming programme when I was on the farm at home in Ireland. There are 75,000 people in this camp who've had no food or water for four days.'

It was the most moving experience of my life. And thanks mainly to the initiative of my colleague, we got back to a Red Cross station, some 60 miles (96 kilometres) away, and made sure that at least one load of supplies was delivered to the camp before nightfall.

Our immediate task from then on was to ensure that food and medical supplies were sent to *all* the camps from central humanitarian supplies.

The camps in Zaïre were frightening places. Rows of tents stood in the mud. The surrounding trees had all been cut down for firewood. Water was in seriously short supply, and what water was available was befouled. The European Union poured hundreds of millions of Euros into those camps – it was the only way to keep the refugees alive – yet we knew that many of the same refugees had fled, or been forced to flee, because of their participation in the massacres. These were Hutus who in many cases had killed their neighbours in response to orders issued over the sinister Radio Mille Collines ('Thousand Hills Radio').

The same camps housed other, more disciplined and generally more comfortably-off, refugees in neater rows of huts and tents, often some distance away. These were the troops of the FAR, the Forces Armées Rwandaises – the army that organised and often supervised the mass murders. They had fled with their arms, their munitions, their artillery, their transport and their command structure. In their lorries they had also brought with them much of the wealth of the Rwandan regime – allowed through the lines guarded by 'Operation Turquoise', the French intervention force that brought an element of peace to the west and south of Rwanda . . . while offering protection to the fleeing FAR.

The morality of our action in the camps in Zaïre is far from simple. It is clear that we had an obligation to save lives and to bring humanitarian relief to the Rwandan refugees living in extreme need. Yet these same camps were, even when we were visiting them, becoming training grounds for the process of destabilisation in the whole of the Great Lakes area of Africa. We all saw what happened subsequently. It was not only due to the arming and military training of the young men in the camps – although that was a part of it. The break-up of the former Zaïre had been coming for years, the internal stresses were reaching breaking-point, but the final catalyst was the displacement caused by the Rwandan massacres and our failure to act earlier. Our humanitarian actions afterwards were too late to avert disaster, and we – the European Union, the European Parliament and the ACP–EU Joint Assembly – must bear our share of the blame.

All the same, I believe that what now seems evident, looking back from the perspective of 2001, could not be perceived in 1994.

For a long time, though, Rwanda and the Joint Assembly's role there continued to exercise my thoughts in moments of contemplation. Could we have done more? Should Europe have acted differently? Could we have avoided the post-massacre horrors and the destabilisation of the whole region, even if we could not have prevented the killings? There was simply not enough manpower or money available to police the camps properly and disarm the FAR troops. At least we made an effort, and we did *some* good, which is always better than doing nothing.

Although the situation in Rwanda has improved, the devastation caused by the turmoil affected any hope of development. I saw the small farms which, despite their tremendous potential for the growth of food, had been abandoned and left totally neglected, and I knew that those who had been farming and living there would never want to go back.

Standing there, feeling the despair and incomprehensible injustice, I was convinced more than ever before of Europe's role as *looking out to the rest of the world*. Funding is undoubtedly the number one ingredient – but to spend and distribute it wisely requires in-depth understanding of the root of the problems, and is difficult to manage when watching the devastation on television from comfortable, one-year-interest-free luxury settees. Are we doing enough? If we add together the total amount of support that goes into developing countries under the Lomé Convention, taking the contributions of the fifteen member states together with the European Aid Programme, the European Union as a whole invests something like $30 billion a year – which is far more than any other country or groups of countries in the world.

And yet we have not made the kind of progress that we should have made, and could well have made. Moreover, where does it end, with a world population that will increase, even double, by the year 2030? This an incredible thought, particularly in view of the fact that there is surplus food in one area of the planet and frightening shortages elsewhere.

I once had a meeting in Brussels with the President of Uganda, Mr Yoweri Museveni. During lunch, he suddenly turned to me and said, 'I understand you are a farmer .. ?'

'Yes, President, I *am* a farmer.'

'So am I a farmer,' he said, and continued as if musing, 'so I suppose you get one good crop a year, and a good harvest?'

'No, President. A farmer never gets a good crop. He might get a *reasonable* crop, but I've never had what a farmer would be satisfied to call a good crop,' I replied.

'Well, I often get two harvests, or even three harvests, or two harvests and three crops. So why are you trying to feed me?'

In fact, he had surplus food in the most fertile, well-watered and productive areas in the south of Uganda, and terrible shortages in the north and particularly in the north-east. His biggest problem was thus not the production of food for his people but the distribution of it. In other words, we in the West, in the industrialized countries – we have the technology, we have the science, we have the know-how, we have the skills and we can produce. And 'food aid' is therefore the order of the day for us. What Mr Museveni was really saying to me was, 'You know we can grow the stuff. What we need from you is the expertise to add value to it, to move it around, to ship it to different areas. It is marketing expertise we need, and fair play in the marketplace.' We should not forget, in considering how to utilise our global agricultural resources more efficiently, just how limited they are.

One of my tasks as Co-President was to preside over the Joint Conferences together with my counterpart, the ACP Co-President – a job we took in turns. During my five years in this role, I worked with three ACP elected Presidents. My first Co-President was Dr Marcel-Eloi Chambrier Rahandi from Gabon, who had already worked for a year with my predecessor, Dr Maria Luisa Cassanmagnago Cerreti. In 1995, the ACP countries elected Sir John Kaputin from Papua New Guinea, now Foreign Minister in his home country. And from 1997 to 1999 I alternated with the Hon. Thebe Mogami from Botswana.

Bringing together some 28 interest groups, each of them working with their respective Chairmen and *rapporteurs* from different states and different political parties, was a fascinating job in itself. Inaugurated in 1979, the Conferences covered a wide range of issues including, for example, industrial co-operation, the environment, human rights, debt, commodities, technology, AIDS, energy, hunger in the world, the place of women, and transport. New interest groups were formed as time went by, and during my Co-Presidency we set up groups to look into the Second Period of Lomé IV (1994), to monitor consistent progress under the Convention, and to examine such topics as sustainable development (1994), industrial development and refugees/ humanitarian aid (both in 1996), urban development (1997), regional co-operation (1998), climate change, and small island states (both in 1999).

Gabon, Mauritania, Senegal

Following my mission to Rwanda, my colleagues and I who had gone there drew up a resolution for the October 1994 session of the Joint Assembly in Libreville, Gabon – the first over which I presided.

Gabon is an interesting country. My ACP Co-President at the time, Dr Marcel-Eloi Chambrier Rahandi, was himself a Gabonese. Gabon has a population of about 1 million, with important reserves of oil. This creates an almost unique situation in Africa. Most of the manual labour there is done by immigrants from all over the continent, while many Gabonese, including my Co-President, are very rich.

This was very clear in my visits to Dr Chambrier Rahandi's private residence, and also in our contacts with the President of Gabon, who had been in power since 1967, Mr Omar Bongo. I will long remember the official dinner hosted by the President and Mrs Bongo in our honour. The lavishness of this event was equalled only by the almost regally formal protocol.

Presiding over the Assembly was less difficult than presiding over the European Parliament. Generally, the ACP members were highly respectful of the President, abided by the rules of procedure, and never challenged the rulings of the Chair. The only excess that had to be firmly taken in hand was a certain tendency on the part of many to go well beyond the allotted speaking-time.

After the Libreville session I returned to Europe via Mauritania, where I wanted to examine some European Union development projects, particularly in the agricultural sector. I was particularly struck by a project – which worked remarkably well, to my surprise – in which rice was grown on desert sand. The project proved that it could be done, but I kept wondering what the cost had been in maintaining the water supply. Is it worth depleting groundwater reserves for so fundamentally unnatural a process? Wouldn't it be more economic to use the same water to produce crops more suited to semi-arid conditions?

Such decisions ought to be taken on scientific, economic grounds, rather than for reasons of national prestige.

The next session of the Assembly that I chaired was in Dakar, Senegal. During it – following a long and heated debate, and a strongly-worded resolution on the human rights situation in Sudan – it was decided to carry out a fact-finding mission to that country, and to visit its neighbouring ACP countries Ethiopia, Eritrea and Kenya.

Sudan

This was a controversial mission. The Sudan is a huge country – the largest in Africa, at 967,000 square miles (2.5 million square kilometres) – with a population of some 28 million. At the time of our going there, the country had for some years been divided by civil war of fluctuating intensity between the predominantly Arab and Muslim north and the ethnically African south which has a mainly Christian or animist population. The army was technically in control, as it had been since 1989, under General Omar Hassan al-Bashir, although many believed that the real power was exercised by Dr Hassan el-Turabi and his National Islamic Front.

We went to the Sudan at the invitation of the President of the Sudanese Parliament, the Transitional National Assembly. Before accepting the invitation we had insisted on getting an undertaking in writing from the Sudanese authorities that our delegation would be free to travel where it wished and to meet freely with whomsoever it wanted. In order to assess the real situation in the larger area we decided to travel also to Ethiopia and Eritrea, neighbouring countries affected by the Sudanese civil war, and to hold meetings in Nairobi, Kenya, with leaders of the Southern Sudanese opposition groups, who were themselves no angels.

The delegation was made up of my first Vice-President on the European side, Mrs Glenys Kinnock, and two ACP Vice-Presidents of the Joint Assembly, Mrs Heather Robinson, a strong, independent-minded and straight-speaking Jamaican MP with a friendly personality, and Mr Jerome Boulle, Parliamentarian from Mauritius and one-time Mayor of Port Louis, a quiet-spoken, serious and thoughtful companion who displayed calm judgement throughout the mission. We also took with us, from the European Parliament staff, our own Arab-speaking interpreter, Mr Laurent Bernhard, because we needed to be sure that the African-provided translation, particularly of opposition interlocutors, was accurate. A representative each of the ACP and of the EP secretariats completed the team.

In a formal letter to the Sudanese authorities we listed all the people whom we wished to meet, and it was agreed – with the single exception of Sadiq al-Mahdi, the former Prime Minister and leader of the opposition Umma Party, who was in prison at the time of our initial request. I sent a follow-up letter strongly reiterating our desire to meet Mr al-Mahdi, and, to my surprise, received a reply to the effect that he was being released from detention, and that a meeting might therefore be possible.

I wonder whether our pressure contributed to the release of Mr al-Mahdi.

The delegation was particularly insistent on travelling to the Nuba Mountains where a largely Christian population was involved in a long-standing campaign for a degree of autonomy, and was being brutally suppressed by the Sudanese army. This was agreed to in principle.

After a flight – for which we paid – to Kadugli, the government-controlled capital of the area, we were informed by the Governor that it would be difficult to visit the particular village we wanted to see, a village specifically selected by Mrs Kinnock. After some time meeting local dignitaries and drinking tea, most of the delegation set out for the village with an escort, despite obvious reluctance on the part of the authorities. In fact, we never did get to visit the village. The narrow bridge over a flooded river was blocked by tractors and a lorry, forcing the delegation to turn back. We still do not know whether or not the obstruction was contrived, but there is no doubt that during our official reception at Kadugli, complete with speeches and refreshments, the authorities would have had plenty of time to radio ahead to the local army post to arrange for the blocking of the drift.

In the event, our visit to Nuba Mountains was frustrating: we met only officials and officially selected representatives. We were, however, shown a remarkably well-kept and well-equipped local village where a European Parliament staff member found some Samsonite suitcases stacked in a hut – hardly usual Sudanese village equipment. One might well wonder to what extent the village had been 'prepared' for our visit!

As well as the usual meetings with various ministers and officials, we were able to speak to representatives of the Christian Churches. They appeared to be both reluctant in what they said, and rather frightened about saying it. Because we had been warned that all meeting rooms would almost certainly be electronically bugged, I made a point at the end of the discussion of informing them that we would maintain contact, and would follow their progress over the coming months – which we did.

Our meeting with Sadiq al-Mahdi, recently released from prison, was fascinating. He was open and unafraid in his criticism of the al-Bashir regime, and was an impressive personality. With his London-educated daughter, he received us for tea in a summerhouse in his garden. I remember the former Prime Minister as a tall, impressive figure dressed in the usual Sudanese white robes. He is a direct descendent of the Mahdi who led the revolt against the Anglo-Egyptian regime that led to the death of General Gordon in Khartoum in 1885 and the subsequent expedition of 1918 under General Kitchener, in which the young Winston Churchill participated as a soldier-journalist. That expedition resulted in British – or officially Anglo-Egyptian – control over the Sudan until the country's independence in 1956.

Sadiq al-Mahdi made a reasoned plea for a return to democratic government, and called for tolerance of the south, opposing the imposition of Islamic law on non-Muslims. I was not surprised when, shortly after our visit, he left the Sudan for Asmara, where he played an important role in organising the anti-Bashir opposition.

The other really memorable meeting in the Sudan was with the suave and silver-tongued leader of the National Islamic Front, Secretary General of the Popular Islamic Congress, Dr Hassan el-Turabi. The precise role of Dr el-Turabi was uncertain. At the time of our meeting he did not occupy any official position in the Sudanese Government, although he later became President of the Parliament. His Popular Islamic Congress was regarded as being instrumental in the spread of Islamic fundamentalism throughout North Africa and the Middle East.

The meeting was in Dr el-Turabi's comfortable villa in suburban Khartoum. On top of the building, the array of antennae would not have been out of place on the roof of the BBC (or CIA or KGB) headquarters. The interior was equally high-tech.

Dr el-Turabi received us courteously. He spoke excellent, cultured English and French, having been educated in both France and the UK. Firmly, he maintained that accusations of human rights abuses and forced Islamisation in Sudan were all part of a Western plot against the Muslim world. But as the meeting progressed and the delegation took an increasingly tough line, he became more agitated, and finished with a diatribe against the West in general and the European Union in particular. We were particularly surprised by his attacks on France, which he accused of supporting the persecution of Muslim believers in Algeria. By the end of the meeting the mask had pretty well slipped altogether, and a more militant Dr el-Turabi appeared from behind the smooth façade.

Compared with Sadiq al-Mahdi and Hassan el-Turabi, President al-Bashir seemed a rather colourless character. He spoke in Arabic, which was interpreted by a Sudanese official into English. Through our own interpreter we discovered after the meeting that parts of his statement had been changed by the Sudanese interpreter in the English version. Why? Was it poor translation, or was he not being trusted to convey the correct message?

At the time it was not clear how much real power President al-Bashir had, or whether he was merely a mouthpiece for the army or for Islamic groups. Recent events make me believe that he was actually much more than just a stooge for Islamic factions or the National Islamic Front, although the power of the army remains hard to assess.

My final memory of the Sudan is of a visit to the womens' prison in Omdurman. Conditions were not bad, but there is something depressingly sad about hundreds of young women in gaol, many there only for selling *merrissa*, a home-made alcoholic drink (illegal in Muslim countries), in order to provide for their families in a hostile urban environment. A great number of these women were Southern Christians who had drifted into Khartoum and other northern cities as a result of the civil war and the economic collapse of the south. We heard them singing hymns and organising a Bible-reading session – hardly the activities of hardened criminals.

My abiding memory of Sudan in 1995 was the sense of aggression, of being subject to surveillance wherever we went, and of not being able to judge what was true and what was not. Political reforms were under way. Some of the 'ghost houses' in which political opponents had been detained and tortured before being sent to prison or executed, including the infamous 'City Bank Ghost House', had been closed down. We were, however, not able to visit the part of Kober Prison that was being run by the security forces, and there was considerable evidence – notably from some courageous women who had been able to meet us at receptions organised by Mr Jean-Claude Esmieu, the EC Delegate in Khartoum – to the effect that beatings and torture were continuing. It was also widely reported that women who did not conform to Islamic clothing norms, even non-Muslim women, were being routinely mistreated.

We strongly pressed for continued political reform and respect for the rule of law, and were gratified to learn that some 30 political prisoners were released just after our visit, as were 37 detained military officers, many of whom had been held since the 1991 attempted coup.

Continued pressure can only be useful, I believe, in such situations. If a country is completely isolated, it will feel free to behave as it wants, with no regard for international norms or international opinion.

Eritrea

From Khartoum we flew to Asmara, the capital of recently-independent Eritrea. A new country that had achieved independence only four years earlier, Eritrea was bursting with enthusiasm for the task of nation-building.

Its young President, Issias Afwerki, made a refreshing change from the usual, rather stuffy, protocol-conscious head of state. We had a long audience, more like an informal chat, in his simple office, in which he condemned Sudan in most undiplomatic terms. Just as we were getting into our cars to leave, dog-tired after our early departure form Khartoum and a day full of meetings, we saw the president climb into the passenger seat of a modest Japanese family car and drive off without escort or outriders.

Asmara was delightful, a little piece of Italy in Africa. We enjoyed the bracing air and a simple but perfectly clean hotel in which we could order a gin and tonic – in stark but welcome contrast with Islamically-dry Sudan – and talk freely without the risk of being bugged.

Eritrea may not have been a model democracy, but it was a dynamic young country proud of its achievements and eager to develop through its own efforts.

It is so sad that pride and obstinacy on both sides later led to the unnecessary and unwanted war between the erstwhile allies Eritrea and Ethiopia. That war, thankfully, has been brought to an end. Let us hope that both sides can now resume the much-needed work of development and nation-building.

Ethiopia

From Asmara we flew to Addis Ababa for a brief visit. This was the first time I had visited Ethiopia since the overthrow of the Mengistu regime in 1991. It was like a breath of fresh air. No longer was the oppressive hand of Marxist-Leninism hanging over what is certainly one of the most culturally exciting countries in Africa.

Meles Zenawi had been in power for less than four years. His Tigrean Liberation Front had driven out Mengistu in alliance with the Eritrean Peoples Liberation Front (EPLF), he had given Eritrea its independence, and he was now embarking on a new approach to African political identity by devolving much greater political power to the ethnic groups that made up Ethiopia. It may be significant that whereas the Emperors and Menigistu had been Amharas, Meles was, like his Eritrean counterpart Issias Afwerki, a Tigrean.

The idea of adopting the ethnic group as the fundamental unit in political society is a stimulating one, but fraught with danger. Many Africans see themselves as primarily members of their ethnic group, or even their clan, rather than as citizens of their country. So it is interesting that this experiment was put in hand in Ethiopia, where there is some genuine understanding of nationhood, at least in the central highland area, rather than in one of the totally artificial states created by European colonial powers during the late 19th century 'scramble for Africa'. But already the experiment is being watered down. Local political parties have come under increasing central control, and many of them are now merely local subsidiaries of the national Government party.

Our talks in Ethiopia were overshadowed by the attempt to assassinate Egypt's President Hosni Mubarak in Addis Ababa on 26 June 1995. Sudan was at once accused of harbouring three of the Islamic extremists apparently involved in the failed attempt, and some Ethiopians even suspected elements within the Khartoum regime of complicity in the attack on the President. As a result, relations between the Sudan and Ethiopia were once more at an extremely low ebb. Sudanese aircraft were banned from Ethiopian airspace. It must be remembered that Sudanese-Ethiopian relations are frequently strained, because there is a long history of Ethiopia's support for the Southern Sudanese rebel movements (which may or may not owe something to Christian solidarity) and of the Sudan's support for Ethiopian dissidents.

After 24 fascinating hours in Ethiopia, which gave us a good insight into the regional ramifications of the Sudanese situation, we flew to Nairobi where we met Dr Riek Machar, Chairman and Commander-in-Chief of the South Sudan Independence Movement and army, and Mr Pagan Anum, the Nairobi representative of John Garang's Southern People's Liberation Army (Garang was at that time in the field in Southern Sudan). We also met representatives of the Red Cross and NGOs active in South Sudan. We were particularly impressed by the relief work carried out by the European Union's Humanitarian Office, ECHO. It ran a major operation from Nairobi and Lokachokio that enabled hundreds of thousands of South Sudanese who had been displaced by war to survive.

I was particularly proud of the enormous relief effort financed and organised by the European Union. It is such a pity that the citizens of Europe are not aware of all that is being done in this respect by the EU – continuing, arduous and dangerous work that keeps millions alive, and for which Europe receives almost no credit, even within our own member states.

The delegation reported back to the Joint Assembly at its next session, held in Brussels in September 1995. This was followed by sessions in Windhoek, Namibia, and in Luxembourg in 1996.

At the Luxembourg session, the ACP states proposed that the next session – in 1997 – be held in Lomé, Togo. At once there was an outcry from many of the European members to the effect that President Eyadema of Togo was far from a model democrat, and the transition to a multiparty system in Togo had been long and hard. In any case, there was a quite legitimate reason for the Europeans to refuse to go: EU co-operation with that country was still partly suspended.

Finally, at an emergency meeting of the Joint Assembly Bureau, it was agreed that the first session of the Joint Assembly in 1997 should be held in Brussels, so that a solution could be found for deciding on the venue of the other session in 1997, which according to the Lomé Convention ought to be in an ACP country. It was meanwhile agreed that a joint delegation, consisting of three ACP and three European Parliament members, should visit Togo to assess the situation.

Togo

Consequently, on 23 May 1997 I found myself in Lomé, the Togolese capital, along with my ACP Co-President, the larger-than-life Sir John Kaputin from Papua New Guinea, and a delegation made up of Mrs Karin Junker, a German Socialist, and Mr Jean-Aubine Giansilly, a French Gaullist from the European Parliament, as well as Mr Andebrhan Weldegiorgis from Eritrea and Mr Aboubacar Somparé from Guinea, both ACP Vice-Presidents.

After four long and full days of meetings with the President of the Togolese National Assembly, the different political parties, the press, the trade unions, representatives of industry and agriculture, the European Union diplomatic representatives, the human rights organisations, the Prime Minister, a series of Government ministers, and a long audience – as well as an unscheduled luncheon – with President Eyadema himself, we came together to draw our conclusions, which we then presented in a written Report to the Assembly.

I quote it in full because I think it gives the flavour of the sort of difficult balancing act often required to overcome complex political problems that arise in relations between European and ACP countries:

> The delegation's mission is to examine the situation in Togo with regard to democratisation and human rights, and to make a proposal to the Joint Assembly Bureau regarding the invitation from the Togolese National Assembly to hold its next session in Lomé.

273

The delegation notes that the human rights situation, while not perfect, has improved over recent years. It further notes that the democratisation process is under way. One of the major difficulties to be overcome is the extreme level of polarisation between government and opposition. Every effort must be made to win the confidence of all constitutional political parties in the Togolese electoral and parliamentary systems. In this regard the delegation was heartened to note that all the parties questioned stated that they accepted the 1992 constitution.

The delegation notes that co-operation between the European Union and Togo is recommencing. Co-operation had been suspended in 1992 by the EU and, on a bilateral level, by the member states, with the exception of France. Similarly the USA and Japan had frozen co-operation with Togo, though Japan made a major payment in 1996. The EU and Germany continues assistance to certain projects concerning the basic needs of the people, without government participation. The resumption of co-operation is to a great extent dependent on the satisfactory preparation of the next series of presidential and parliamentary elections, which should begin in 1998. The EU should be fully involved in the forthcoming electoral process, through the provision of technical and financial assistance. It is most important that the opposition parties, including those that did not take part in the last elections, should participate in all future ballots. For this the concerns of the opposition should be addressed, notably with regard to security, an impartial electoral commission, an independent complaints procedure, and fair access to all aspects of the media.

In conclusion, the delegation proposes, with reservations on the part of one of its members, that the Joint Assembly accept the invitation from the National Assembly of Togo to meet in Lomé. The Bureau should decide whether the 25th session, in October 1997, be held in Lomé, or whether it would be preferable to meet in that city in the spring of 1998 when the democratisation process is further advanced and when EU co-operation would, hopefully, be fully operational once more. This alternative is favoured with some insistence by one member of the delegation.

The Assembly Bureau, meeting in Brussels, decided by a very large majority to hold the next session in Lomé.

This session, from 27 to 30 October 1997, was politically rather tense. The Togolese authorities went out of their way to ensure that everything was impeccably organised, and the opposition took full advantage of the occasion – particularly the presence of so many foreign politicians and journalists – to publicise their case.

The former Prime Minister of Togo, Mr Joseph Koffigoh, made an eloquent and well-reasoned appeal, in a memorable speech, for tolerance. Let Togo prove itself as a democracy, he argued. Many European members remained sceptical.

As Co-President, I replied to Mr Koffigoh in a concluding speech in which I undertook that the Joint Assembly would reserve its judgement until it had observed the forthcoming presidential elections to be held in June 1998.

My dismay can well be imagined when the Conference of Presidents of the European Parliament, taking no account of the political exigencies, refused to approve a mission to observe these elections, on the grounds of expense.

In the event, the elections were a shambles. The independent electoral commission resigned, and General Eyadema declared himself the winner even before the final results from Lomé, the capital, had been announced.

Here was an election that we should have observed, but were prevented from observing by a shortsighted policy on the budgetary front. This was one of the most unsatisfactory events to have occurred during my Joint Assembly Presidency. My annoyance was compounded by the fact that the Assembly in fact never got round to spending all of its annual budgetary allowance. There would have been more than enough funds in our budget to have covered the observation of the 1998 Togolese presidential elections.

Bougainville

I 998, was a particularly interesting year for the Joint Assembly, which for the first time played a part in a little-known but devastating conflict on the far side of the world from Europe.

The island of Bougainville lies to the east of Papua New Guinea (PNG). It is a mountainous island 120 miles (208 kilometres) long and 60 miles (96 kilometres) wide at its widest point, with a population of under 200,000.

Before the coming of the Europeans it appears that Bougainville – including Buka island, along with Choiseul, Shortland and Isabel – were all governed by one chief. In 1899, in an agreement between Germany and the UK on a land settlement in Western Samoa, it was agreed that Bougainville and Buka would continue to be ruled by Germany, while what are now the Solomon Islands would be ruled by Britain. Following Germany's defeat in World War I, Bougainville, with the rest of New Guinea, became a League of Nations Mandate Territory, administered by Australia, which already controlled Papua. Bougainville was then occupied by Japanese forces from 1942 to 1945. In 1947 Bougainville, with the rest of PNG, became a United Nations Trust Territory, again administered by Australia.

In the early 1960s rich copper ore deposits were discovered, leading to the start of work on Panguna Mine in 1966. Until this time the main economic activity on Bougainville had been coconut and cocoa plantations. Panguna Mine is owned and was operated by Bougainville Copper Ltd (BLC), a subsidiary of Con-Zinc Rio Tinto Australia, which in turn is majority-owned by Rio Tinto Zinc of the United Kingdom.

The mine started commercial production of copper in 1972. Within two years annual production amounted to 640,800 tonnes of concentrate. By the mid-1970s Panguna Mine was the PNG government's most important source of revenue. The mine produced 3.1 million tonnes of copper, 783 tonnes of silver, and 306 tonnes of gold.

In 1975, when PNG became independent, Panguna accounted for 44 per cent of national exports and 17 per cent of GDP. Already Bougainvilleans were expressing dissatisfaction with central Government. The PNG constitution, affording considerable powers to the provinces, was specifically designed to appease Bougiainvillean aspirations towards greater local autonomy.

But although the mine contributed revenue and led to the improvement of the island's infrastructure and local services, it also caused serious environmental damage. Forests were cleared and a hole measuring 4 miles (6 kilometres) in length and 2+ miles (4 kilometres) in width was excavated to allow the extraction of copper. Huge quantities of overburden and tailings were disposed of on the banks of the Kawerong River and washed into the Jaba River, changing its flow.

The workings also required the relocation of families from the Panguna area. Yet although compensation was paid for the upset, and a small proportion of royalties went to the landowners, this was considered insufficient, and arguments arose over precisely who was entitled to what (especially in relation to the royalties). In 1987, a group led by Francis Ona set themselves up in opposition to the traditional landowners' association (the Panguna Landowners' Association) which they accused of being too conciliatory towards BCL and inadequately representing the interests of local residents. This breakaway group demanded 10 billion kina (6.3 billion Ecu) in compensation, 50 per cent of BCL profits, and much better environmental protection.

Failure to reach a compromise led in November 1988 to a programme of disruption of the mining operations. By now, the dissident group had formed the Bougainville Revolutionary Army (BRA). In January 1989 violence broke out and riot police were called in. The police were then accused of using excessive force and, indeed, of brutality, including the destruction of some of the dissidents' houses. The situation deteriorated further in February and March, and the PNG Defence Force (PNGDF) was sent in. Finally, the mine was forced to close, on 15 May 1989, and the BRA took over effective control of Bougainville.

From then on the island of Bougainville was outside the control of the Government of PNG, and was run by the 'Bougainville Interim Government' (BIG), the political wing of the BRA, headed by Francis Ona. The military arm of the BRA was under the command of Sam Kauona. In the meantime, the infrastructure on the island began to crumble.

In October 1992 Government troops began a major offensive against certain rebel held areas of Bougainville, including the capital Arawa. In the ensuing fighting most of the town was destroyed.

In June 1994 further talks were held in Honiara, and in September 1994 Prime Minister Chan signed a cease-fire agreement with Sam Kauona, under which the economic blockade was to be lifted. In October 1994 Chan also signed an agreement, known as the Charter of Mirigini, with a group of non-BRA Bougainville leaders. This provided for the establishment of a Bougainvillle Transitional Government (BTG) – which was opposed by the BRA. In April 1995 the BTG was sworn in in a ceremony in Buka. Theodore Miriong, a former legal adviser to Ona, was elected Premier of the BIG. An amnesty declared in May 1995 by the BTG and the PNG Government was rejected by the BRA . . . and violence escalated.

The troubles continued, despite several unsuccessful attempts at mediation, until 1997, when new Prime Ministers came to power in both PNG and the Solomon Islands. The new PNG Prime Minister, Mr Bill Skate, despite a rather dubious past and a violent youthful period during which he was alleged to have been involved in violent crime, decided to do all in his power to bring peace to Bougainville. In this he was actively supported by Bartholomew Ulufa'alu, the new Prime Minister of the Solomons.

The northern Solomon Islanders are related ethnically to the people of Bougainville, and there is considerable sympathy on their part for the Bougainville cause, notably on the islands of Shortland (only 5+ miles/9 kilometres from Bougainville) and Choiseul. The Bougainville unrest had had a serious effect on the Solomon Islands' economy, so it was also in Mr Ulufa'alu's interest to bring about an end to the Bougainville troubles.

Mr Skate and Mr Ulufa'alu decided to give their full support to a new Bougainville peace initiative by the Foreign Minister of New Zealand, Mr Don McKinnon (later to become Secretary General of the World Trade Organisation).

This initiative started when Mr McKinnon contacted Mr Martin Miriori, then living in exile in the Netherlands. Informal meetings between the BIG and BTG representatives and the New Zealand Government had been held in June 1997 at which it was decided to pick up the peace process from where it had stopped after the talks in December 1995. The PNG Government agreed to participate in a major meeting in Burnham, New Zealand, in July 1997, with Bougainville leaders from the different factions. This resulted in the signing of the Burnham Declaration calling for peaceful settlement of the conflict, reconciliation between the parties, and negotiation with the national Government. The 'Burnham Truce' thereupon came into effect.

Follow-up meetings were held in New Zealand in September and October 1997. These meetings paved the way for a meeting of leaders, with representatives of all involved parties – PNG government, BTG, BIG, BRA and resistance movement – as well as representatives of civil society and representatives of the Government of the Solomon Islands.

On 23 August 1997 Mr Skate made an official visit to Bougainville, or, more precisely, to Buka, on which the BTG is based. During this visit he made statements reassuring the Bougainville people of his commitment to the peace initiative. Furthermore, both Mr Skate and Mr Ulufa'alu went to Bougainville for Christmas 1997.

At the same time, at the invitation of the parties to the Burnham Truce, New Zealand co-ordinated the formation and deployment of the neutral regional Truce Monitoring Group (TMG) composed of both military and civilian personnel from New Zealand, Australia, Fiji and Vanuatu. At present there are 89 Truce Monitors and 236 support personnel, all of whom are unarmed. They took up duty in Bougainville in December 1997, and are based in Buka, Buin, Tonu, Arawa and Loloho, where they maintain port facilities and a logistics centre.

In January 1998 the Leaders' meeting was held in Lincoln University, New Zealand, attended by some 190 participants from the National Government, the BTG, the Bougainville Resistance, the BIG and the BRA. Church and Womens' representatives also attended. At the invitation of the parties, the UN Secretary General sent a representative. Although invited, Francis Ona decided not to attend the Lincoln meeting. It was chaired by Prime Minister Ulufa'alu of the Solomon Islands, and was opened by Prime Minister Shipley of New Zealand. The Lincoln Agreement on Peace, Security and Development on Bougainville was signed on 23 January 1998 by Sir John Kaputin, Chief Negotiator for the PNG Government, Mr Joseph Kabui, Vice-President of the BIG, Mr Sam Kauona, Commander of the BRA, the former Co-President of the Solomon Islands, and others.

Without this background to the situation, little known outside the region, it would be difficult to understand why we set out to visit Papua New Guinea and the Solomons in February 1998. Our aim was to see the situation on the ground, to encourage reconciliation among the antagonists, and to monitor the use of European Union assistance, which was deemed to be of considerable importance by those closely involved in the situation.

After a long flight via Australia, I arrived in Port Moresby, PNG, on the morning of 23 February 1998 and immediately went into a series of meetings with Government ministers and police and army officers responsible for Bougainville. The next day we had discussions with all shades of political opinion, including a long exchange of views with Prime Minister Bill Skate, and meetings with religious leaders.

Before going to Bougainville Island we went to Raboul, New Britain, which had been very largely destroyed by a volcanic eruption. Most of the inhabitants had been resettled some 12 miles (20 kilometres) away, in an operation partly financed by European Union aid.

Near Rabaul we held talks with the Roman Catholic Bishop responsible for Bougainville, who gave us his personal view on the peace process. He believed that the people deeply desired peace, and that the impulse for peace came mainly from the women of the island.

That evening we were entertained by local people, who, as well as inviting us to traditional food, performed dances in their bare feet on glowing red embers, without any apparent discomfort or ill effects. I still do not understand how.

Then to Bougainville, in pouring rain. We began in Bougainville with a series of briefings on Buka island, north of the main island, given by the politicians and the local Commander of the International Truce Monitoring Group, a most impressive Fijian officer, Colonel Meli. Then using two helicopters, one PNG and the other provided by the New Zealand Air Force, we went to Bougainville island.

Helicopters were the only possible means of transport because the road infrastructure had fallen into total disrepair since the start of the conflict.

The helicopters themselves were memorable. I travelled in the PNG helicopter, an old Huey of US Vietnam War vintage, with open side-doors and rain coming in through the roof. It was a wonderful way to see the countryside – including the environmental devastation caused by the Panguna Mine – over which we flew. Damage, destruction and pollution was visible everywhere, including the waste failings, which had affected a river almost down to the sea.

We travelled all over the island, speaking to local groups and observing the situation. On one occasion we heard that a reconciliation ceremony was about to take place in a village some 6 miles (10 kilometres) distant from where we were. So off we went to it. It was a fascinating experience, seeing the dancing and the speeches. Apparently the two villages had become enemies during the Bougainville fighting and now they were making peace. Sir John Kaputin, travelling with us did not miss the opportunity to make a long and passionate speech to both sides, in which we caught the two expressions in Pidgin (which everybody speaks) with which we had become familiar: *buggarup*, meaning 'troubles', including the civil war, and *tok-tok*, 'talk-talk', meaning just that – negotiations.

Perhaps the most significant contact we made was a long session, in a dusty local church in a remote village in central Bougainville, with Joseph Kabui, Vice-President of the Bougainville Interim Government and Sam Kauona, the Military Commander of the Bougainville Revolutionary Army, the senior guerrilla fighter on the island and probably the most influential figure after Francis Ona. He looked tough and effective – but not very military, in an old T-shirt advertising Guinness.

The setting was extraordinary. We had started in the local primary school and moved from there to the simple earth-floored church, which had no glass in its windows. The whole village gathered around, many armed with long *panga*-type knives. Yet the message was most encouraging. The people of Bougainville wanted peace as well as the setting up of their own administration (no precise details were given of the degree of autonomy sought) and police force. Significantly, they did not want any more pollution from Panguna Mine.

Night in Arawa, the almost totally ruined capital of Bougainville, was a truly weird experience. The whole mission slept in three cramped bedrooms, each person almost on top of the next. Only Maartje van Putten, our sole woman member, had a room to herself. Some of our delegation did not have mosquito nets and accordingly suffered horribly from insect bites. An Irish colleague, a friend from my NFU days, when he had been President for the Irish Farmers' Association, Alan Gillis, suffered this misery throughout our entire stay.

Wherever we went in Bourgainville we were most impressed by the work of the Truce Monitoring Group (TMG), consisting of Australian, New Zealand, Fijian and Vanuatu troops. The commander of the force in Arawa, Colonel Mataparae, a New Zealand Maori, gave us a most encouraging analysis of the situation, and as we travelled around the island we became increasingly conscious of the excellent work being done by the Group. In one village I remember a tiny, pretty New Zealand Maori woman officer who seemed to have built up a really cordial relationship with the local people. It was like that throughout the island.

Everywhere we went we met women who were active in the peace movement. Usually working through Church structures, both Catholic and Protestant, it was they who had started the peace process and it was they who sustained it at difficult moments. It is clear that without the determination and force of character of these women, the war would still be going on.

After journeying around Bougainville we went on to Honiara, the rather sleepy capital of the Solomon Islands. Here we were shocked to learn just how badly the Solomons had been affected by the Bougainville troubles. The material costs for a very poor country amounted to some 22 million US dollars, in addition to the US$10 million involved in maintaining the 5,000 Bougainville refugees that had sought refuge in the Solomons. About 1,000 were left when we were there. But as we were soon to learn, many of these were hardliners or people who had taken part in specific guerrilla activities and were afraid to return. We had a highly instructive meeting with some of these remaining Bougainville refugees in the Tanagai Care Centre just outside Honiara.

The Solomons also experienced political instability as a result of the Bougainville crisis. The former Prime Minister, Solomon Uawaloni, a notoriously corrupt figure, had been forced to resign because of his involvement in a scheme to import arms and military equipment, almost certainly for use by the Bougainville rebels, from which he presumably would have earned a profitable commission. The new Prime Minister, Bartholomeu Ulufa'alu, was a much more pleasant, sincere and well-meaning person, and a devout Christian who started every meeting with a prayer.

The Solomons is a profoundly religious society. With some of the delegation I went to church in the Anglican Cathedral in Honiara on Sunday 1 March 1998 – a huge, typically Melanesian building with the sides open to the elements. The music was exceptionally beautiful, a mixture of local Pacific tunes and rhythms, and Anglican liturgical singing. It was a memorable service, made all the more so by a sermon that referred not only to the Bougainville peace process but also to the question of fair prices for commodities from developing countries on the markets of the industrialised world.

Our conclusions on leaving the Solomons via Vanuatu was that the peace process, and notably the Lincoln Agreement, had given rise to real hope. All international actors, including the European Union, had their role to play.

We identified the economy (notably the rural economy), road infrastructure, education, school rehabilitation and health (notably primary health care) as priority areas for EU assistance. I am pleased to state that the European Union subsequently did play a useful role in the long task of rehabilitating Bougainville – a marathon task that is not yet complete.

After the Solomons I went on in an unofficial capacity to Fiji. Here I had talks with Government ministers and the private sector, particularly on the future of the sugar industry, the islands' second foreign-exchange-earner after tourism.

The Sugar Protocol annexed to the Lomé Conventions was under threat from the World Trade Organisation, and it is clear that the guarantees given by the European Union to buy Fijian sugar under specially privileged arrangements cannot continue indefinitely in the face of such pressure.

Kenya

My last special mission as Co-President of the Joint Assembly was to Kenya in September 1998. I went at the invitation of the Kenyan Ambassador to the EU, Mr Philip Mwanzia, and President Daniel Arap

Moi, whom I have known for years. The purpose of the mission was to review the situation in Kenya and to monitor the European Union's co-operation programme with that country.

When I arrived in Nairobi on 23 September 1998 the city was still in a state of shock, following the bomb blast on 7 August 1998 that had destroyed the American Embassy and several nearby buildings, including Kenyan Government buildings, killing 255 people and injuring some 5,000, many very seriously. A similar attack had been made on the US Embassy in Dar-es-Salaam. Islamic extremists – in particular, the followers of Osama Bin Laden – were suspected of having perpetrated this appalling crime.

The effects of the blast scarred a good part of the city centre. There was a huge hole where the US Embassy had been, and the neighbouring buildings were either totally destroyed or badly damaged. Even ministries where we met, several hundred yards away, had had their windows blown out and staff injured by flying shards of glass.

The most positive aspect of this devilish crime was that it gave rise to a great sense of solidarity among the Kenyan population. People from all walks of life had clawed at the rubble, often with their bare hands, in an attempt to save those buried, and to a certain extent that spirit lived on while we were there.

There were the usual problems regarding corruption. Some of the new ministers, notably the Minister for Finance, were trying valiantly to clean up corruption, while some of the old ministers noted for having their fingers in the till were still in place and determined that there should be no radical transformation in a system that had served them – but not the country – well.

On the other hand, the press continued to be remarkably free. The political opposition operated openly and without serious harassment. Kenya also had an admirable record in foreign policy. It did not interfere with, or invade, its neighbours, and it had accepted a huge number of refugees from Somalia and other countries in the region.

I noted with approval that constitutional change was under way, with the collaboration of the Opposition.

I travelled to the Rift Valley to see the areas where the inter-ethnic clashes had occurred in December 1997, and was pleased to note that these had been much more firmly dealt with by the Government than had the politically-inspired clashes of 1991–92, when Kikuyus living in the west, in areas traditionally loyal to President Moi, had been driven out in a form of ethnic cleansing. This time ethnic clashes had been handled strictly, and the situation soon returned to normal.

My meeting with President Daniel Arap Moi was interesting – as always. I knew him of old, and shared his interest in cattle. I had even judged some of his livestock at the Nairobi Show some years earlier, presenting them, unknowingly, with eight firsts and a Supreme Champion!

He was as alert as ever, and I got the impression that he was willing to go along with a degree of reform if it was the precondition for further IMF and World Bank assistance.

Throughout my visit I was accompanied, as usual, by the staff of the European Union delegation, and one point they insisted I made, and that I duly raised with President Moi, was that the EU could not continue to finance projects to improve transport infrastructure – including the vital Mombasa–Nairobi road – unless the police rigorously enforced regulations fixing maximum axle weights for lorries. Excessive weight on overloaded lorries quickly degraded road surfaces. The President agreed to see to this via the competent authorities.

After my return from Nairobi I drew up a comprehensive resolution that was adopted by the Joint Assembly at its meeting in Brussels on 24 September 1998.

The end of the Co-Presidency

My last session as Co-President of the Joint Assembly was in Strasbourg from 29 March to 1 April 1999. It was in many respects a highly emotional session. I thanked all those who had contributed to what, I was informed by many, had been a highly successful Presidency. My charming Botswanan ACP Co-President, Thebe Mogami, was also coming to the end of his mandate, and he thanked me warmly for the closeness of our collaboration. It had been a pleasure to work with him, and with so many members, even from opposing political tendencies, in the common cause of North-South brotherhood.

As I looked back then, I had very mixed emotions. Some of my happiest memories in the European Parliament – or indeed anywhere else – were from my ACP days. I had enjoyed meeting so many interesting people from so many contrasting backgrounds in the African, Caribbean and Pacific countries. And I had been supported by a wonderful team from the European Parliament, led by Bryan Rose, who was a veritable walking encyclopaedia on African affairs and who became a friend for life. I also had an excellent relationship with the European Commissioner for Development, João de Deus Pinheiro, and his British Director General, Philip Lowe. They listened attentively to the Joint Assembly, and in this interaction it was not difficult to feel that the views emanating from the Assembly were influencing ACP-EU development policy.

At a pleasant and moving ceremony attended by members and the staff of the Joint Assembly, I was presented with a photograph of myself, speaking from the Chair at one of the most sensitive moments of my Co-Presidency – the session in Lomé, Togo, in October 1997, in which Togo's democratic legitimacy was being criticised by some European members and defended eloquently by Togo's former Prime Minister, and subsequently Minister of Foreign Affairs, Joseph Koffigoh. Even now when I look at this photograph it brings back fond, and exciting, memories. And I particularly remember the tributes paid by two women Socialist members, Glenys Kinnock and the Dutch MEP Maartje van Putten.

I had enjoyed being deeply involved in specific issues such as the long-running dispute between the USA and the European Union over banana imports, in which we battled for years to defend the livelihoods of small producers in the Windward Islands and other parts of the Caribbean, who had a privileged access to the EU market, against the actions of the US and some Latin American countries, through the World Trade Organisation, who wished to remove this privilege in the name of free trade. The US argument was strong in terms of economic doctrine – and eventually won the day – but we struggled on behalf of the 'little men' for as long as we could, because of the practical consequences to their family businesses.

I also felt involved in the tragic, and so unnecessary, war between Ethiopia and Eritrea, during which delegations from both sides used to come to see me every few weeks. We tried to play an even-handed and calming role, encouraging both sides to go to the negotiating table. Such direct personal involvement was a satisfying experience, yet overall I could not be at all satisfied about the ACP situation or what was to become of it. Indeed, the more I had come to learn about the realities of the developing countries, the more disturbed I had become about the general Western approach to these problems.

I found the visits I made to ACP countries in my capacity as Co-President of the ACP–EP Joint Assembly an essential complementary experience to what I had previously known of the so-called Third World through my activities in the NFU, the European Parliament and as patron of the charity Farm Africa. There is an insuperable difference between 'knowing about', for instance, the situation in an African country when one is sitting in London or Brussels, and experiencing that situation at first hand, on the ground. As ACP President, I had privileged access to the major actors on both European Union and ACP sides of the equation, and, equally importantly, to the realities of how EU and other Western assistance was affecting the local people to whom it was directed. I thus had the opportunity to draw up a sort of balance sheet and to reflect on the impact of Western aid to the ACP countries in the post-colonial period.

I must frankly say that the balance sheet is not a positive one. It is true that I have witnessed some examples of excellent work achieved and of well-directed work carried out by extremely devoted individuals. To see the benefits of a successful clean-water scheme for a village or a new regional medical centre or secondary school is a satisfying experience. And to meet a nurse or teacher who has given decades of his or her life to the service of an African community is not only humbling but inspiring. However, we must look beyond such individual experiences to the wider picture and at what has been achieved overall.

One of the most depressing conversations I have ever had was with an aid worker in Africa who was coming to the end of a 30-year career in a senior administrative position, with responsibilities for channelling Western assistance, under several programmes, to a vast region of that continent. I asked him what had fundamentally changed in those 30 years. His answer was, 'Nothing in the slightest!'

No doubt that was an exaggeration, and we can never know what would have been the situation in ACP countries, had not the European Union and, to a lesser extent, the USA and other donors not made their contribution. Nevertheless, it is impossible to escape the conclusion that we could all have done a great deal better – and that we must all do a great deal better in the future.

Consider the inputs that have been made, in terms of aid, to the ACP countries since the 1960s. The European Union countries have annually – annually – been pouring in some 30 billion Euros. To this must be added some part of the 10 billion Euros that the USA spends on overseas aid (although most of that money goes to non-ACP countries such as Israel and Egypt, a fact that frequently surprises those not directly involved in aid issues). As a percentage of our Western wealth, that is not an over-generous contribution, but it is still a vast injection of resources, for which the taxpayers who provide it are entitled to expect significant results.

And yet when we look at the ACP countries, particularly in Africa, we see a bleak overall picture. Several regions of that continent are still periodically subject to pitiless famine. In virtually every country there is widespread suffering through poverty, inadequate medical care and the systematic abuse of human rights. Very few countries have managed to achieve an adequate basic infrastructure of such elements as roads, schools, electricity supplies, water and sewerage services, nor the qualified personnel to run and maintain them. The life expectancy of our fellow men and women in most African countries is barely half of the European average – and it is a life most likely spent in what we would consider misery.

Whose fault is it?

It is easy to place a large part of the blame on corrupt and inefficient dictators – and certainly there is no shortage of them in Africa. It is true, also, that corruption and inefficiency in many countries are not restricted to the men at the top but permeate the very warp and woof of the social, commercial and administrative fabric of society. This is something that holds back internal progress and also diverts outside aid from its intended targets into numbered Swiss bank accounts.

But the blame does not stop there. We in the West must also look at ourselves.

There is no use, of course, our beating our breasts and bemoaning the evils of the colonial era – although honesty obliges us to admit that some, at least, of today's problems can be traced back to Western exploitation of the continent's natural resources and to the arbitrary drawing of lines across the map in the course of the 'scramble for Africa' of the 19th century, without regard for the interests or natural territories of the indigenous peoples. The Third World debt problem, which has crippled the economic recovery of many ACP countries and which is only now being seriously addressed in practical terms, can also be traced back to that time.

Nor can we be proud of the conditions under which we granted independence to our former colonies in the post-World-War period. To say that many of them were ill-prepared for such a change would be a vast understatement. In more recent times, during the Cold War, the West was also guilty of turning a blind eye to the multiple evils of dictators such as Mobutu, provided that they were willing to be 'anti-Communist'.

We must face up to our share of the blame for all these unhappy aspects of the past. But what is much more important, in practical terms, is that we, at the same time, analyse our shortcomings in the present and try to rectify them.

By that I mean, specifically, that we need to examine development aid to Africa, fundamentally and comprehensively, *and to make a fresh start*. I have come to the conclusion that there is no point in attempting to tinker with the mechanisms already in place: there is simply too much chaos – duplication of effort, lack of clearly-defined objectives, inadequate co-operation with people on the ground, unsatisfactory control systems and poor accountability – for worthwhile improvements to be possible without a radical re-think of our whole approach to this set of problems. And I believe that we owe such a re-think to our own taxpayers and to the ordinary citizens of the African countries.

From my first-hand experience, I know that such an approach is likely to be bedevilled by what I can only call the 'neo-colonial complex'. We in Europe have in recent decades been so inhibited by the fear of being branded 'neo-colonialists' – and others have been so keen to accuse us of that outlook whenever we raise issues of accountability or good governance – that the entire ACP-EU relationship has, in many ways, been the victim of fashionable political correctness. If we seriously want to make progress, to eliminate waste and to benefit the African peoples, we must shake off that complex and approach the relationship anew, with lucidity and realism. Of course, we must be sensitive to issues that touch upon the national dignity of our ACP partners – but on the other hand, we must not allow ourselves to be trapped into a situation of seeing only through a glass darkly and playing only the role of paymaster.

What I am advocating is a new concept I would describe as open, global partnership. The application of this concept presupposes, on the part of the 'donor communities', an initial, integrated approach, embracing the European Union (and I firmly believe that the 15 member states should abandon the division of their aid budgets into national and European programmes), the USA, the World Bank and other governmental agencies, along with an attempt to persuade the Non-Governmental Organisations, to subscribe to the same policy, so that the individual recipient countries would have opposite them a co-ordinated set of interlocutors.

Each country (with an encouragement towards trans-national, regional co-operation, where appropriate) would be encouraged to carry out, within the framework of its own national budget and development programme, and in partnership with the European Commission, a joint analysis of the needs of the country and of a realistic programme of specific projects to which the donor community could make a positive and practical contribution, in complementary and supplementary ways, within the constraints of the available human and financial resources.

Such programmes would be aimed not only at physical development projects but at measures designed progressively to improve the level of 'good governance' – including, for example, respect for human rights and the rule of law, and the furtherance of democratic principles and organisational structures within the country concerned.

At the stage of implementation, these programmes would enjoy the benefit of European Union management support, and would be subject to the same controls and standards of accountability applied to EU funding in Europe.

I am acutely aware of the likely opposition and objections to such ideas.

Firstly, I have no doubt that a number of 'recipient country' governments would loudly complain that Europe was trying to interfere in their internal affairs – in other words, the 'neo-colonialist' argument would immediately surface. Furthermore, some European Union member states would be reluctant totally to submerge their national development aid within an EU programme. Similarly many NGOs would not wish to sacrifice what they see as their independence of action to an overall framework. Non-EU Governments and other organisations might well resist the idea of playing second fiddle to Brussels in this respect. And critics of the Commission would undoubtedly complain that my proposals would lead to more paperwork and to an increase in the number of Eurocrats.

However, I would respond to such objections in the following way.

To the African government bent on resisting 'interference' I would say that the political and financial reality is that there will only be limited resources available for development aid, and that these will have to be concentrated in those countries and in those ways in which the taxpayer donors can be satisfied they are being used to best effect, in an open and transparent way.

I would remind member state governments that recent opinion polls in Europe indicate an increasing reluctance on the part of individual citizens to support development aid precisely because of a (to my mind, well-founded) perception that the present fragmented nature of such assistance is wasteful.

To the NGOs I would say that the diversity and flexibility of their contributions are appreciated, but that there is no reason to suppose that these could not be further enhanced through their being carried out within an overall, coherent programme of development.

I can understand the instinctive objection of the Americans, in particular, to allowing the European Union to take the lead in this field, but I would point out that it would be realistic and would be the mirror-image of what already takes place within the realm of defence, as between the USA and Europe.

I do have sympathy with those who do not wish to see bureaucracy or staff numbers increase within the Commission, but to them I would make two points. I believe that in the past the European Parliament and Council of Ministers have all too often given a mandate to the Commission to carry out certain tasks, and have provided considerable budgetary resources to be used in the implementation of such tasks, but without providing adequate personnel resources, particularly 'on the ground', to manage and control the practical work in a proper fashion. I would advocate that all budgetary allocations to the Commission, certainly in the field of development, should be accompanied by an assessment and provision of the manpower necessary to ensure an efficient and accountable fulfilling of the mandate concerned.

My second point is this: some administrative situations have become so chaotic – and I would submit that this is indeed the case with the development aid programmes in Africa – that only by deploying a determined trouble-shooting taskforce can we hope to solve the problem.

So much for the objections to the concept of global partnership. To me, there is one overwhelmingly important advantage to the concept – that its visible application would quickly help to convince all those involved in the process (taxpayers, charity donors, governments, NGOs and beneficiaries at the point of delivery) that it was well directed, efficiently managed and transparently accountable. That would go a long way to overcoming 'donor fatigue' and, as a useful political by-product, to improving the image of the European Union.

14

ON THE HORIZON

> To see should be easy, but to *foresee* –
> that is the difficult thing.
> (Rural saying)

How do I see the future in the three overlapping spheres I have been closely involved in – agriculture, development aid to the Third World, and the European Union?

In all three of them I take a strictly non-deterministic view. There are, I think, excellent opportunities ahead for progress, but there are no guarantees of success – and there are many dangers, some of which will only be avoided by the exercise of considerable wisdom and courage on the part of our leaders.

The future of agriculture

So where, firstly, do I believe agriculture in Britain and the European Union is going?

There is, of course, a temptation to dwell on the crises of BSE ('mad cow disease') and foot-and-mouth disease, which have caused so much devastation in the recent past. Quite apart from their immediate cost and negative impact, they have obliged the public – and therefore the politicians – to reflect on the complex issues of food production and its economics at all stages from farmgate to plate, on the importance of the wider environmental and economic aspects of agriculture, and on the regulatory role of Government at national and European levels. BSE and foot-and-mouth have put agricultural and rural issues on the front page of the media for months on end, and there is no doubt that these dramas will act as a catalyst in the policy reviews that will follow in these fields.

However, I believe we should look beyond these (admittedly serious but) short-term problems.

The three main factors that will determine farmers' incomes over the next few years – apart from the ever-dominant but increasingly unpredictable forces of the weather – are the value of the pound Sterling (for as long as it remains outside 'Euroland'), the state of the world economy, and whatever changes are made to the Common Agricultural Policy, especially in the light of European Union enlargement.

The value of the pound, then. As many UK bankers have learned in recent years, future currency movements are unbelievably difficult to forecast – and I see little point in trying now. It seems probable that we shall never see the extraordinarily low pound values of the mid-1990s again. While the pound remains outside Economic and Monetary Union, however, we must anticipate continued volatility, and the UK agricultural industry certainly can't bank on any definitive improvement in incomes from a consistent strengthening of the Euro relative to the pound.

Secondly: the state of the world economy.

Although the European Union agricultural economy is still somewhat insulated by trade barriers, world market forces can nonetheless have a significant impact on European Union and UK farmers' incomes. When world prices are high, agricultural products can be exported without subsidy. In addition, stocks in intervention stores (built up as a result of intervention buying, through which the European Union buys certain agricultural commodities to support prices when they fall below a threshold level) can be reduced or eliminated – thus taking away an overhanging threat to prices within the European Union. Demand for food outside Europe is related to the rate of world economic growth and, in particular, growth in the developing economies of Asia and Latin America. As demand increases, prices rise because the supply response – more land being brought into production worldwide or extra inputs being used to increase yields per acre/hectare – lags.

After an extremely depressed period, which was at its worst in 1998–99, world economic growth recovered strongly – and the prospects are still good, despite some warning signs in the USA that growth there may slacken. During 2000, European Union intervention stocks of skimmed-milk powder, for example, fell from around 175,000 tonnes to virtually zero. Grain stocks – although much greater than milk – are reducing. In dollars – the currency of most trade in these agricultural commodities – world prices increased, and Europe benefited additionally by the fall in the value of the Euro and the pound against the dollar.

This stronger world market should last for a couple of years, unless high fuel prices substantially reduce world economic growth rates. After that, most forecasters anticipate a slowing of the rate of growth of the world economy even without a major oil price shock. Also, the higher world commodity prices will quickly stimulate a supply response in South America, Oceania and Eastern Europe, where unused or under-utilised land is available, costs are low, and there are no such constraints as quotas.

Further liberalisation of world agricultural trade will no doubt occur, but the various conflicting views – as witnessed in Seattle in 1999 – will ensure that the pace is slow.

The third main factor is the evolution of the Common Agricultural Policy.

The Agenda 2000 changes to the CAP were, frankly, disappointing. They did not look far enough ahead. The original Commission proposals took positive steps in the direction of reducing export subsidies and price support, but the Council of Ministers watered these down greatly for the final agreement. The result will be continuing strains in the European Union to meet the GATT agreement, a reactive rather than proactive position in relation to likely future WTO agreements, continuing pressures on the European Union budget, and added difficulties in the programme for expansion of the European Union.

The failure to grasp the CAP nettle will not have directly quantifiable impacts on UK farmers over the next few years, but it will be a negative factor in relation to prices – if only because of the pressure on 'intervention buying'. The EU Commission sees intervention now as a cumbersome and fraud-prone method of supporting farmers, and in its actions is discouraging it. This is especially clear in the case of grain, for which new rules introduced in early 2000 act as a significant deterrent. The same philosophy of discouragement by deterrent rules can also be seen in respect of milk.

The reality is that the European Union does not have the funds to provide full compensation to move to world prices as tariff barriers are removed, and the forthcoming first wave of enlargement to the East (which would under current arrangements almost triple CAP expenditure) has forced the European Union in the direction of a partial 're-nationalisation' of the policy. I don't see this as an abandonment of the CAP – rather, I believe it is a necessary move, in keeping with the policy of subsidiarity, to allow the flexibility for direct payments to be set at different levels in individual member states, according to regional priorities.

I expect we will move towards a form of voluntary modulation, so that direct payments above certain thresholds can be reduced. The money thus saved could then be used for rural development projects, with matching assistance from national treasuries.

On a lower level than these three major issues, a factor that has some significant bearing on UK agriculture's competitive position – and hence its incomes – is the negative attitude of the British public and even, to some extent, the British Government, towards biotechnological developments, compared even with other European countries, and certainly compared with rest of the world, especially the United States. There is no doubt that the recent developments in plant-breeding technology can reduce costs, can increase production for a world still plagued by hunger, and, by reducing the need for pesticides, can have a beneficial effect on the environment.

The UK public has not yet accepted these *facts* – perhaps because a sensation-seeking press has not allowed the facts to be communicated properly and objectively. It now seems certain that the next phases of genetic research will lead to developments in food quality for health and in pharmaceuticals from farm crops. These developments will give huge and more obvious benefits to humankind, and should thus gradually change UK attitudes. If they don't, the lack of genetic research and development in the UK will be a permanent constraint on the competitiveness of our agriculture and will further diminish it.

I see the bio-tech controversy as part of a wider problem – the alienation in recent years of the vast urban population of our country from the interests of farming and rural life generally. This can be seen also in such contexts as the hunting debate and animal welfare issues generally. It will take a sustained effort of mutual understanding – and above all, a much greater PR awareness on the part of those of us who live and work in the country – to heal this dangerous rift. It is up to us who know, love and understand the countryside to show that we care about its future.

I was once accused at a public meeting, by a member of Friends of the Earth, of being a greedy farmer who raped the land and destroyed the landscape. I replied, truthfully, 'I am the descendant of at least five generations of farmers. My motto is to leave this Earth in better shape than I found it. So I have been a friend of the earth longer than you!'

'You couldn't have,' was his fatuous retort. 'Friends of the Earth haven't been going that long!'

As if only the members of his organisation could be planet-friendly!

It is vital that conflicts about the role of science and technology in agriculture be resolved in a rational way. I am convinced that only through the proper application of science – and by that I mean not just the blind following of every laboratory advance, but the balanced use of scientific progress, taking into account the welfare of humankind, the animal kingdom and our environment – will British and European agriculture be saved in the long run.

An important aspect of this is the need to restore an emphasis on education in the agricultural sector. We must recognise more clearly the crucial role our universities and agricultural colleges have to play in the future of our industry, and reverse the recent negative trends in that respect.

Another new development, if oil prices remain high, will be the use of crops for fuels. The production of bioethanol already accounts for about 5 per cent of the US corn (i.e. maize) crop. Further depletion of fossil fuel stocks and the popular reaction against nuclear energy will provide further stimuli for research into and development of crop-based fuels.

If this development does come about, it will be an extension to the set-aside measures already in place. The public initially found these hard to understand – and it is true that there is an apparent paradox in paying farmers to produce goods, then paying them for not producing them. But it has been an effective method of putting the brake on the production of unwanted volumes of certain commodities while allowing land thus taken out of, for example, wheat production, to be used for the growing of oil-seed rape. I am sure that, quite apart from the macro-economic aspects of set-aside, the practical rotation of land use is beneficial in itself.

It reminds me of the old 'four-course Norfolk rotation' used by earlier generations. As my father used to say, 'Take 10 per cent of the land out of use every year and give it a rest. It needs a rest now and then, just like you!'

What will be the impact of all these trends on farming in the UK?

It will be to continue to reduce the number of producers. Co-operation between neighbours to share labour and machinery will continue, and there will be more examples of complete amalgamation of farming operations. There will simultaneously be an increase in the proportion of farmers who augment their income from outside work or other businesses. In the past this income augmentation has traditionally derived from part-time manual work or support from a wife who might work full-time or who might be responsible for 'on-site services' like bed-and-breakfast. Increasingly, incomes will also be augmented through recourse to the professions and other non-farm businesses that can be carried out from a rural home as a result of modern developments in information technology.

The pressure of low incomes will continue to force down those costs specific to UK agriculture (e.g. land rents), but not those where the supply and demand factors, which affect price, are European or worldwide (e.g. fertilisers, agrochemicals and fuel). Most costs will thus be unaffected – and the inevitable result will be further amalgamations and contract farming agreements on a substantial scale.

Some farmers express concern that 'corporate farming' will thus take over the management of land in a big way, just as pig and poultry production is increasingly in the hands of vertically-integrated businesses. I am not too worried about this, however. Although there will be a place for a few professional farm management companies – and they will probably expand – it is likely that the larger, more successful, family farm operations will simply expand further through contract farming operations to gain further benefits from economies of scale.

Despite the relative pessimism I expressed in Chapter 10 about the British experience in cooperative exercises, I would hope that the arguments in favour of them – especially when the economies of scale become even more important than they are today – will find more practical support in the future than they have hitherto.

Development aid to the Third World

I now turn to the issues involving our relations with the developing countries – in which, of course, agriculture and food production loom large. One of the major obstacles in the way of bringing assistance, in the widest sense of the word, from Europe to the ACP countries, especially those in Africa, is fragmentation of both interest and effort.

First of all, the fact that European Union aid is not deemed, overall, to have been an outstanding success story has led member state Governments to divide their assistance in two: a contribution made through the European Union, and one made through their own national aid programmes. The latter contribution, moreover, tends to receive much greater publicity, as the national media give extended coverage, for example, to ministerial visits to projects funded by the individual member state. Despite attempts to co-ordinate the fifteen national efforts, plus those of the EU Commission, common sense would suggest that an integrated European programme would produce better results and better value for the taxpayers' money.

It is important to be specific here about what I mean by an 'integrated' programme, for there is another aspect of fragmentation that ought to be tackled: the fragmentation in the conceptual approach to aid, and our overall relations with the ACP countries.

Too often those most interested in development projects are not interested enough in topics such as human rights or good governance, believing them to be something of a luxury 'Western-inspired frill' compared to the 'real' on-the-ground problems of hunger, poverty, low living standards, poor infrastructure and inadequate health care suffered by the local populations in their everyday lives. They are to some extent encouraged in this view by undemocratic governments who are keen to accept responsibility for the running of European-Union-funded projects and who resist the notion of control and management by the Commission on the grounds that it is 'neo-colonial interference' in their internal affairs.

But I am convinced that good governance in individual countries receiving European Union aid is not only desirable for its own sake but is a catalyst working to increase the cost-effectiveness of the aid process in each country.

There is all too much evidence available to show that undemocratic countries are corrupt, inefficient and wasteful in their normal functioning. In their dealings with European Union aid programmes, left to their own devices, they will be no less corrupt, inefficient and wasteful. That is why I have advocated an approach at European level that would be in partnership with the ACP country concerned, but that would be free from any post-colonial guilt complexes on our part. It would involve a joint assessment of the totality of the country's needs in areas in which we could be of assistance, and the drawing up of a pluri-annual aid and development programme aimed at strengthening all the country's structures, both physical and organisational.

Most important of all, there should be prior agreement on the degree and level of European monitoring and management of individual projects, from start to finish. That will require a quantum leap of faith and methodology on the part of both the recipient country and the European Union. For the former, it will mean an acceptance that European taxpayers' money will only become available to help them if those taxpayers can be sure that the money is well spent. And on the European Union side, the Commission must be given the human and financial resources necessary to carry out the sort of mandate I have outlined. It will initially be expensive, but I believe that in the longer run, proper project conception and implementation will both save money and ensure that the objectives of European aid are met.

Frankly, without such a new and radical approach to the problems of European Union aid to the ACP countries, I cannot see how our policies can be sustained – particularly in the light of the pressure on our resources from the needs of Eastern Europe in the next two decades.

The future of the European Union

Undoubtedly the most important issue we must consider as we look at what is on the horizon is the future development of the European Union itself, for – whether Eurosceptics and Eurofanatics like it or not – that is the framework within which all the other issues will inevitably be addressed.

As at any point in time in modern European history, there are many uncertainties ahead. That should not, in itself, alarm us, since the European dynamic has succeeded in carrying us along now for four decades, in each one of which major problems have been encountered and, to a large extent, solved. Yet there is a daunting set of challenges to be met over the next few years.

Firstly, there is the consolidation of the Euro. This will be largely a question of how well the collective economy of the 'Euroland' states perform, coupled with public and investor confidence. The policy attitudes of the two main British political parties to this issue are revealing. Press comment tends to focus on the differences in the stance of each of them: Labour gives the overall impression (not without internal divisions) of basically wanting to join, but waiting for the right conjunctural moment; the Conservatives, while (just about!) refraining from saying 'never', give the impression that if they ever did come to support the UK's joining, it would be with great reluctance and because the case for doing so had become economically irresistible.

In the knockabout world of Westminster and the attendant media, these perceived differences are useful to both sides, who seek to differentiate themselves as much as possible, within the traditions of confrontational politics.

But what is of most significance is the underlying assumption common to both these approaches, that in important European developments, while Britain may sooner or later – usually later – tag along, we will not be numbered with the innovators.

This non-participating reflex has characterised our national position from the very start, and with baneful consequences. It strikes me forcibly that we have suffered – and are still suffering – from a national miscalculation over the intentions and resolve of our continental neighbours, particularly the 'locomotive' of France and Germany, in respect of the European mainstream.

We seem to live in a time-warp, in which we are retrospectively reconciled to where European integration was ten years ago, we are vaguely unhappy about the stage Europe has currently reached, and we are profoundly unhappy about where it might be going next. Whenever our partners propose an 'integrating' change, our first reaction tends to be to dismiss the goal as a pipe-dream. As the change then takes practical form, we then pour a modicum of scornful doubt on the ability of the pioneers to make it work. And when it does finally work, more or less, we reluctantly join up as an inevitable 'Johnny-come-lately'. Paradoxically, this 'semi-detached' approach is always more likely to result in our being *shaped* by the European Union, rather than our being involved in the *shaping* of the Union.

It is also the basis for our reputation of being 'not very good Europeans' – a reputation that is otherwise entirely undeserved, since the UK has one of the best records in terms of compliance with European Union law and policies. The continental criticism is utterly understandable, however, since it would be absurd if the other member states were to adopt a policy of staying on the sidelines until new policies were seen to be working in practice. 'Europe', in its modern form, could never have been begun, much less developed, in such circumstances.

One of the ironies of the present situation regarding the Euro is that the single currency's final success is likely to be assured, almost overnight, as soon as the UK joins the system. For although it is true that the Euro must succeed in economic-monetary terms, we cannot ignore the fact that it is, just as importantly, political in its inspiration and nature. Those who decry this fusion of the political and the economic overlook the fact that the original 'Common Market' (the EEC) was as much a political as an economic creation. The gains that have been made for the peoples of Western Europe in terms of living standards and economic advancement could not have been achieved without the political focus provided by the treaties.

To me the success of the Euro is only a matter of time. It is so central to the whole concept of the Union, not only as the primary instrument in completing the single economy but as the major factor at present in the 'Europeanisation' of the member states, that I cannot conceive of its failure.

'Enlargement' has always presented a challenge to the European enterprise, but it must be acknowledged that the enlargements that now loom on the horizon present a whole series of challenges wider in scope and more complex in their degree of difficulty than anything that the EEC/EC/EU has hitherto had to grapple with in earlier expansions.

No fewer than thirteen countries have applied for membership, and of them Poland, Hungary, the Czech Republic, Slovenia, Estonia and Cyprus are regarded as front-runners. Beyond even the thirteen, there are half a dozen other states in which ambitions to join at some point in the future have been seriously expressed. So the potential expansion could eventually lead to a Union of more than thirty states.

Each one of the applications will have to be considered separately, of course, but we must nevertheless face up to the issue of the sheer scale of the likely enlargement of the European Union over the next few decades, and plan organisational and constitutional changes not only to take account of the needs of a Union of twenty member states, but already to anticipate one of thirty or more. The Union is not just approaching a moment of some enlargement – it is on the threshold of a whole new era in its development, in which its sheer scale will, by itself, impose fundamental transformations.

The bulk of the applicant countries, and of the aspiring states, are former satellites of the Soviet Union who had been locked up for almost five decades in a system of controlled economies under a totalitarian order. Much has been achieved over the past ten years economically, socially and politically to bring these countries towards conformity with the Union's criteria for economic performance and democratic stability. But clearly, the successful absorption of a country like Poland, for example) will be more difficult than was the case with (for example, Denmark or, more recently, Sweden.

The timescale of new entries is a particular problem. Several of the newly-liberated states of Central and Eastern Europe were keen to join the European Union at the earliest possible moment, inspired by desires for security and material prosperity, and above all by the desire to escape from the potentially dangerous vacuum left by the collapse of the Soviet system.

I can understand how the prospects held out to them were over-optimistic – I recall that in 1997 President Chirac publicly told the Poles that he hoped to see their country admitted to membership by 2000 – and I can also understand the growing impatience and disillusionment of the populations in the leading applicant countries at the fact that they are *still* outside. But it is an operation that must be got right. It would not be in the interests of a particular state – and it would be disastrous for the European Union as a whole – if the timing were rushed or corners were cut. In each and every case there must be an insistence on the full and practical acceptance by the applicant country of the *acquis communautaire*, compliance in detail with the criteria for membership and realistic arrangements made for a period of transition. There will be a temptation to lower some of these hurdles, on account of the pressures I have outlined, but that temptation must be resisted.

Preparations for the enlargement to come in the medium-to-long term are inextricably linked to the need to reform the institutional and constitutional arrangements of the European Union, along with many of its working practices and procedures. Obviously, a Union of thirty member states could not be run using the structures of the fifteen-member Union of today – even if the present functioning was satisfactory, which is certainly not the case.

There are other important reasons for change. The last two revisions, at Maastricht (1997) and Amsterdam (1999), were both the products of messy compromises between the national governments. To take but the two most unsatisfactory aspects of these proceedings:

> · in the Maastricht text, the 'pillarisation' that kept necessary, but controversial, spheres of action in play as inter-governmental *but not community* matters, relating to defence and foreign policy (the 'second pillar') and justice and home affairs (the 'third pillar'); and
> · in the Amsterdam text, the inadequate tackling of the decision-taking procedures.

Much was hoped for in this respect from the European Council meeting held in Nice in December 2000, which was billed as the summit to prepare Europe for the next wave of enlargement. To those who believed that this was the golden opportunity to tidy up the complications of the existing treaties, and to take the bold decisions necessary to streamline and to restore an element of dynamism to the workings of the Union, Nice was largely, if not entirely, a disappointment.

The press briefings that emanated from several national capitals, including London, Paris and Berlin, in the run-up to the summit were not propitious. Several government leaders were at pains to lay down what became known as their 'red lines' – that is to say, the no-go areas, the matters on which they were unwilling even to contemplate compromise. For example, one of Mr Blair's 'red lines' was 'no surrender of the British veto' – a slogan that was a gross, but convenient, oversimplification aimed at anaesthetising Eurosceptic elements in the electorate.

In the event, some modest gains were achieved at Nice, and matters requiring decision at some later stage were defined and timetabled in a way that had not hitherto been accepted.

The scope of majority voting expanded almost imperceptibly, and certainly without registering a significant breakthrough. But in the same order of technical regulation, an overall compromise was finally found, after protracted haggling, on the weighted voting points system to be used once the next new member states have joined. That was a solid achievement – one which did not, however, receive much coverage in the popular press.

Much more attention was paid to the decision to set up a European Rapid Reaction Force in the light of the practical difficulties encountered in the early days of the crisis in what used to be Yugoslavia. There was considerable debate over whether this force would be the embryonic army of the European Union, a rival to NATO, or merely a NATO-minus-USA unit for use only in situations in which Washington wished not to become directly involved. Politicians of various parties and virtually every member state have been able to find scriptural support in the Nice texts for whichever interpretation suits their particular book – an example of masterly drafting. The true significance of this decision remains to be seen in the use to which it is put in the future.

Perhaps the most far-reaching – in potential, at least – of the decisions taken at Nice are reflected in the passages of the Conclusions devoted to 'Enhanced Co-operation'. These provide for the possibility of eight or more member states' moving ahead down the road of European integration *without the consent of the others*. This can be seen as a positive measure, aimed at relieving the frustration of the more 'European-minded' countries and allowing them to be trail-blazers for the others, who can join in later.

On the other hand, it has the danger of a 'two-speed' Europe written all over it, and it is a provision we in Britain will have to bear constantly in mind in the years ahead. 'Join in later, if it works' could become a particularly seductive and besetting temptation, given our recent history in Europe.

To yield to that temptation, though, is fraught with all manner of dangers. For I am convinced that the countries who will emerge as the practitioners of 'enhanced co-operation' – probably the original six member states of the EEC, along with Spain, Ireland, and some of the new members after the next enlargement – will in effect, shape the Europe of the future for all of us in their own image. It will be to our long-term detriment if we are not among them.

It was especially disappointing that a number of pressing issues involving the tidying up and clarification of the existing treaties were not substantively tackled at Nice – but at least they were identified and deferred for only four years. In the interval, a lot of work will have to be done, for example on the practical application of subsidiarity and the relative competences of the European Union and the member states. And public opinion will equally have to be prepared if the necessary decisions – deferred now for more than a decade – are to be taken and ratified in 2003–2004 that will create a Union capable of carrying out its present and future tasks efficiently.

At the conclusion of the Nice summit, President Chirac claimed that it had achieved what was possible in the circumstances, and what was necessary for the next steps towards enlargement. That was just about true. But the crunch is still to come – and it is the looming realities of enlargement that will finally cause it.

In the context of enlargement it is interesting to note that the extreme protagonists over Europe – the sceptics and the federalists alike – welcome the prospect. The sceptics welcome it because they believe that enlargement will lead to a dilution in the integration process; the federalists because they believe a European Union of more member states will in practice require a stronger centre and more streamlined decision-taking mechanisms.

A third major need for reform arises out of the recent failures in the institutional operations of the European Union – failures that have had a badly negative impact on public opinion. Such failures have not been confined to the Commission, but it was undoubtedly the drama surrounding the fall of the Jacques Santer Commission that highlighted important weaknesses.

Media coverage in the period December 1998 to June 1999 centred on the personal conduct of one or two Commissioners and drew attention to several management failings in the operation of the Commission's systems. But from a constitutional point of view, the real inadequacy was the lack of legal power on the part of both the European Parliament and the President of the Commission to dismiss an individual Commissioner. Had such a power been available under the treaties – and it had often been demanded by the European Parliament – I'm sure that the crisis would have been quickly defused. Instead, it dragged on, causing a great deal of damage.

I personally had some sympathy for Jacques Santer, both as a man and as a President of the Commission who had set out to implement what I considered to be the right policy for his period of office: 'to do less, but to do it better'. His mistake – which was out of character, since he was usually an astute reader of the political mood – was to misjudge the tone of his reply, on 17 December, to the Parliament's criticism of certain aspects of the Commission's operations. The Parliament, freshly reinforced in its role (although, as always, not to the degree it had hoped for) with the coming into force of Amsterdam, now had the bit between its teeth and pushed on, threatening to use the blunt instrument it *did* have at its disposal: dismissal of the Commission in its entirety. It was that threat which finally forced the Santer Commission from office.

More recently, the inadequacies of the aid and development programmes under the Commission's responsibility (which I discussed in Chapter 11) have shown up areas of structural management that need to be overhauled.

The European Union and the electorate

All these are reasons for reform. But undoubtedly the most important reason for the reform of the European Union is the need to gather political support for the Union throughout the European electorate. Nowhere is that need more acute than in Britain – but it is by no means confined to our shores, as opinion polls in all member states have been consistently showing for several years now.

There are several layers of significance to this. Media coverage – particularly in its tone – of inefficiencies, waste and high-handedness on the part of the Commission or of Parliament has created a widespread impression that 'Brussels' is an overblown, unaccountable bureaucracy. Some of this criticism is undoubtedly valid some of the time (although the question of the size of the administrative machine is one in which myth has proved far stronger than fact – the total number of European civil servants is less than 30,000, the size of the administration of an averaged-sized municipality.)

But the quality of administration at the European centre, important though it is, both *per se* and as a source of voter dissatisfaction, does not in itself explain the dangerous alienation of large sections of the European electorate from the concept of the Union. The major benefits that have flowed from the integration process – sustained peace, stability and prosperity – are nowadays largely taken for granted, especially by the younger generation who have no direct memory of the horrors of war or the uncertainties of the pre-EEC era.

The EEC/EC/EU has always been essentially the preserve of a European elite, right from the earliest days of the very concept. It could be argued, of course, that this criticism could equally be applied to national politics in most countries. But whereas at national level there is frequently, perhaps increasingly, a certain amount of public cynicism about the political process and its practitioners, the malaise at European level is of a different order. It is my personal view, having shuttled between Brussels and my home base for more than 30 years and having pondered on grass-roots attitudes over that period, that the fundamental problem is centred on the issues of sovereignty and national identity and the perceived links between the two. Both are perceived by the populace at large to be under threat from 'Brussels'.

This feeling is reflected in, and of course fanned by, the tabloid press. Responsibility for legislation is viewed as slipping away from the national parliament; new policies are thought to be dictated from, and all-important decisions taken by, the European centre; and there is a widespread belief that attempts are constantly being made to turn the British people into continental identi-kit Europeans. (The same sort of views, in varying degrees of intensity, can be detected in most of the other member states, although the UK is perhaps the prime example.)

To get to the bottom of this alienation and what to do about it, we must analyse what constitutes 'national sovereignty' in the modern world, and examine its links to, and difference from, the concept of 'national identity'.

The phrase 'national sovereignty' has a splendidly patriotic ring to it, conjuring up – for the British above all – the heady days of the Empire. But quite apart from the precise circumstances of the European Union, the idea of complete national sovereignty as it would have applied, for example, in the late 19th century is simply no longer tenable as an absolute. The forces of globalisation and inter-dependency, as I have already touched upon, have overtaken it. For a country nowadays to be completely 'sovereign' would mean that it was completely isolated.

It must not be forgotten that countries participating in *any* international agreement or treaty thereby give up a piece, however great or small, of their sovereignty, in that their future actions in the sphere governed by the agreement must take account of the rights of the other participants. Within the European Union this process of pooling sovereignty has already reached an advanced degree.

But the real question to be posed is not to what degree national sovereignty has been 'sacrificed'. Rather, the key political question is, what benefits have we derived from this pooling of sovereignty? In my mind, the answer is resoundingly positive.

It is worth remarking that in the two major 'absentee states' – Switzerland and Norway – there are increasing complaints from various important sectors of industry and commerce that the price they pay for a somewhat sham sovereignty is that they are, paradoxically, obliged to accept norms and standards decided on by the European Union, of which they are not (yet) members.

I have already expressed my criticism of ministers, and of national parliaments generally, for the way in which they contribute to the mythology surrounding sovereignty and the alleged threat to it from Brussels. The sooner there is practical recognition that the European framework – which is not the same as the European centre, for reasons I will explain – is the overall structure within which our lives are ordered, the better for all concerned.

Both major parties in the UK have been tortured at one time or another by the European question. Both still flirt from time to time with the temptation to (mis)use this issue for short-term party political advantage. We must stop pretending that 'Europe' is something that crops up periodically as a crisis, and demonstrate to the electorate that it is a day-to-day reality, affecting all our ways – a reality that requires close attention at governmental and parliamentary levels in an open and transparent manner.

What does that mean in practical terms?

Firstly, there is the role of national parliaments generally within the European Union. Too often in the past national parliaments have been thought of as being in a state of rivalry with the European Parliament. I have never believed that. I see their respective roles as complementary. As a European Parliamentarian, I strongly advocate a *more powerful* role for all national parliaments within the European Union system.

This role should be *chronologically* different from that of the European Parliament. By that I mean that national parliaments should structure their business in such a way as to familiarise themselves with European legislation at the earliest possible stage – that is to say, at the stage of the formulation of national policy. In other words, national parliaments should be able to make an informed input into the determination of their Minister's policy guidelines and positions on any particular subject *before* the Minister goes off to Brussels for negotiations at the European level. In many member states that would call for quite profound changes in the way Parliament is organised, and indeed in the relationship between government and parliament.

I recognize both the increasing pressures on parliamentary time in all our countries, and the progress that has been made, not least at Westminster. But I believe that there is still a tendency to push the consideration of European-Union-related legislation towards the margins of the parliamentary timetable and activities. This inevitably creates the impression in the media, and therefore in public opinion, that Europe is somehow a 'side-show'.

Secondly, there is the role of the European Parliament, and attitudes towards it. I have outlined the evolution of the European Parliament from consultative assembly to the position of co-legislator almost on a par with Council in the sphere of law-making and an increasingly powerful 'scrutineer' of executive policies and actions at European level. But there is still a long way to go in terms of attitudes *towards* the institution.

I believe that one of the positive by-products of the Santer Commission crisis has been that that institution is unlikely to treat the European Parliament in the future with anything other than a co-operative attitude. National ministers, especially when it is their turn to act as President-in-Office of the Council, must do likewise. Too often previously the European Parliament has been fobbed off with stand-ins for the appropriate Minister, or with a quality of information and reaction that the Minister would not have dared present to his or her national parliament.

Thirdly, at ministerial level the work of the Council must be more efficient and make a bigger impact on public opinion. In recent years there has been a general acknowledgement of a lack of co-ordination and coherence in Community action. In particular, there would appear to have been a progressive slippage over the years in the co-ordinating of the specialised Councils, such as those specialising in agriculture and the environment. Even the European summit meetings often show signs of being ill-prepared.

Now, I appreciate the other heavy demands, day by day, on the ministers concerned, and I realise that the internal mechanisms of the Council are of no great interest to the general public. But the news media cannot convey an understandable picture of what is going on at the European centre if these nuts-and-bolts structures are not both transparent and efficient. Above all, there must be a clearer set of procedures for decision-taking, in order to improve the quality of those decisions as well as to make them more comprehensible to the European citizen.

Equally important is the presentational aspect of this activity. Too often the ministerial spin gives the impression that 'European' activity is a sort of 'moonlighting', away from the 'real job' in the national ministry and parliament. Frequently, the only publicity sought, or given, about what a minister does in Brussels relates to a hyped tale of how he or she defended national interests against the schemes of the bureaucrats or the wiles of the foreign politicians. It is, I believe, in all our interests to get away from the fictional approach to the relationship between member states and European Union and to align political behaviour with political reality. What happens in Brussels – whether in the Council, the Commission, or Parliament – is not 'foreign' but *part of our way of organised life*. The Council is *our* Council as much as it is anyone else's – and the same goes for the other institutions.

Since I had the opportunity to spend more time in the House of Lords, I have been impressed with the work of the Select Committees and the chance we have in the Chamber to debate all issues relating to European affairs. The House of Commons is, of course, the pre-eminent Chamber of Parliament, but in the Lords we have the comparative advantage that there appears to be more time to scrutinise Bills.

Having served for twenty years in the youngest parliament in the world and now in one of the oldest, I realise that the shelf-life of knowledge is extremely short, and that the benefit from contributions made by members of the House of Lords comes from long-term experience and wisdom. In a world becoming more 'open-plan', governments will take more action that, either *de jure* or *de facto*, is legislative. This will happen in or out of Europe, and I believe that policy areas traditionally considered domestic will become subject to wider legislation. The House of Lords should develop its system of scrutiny that is already highly regarded by specialists and experts, and extend it to all areas in which our Government is negotiating outside its jurisdiction to legislate or spend taxpayers' money.

I am convinced that a key factor in the development at the European centre is 'subsidiarity'. That rebarbative, but meaningful word for the concept of carrying out all actions at the most appropriate level, must progress from being a theoretical concept – albeit one now enshrined in the treaties – to a much clearer statement of practical realities. An explicit codification attached to the treaties that sets out the 'subsidiarity spheres' would, at political and public-opinion level, serve as a guide to the European citizen as to who should be doing what, at which level, within the European Union, whether at the European centre, nationally, or regionally. The underlying principle is that the European centre should be directly handling only matters that can appropriately be dealt with there.

Such a formal constitutional division would not, of course, guarantee that there would never be disputes about the appropriate 'levels'. Even in the Federal Republic of Germany, regarded by many as a model of subsidiarity in practice at national and regional level, the Constitutional Court is frequently called upon to arbitrate in issues involving competency disputes between the *Bund* and the *Länder*. But it would provide a clearer picture of the relationship between member state and the Union, to the benefit of the administrators and, more importantly, the man and woman in the street.

I believe it would thus do much to calm the fears of those who believe that European integration must inevitably mean that all Europe will somehow be run from Brussels.

I turn now to the other great *bête noire* of public opinion – the perceived threat to 'national identity'.

National identity is sometimes seen as being almost synonymous with 'national sovereignty' – but it is important to disentangle these two threads. Clearly, there are points at which the two concepts impinge one upon the other. For example, the history of the acquisition of national sovereignty in any country is also a vital part of the development of the national identity of its people. We look back at our constitutional history to help give us a sense of who we are.

But that emphatically does not mean that whenever an element of national sovereignty is pooled with our partners, an element of our national identity somehow slips away from us. What we *are* far transcends the constitutional definition of our state: it encompasses our culture in its widest sense, our customs, even our national and regional idiosyncrasies. I can fully understand the man or woman who says 'I'm British, and I want to *stay* British' – but if they imagine that anyone involved in the European integration process has any desire to take away, or change, their British identity, they are mistaken.

It is true, of course, that over the past two decades the peoples of the European Union have had closer contact than ever before. We trade more with one another than ever before, we have far greater opportunities to visit one another's countries, and we know more about one another than our forefathers did. This has resulted in our borrowing from one another things that formerly did not 'travel' from their place of origin, from traditional foods to Premier League footballers. To that extent we have all been 'Europeanised' – but in an enriching way. We have not been pushed towards becoming some theoretically standard 'European citizen'. Nor has any single national identity become – or attempted to become – dominant in the way in which past efforts to create a united Europe by force inevitably led.

The European Union has given us an *additional* layer of identity, without diminishing our own. The proof of that is staring us in the face. Since 1958 the French have not become one whit less French, the Germans less German, or any other of the European Union nationalities less themselves.

The 'threat' to national identity is therefore a non-issue in reality. As a psychological barrier it can only be dismantled over time, through a more self-confident performance by political leaders not afraid to put national identity and the European Union into perspective.

Those are the challenges facing the Union.

What do I think is the realistic outlook?

As regards the Euro, I am optimistic in the medium term. I believe that the underlying strength of the Euroland economy, coupled with its sheer size and the political commitment to the currency, will establish it as a permanent feature in Europe and in the world's money markets, at an appropriate rate. It will prove to be one of the most potent Europeanising forces within the integration process. British membership, however late, is bound to come.

As for enlargement, I believe that inevitable complexities will lead to some slippage in the timetable we would ideally like to see.

Turkey has always been a special problem – and I confess I cannot see a solution to it at present. I have a certain amount of sympathy with the Turkish point of view, which holds that there is a fundamental and discriminatory difference between the European Union's thinking on their application on the one hand, and its thinking on applications from such countries as Poland or Estonia on the other. It was convenient for Western Europe to have Turkey as a NATO member and bulwark against Soviet expansion during the Cold War, but now, so runs this argument, there are doubts about the country's degree of 'European-ness', its Muslim religion, and the size of its population – doubts camouflaged behind exaggerated concerns over human rights issues and the degree of sound economic development thus far achieved.

I remember leaving Turkey after one of my Presidential visits. I had to face a very large press conference at Istanbul airport. After a bombardment of questions on the possibility of Turkey's membership of the European Union, a lady journalist said, 'Can I ask you a personal question? I understand you are a Christian. How can you personally accept a country into membership where over 90 per cent of the people are Muslim?'

I gave the usual answer – that there was no religious bar to membership. And then I stupidly added, 'But I have to say that many people in my country raise the same question.'

The headlines of leading Turkish newspapers the following day read 'Plumb Says 90% of British People Reject Turkey as a Member' – a classic example of misleading and/or mischievous misinterpretation!

It would be deeply, deeply regrettable if this country, which occupies a position of considerable geopolitical importance, were to feel rejected by the European Union. Yet I find it hard to envisage full Turkish membership of the European Union within a foreseeable timescale, if for no other reason than the improbability – despite recent improvements in relations between Ankara and Athens – of the Greeks' agreeing to admit them, which is a *sine qua non* under the treaties. Turkey already enjoys a special relationship with the European Union – for example, through customs-union-type agreements. Perhaps in the longer term a new category of 'permanent quasi-members', going beyond current Association agreements, will be devised to solve the Turkish problem. Such a solution might conceivably also be of use to other possible applicant countries like, in the more distant future, the

Ukraine or Georgia, both of whom have expressed an interest in eventually joining the European Union but who are in a grey zone in respect of the definition of 'European'.

As for likely improvements in the performance and public appreciation of the European institutions, I am optimistic that the Commission, in particular, will make good progress in the short term. An internal management overhaul of the Commission's staff structure and procedures is already well under way, and the initial proposals put forward by the Commission for the realisation of the European Union's development and aid programmes – to my mind not nearly radical enough – are at least a good starting-point for the new beginning that is absolutely necessary, in my view, and in the view of all who have looked closely at the problems.

The standing of the European Parliament should rise as its role as co-legislator becomes more publicly evident in the procedures put in place by the Amsterdam treaty.

One of the most important aspects of this enhanced role is the part played by the Parliament in 'conciliation' with the Council – that is to say, the face-to-face negotiations between representatives of the two institutions over the draft texts of a wide range of proposed legislation. This is not, by definition, a highly visible sphere of parliamentary activity, but one that ultimately has a profound effect on the shape and detail of European law. Over time, the quality of the input made by the European Parliament team, ably lead by a British Conservative Vice-President, James Provan, will make an impact that will be to the benefit of Parliament's reputation.

I am less sanguine about the prospects for an improvement in the Council's performance, if only because the individual ministers and prime ministers involved are, as the constitutional position now stands, constantly torn between their European responsibilities and their duties (and electoral preoccupations) at national level. One glimmer of hope is that when the heads of Government are obliged to contemplate – as they soon will be – the challenge of bringing the requisite legislation to ratify the next package of European constitutional reform through their respective parliaments, they will begin seriously to send out more positive signals about the integration process.

The Irish referendum campaign in June 2001, its low turn-out figures, and its negative result underline the need for even the most enthusiastically pro-European governments and parties not only to be positive in their approach when acting in Council, but to educate and inspire their own electorates, month by month and year by year.

And what of the institutional reforms themselves, in the light of the anticipated enlargement?

Between the two extreme schools of thought – the ultra-federalists and the Eurosceptics – I believe that enlargement will tend, out of practical coordinating necessity, towards 'more Europe' rather than 'less'. I believe that, paradoxically, some of the spheres that have traditionally appeared to be the most 'nationalistic' in context, such as the administration of justice and the asylum policy will quickly come to be seen as suitable spheres of European Union action. Confronted with the problems of international crime, drug-trafficking and illegal immigration, the man in the street can see that these are more effectively tackled if.there is not just inter-governmental co-operation but integrated European policies and agency action deployed against them.

On the other hand, I feel sure that it will be a practical impossibility to get twenty, twenty-five or thirty states to move forward together and uniformly. There will have to be some flexibility. Some new developments will take place in common – that is to say, will involve all member states – and others will take place involving only some states. (This already happens to some extent. For example, the UK and Ireland are not part of the Schengen Agreement on inter-state travel controls.) I say that with great reluctance, for there are grave dangers in eroding the fundamental tenet of commonality. The biggest challenge will be to retain as large a core as possible of things-in-common, whilst ensuring that the things-not-in-common are kept to a minimum and do not create conflicts or contradictions.

Above all, the European Union must not drift towards a 'two-speed' Europe, in which some member states would gravitate towards common action, and others towards opt-outs or bilateral inter-governmental agreements on things-not-in-common. There must be an overall balance so that each member state is, broadly speaking, as 'European' as its European Union partners.

The idea, or threat, of a 'two-speed' Europe has already raised its head from time to time. I can only hope that the thought of travelling second-class will act as a spur to those who might be disposed to be cool towards the prospect of further progress on the path of 'ever-closer union'.

As a Conservative, I worry about the risks currently being taken by the Party on European issues. I entirely endorse criticisms of the genuine shortcomings of the European Union institutions and of the British Government's Brussels-related mistakes from time to time. That is the legitimate role of a parliamentary Opposition. But in recent years the general aura emanating from the Party in respect of Europe has been increasingly negative in nature. It is as if the Conservative approach were based on the assumption that the current process of integration was bound soon to grind to a halt, and would then have to be re-thought. Party policy is hardly 'Stay out of the present game; there 's a new one on the way' – but that is nonetheless the impression being conveyed. I believe it is dangerous to appear to be betting on failure. Nor is such an approach in the traditions of our Party.

The reasons for our second successive, massive defeat at the polls in June 2001 were many and varied, some of the most important of them falling outside the scope of this book. Yet it is clear that our European stance was one of them. Its most striking element – the 'Keep the Pound' slogan – may have been thought to have had a stirringly patriotic ring to it, but the fact that the commitment was (perhaps thankfully) limited to the next parliament made it sound like yet another variation on the Augustinian prayer: 'Lord, give me chastity and continence . . . . but just for five years!' It was simply not credible. And in general, the flavour of our European policy was one of out-of-date Little Englander-ism.

One consolation we can draw from the sheer scale of the defeat is that it presents us with a *tabula rasa* on which to start again. We can, and must, re-think all our policies. And I would suggest that our overall approach to European affairs is one of the most important, if we are to move back to the central ground, on which, it is now more than ever plain, elections in modern Britain are won. It is no use merely rallying the Party faithful round a number of ideological mantras. We have to reach out to the electorate at large with policies and attitudes that take account of today's realities in the world, and that appeal to young people in the future.

We need to come across as an alternative government, not a nostalgic protest party. We must convince the voters that we are capable not only of running the economy and providing adequate public services, but of giving our country a permanent and confident place in the changing Europe of the future.

In the short term we must move away from the recent voodoo attachment to the pound. Otherwise, we will fall into the trap of the proposed referendum that now yawns before us. We should not forget that the Labour Government has control both of the timing of that referendum and of the interpretation of its own criteria for judging that the moment is right to join the Euro. They therefore enjoy the huge advantage of being able to put the issue to the public only when – thanks to the sophistication of the opinion polls – they are sure of winning. Were we in the Conservative Party to persist in outright opposition to the Euro, we would in effect be presenting the Government with a golden opportunity to inflict on us another defeat and have our new leadership branded 'Failure'.

It would be equally risky, in my opinion, to yield to the temptation dangled before us by some pro-European members of the Party who would like to leave it to the Labour Party to provide 'solutions' to the big European issues, before the Conservatives regain power and simply accept these as *faits accomplis*. I believe that we should re-engage with the European debate in a constructive way and radically review our policies in relation to the European Union. That does not mean accepting everything with a 'European' tag as essentially positive – but we must escape from a largely self-inflicted position of 'dog-in-the-manger'.

Europe as an issue will not go away. On the contrary, it will increasingly be understood as the basic political framework for the future. There will therefore be a need to present to the electorate an image of a party willing and able to play a participatory role, a party with sensible, realistic and positive policies to offer on Europe.

That would be a return to our roots.

ENVOI

Ben N Gill, President of the National Farmers Union

How to describe Henry Plumb? It has never been easy and, I guess, never will be, for throughout his life he has done so much and met so many people requiring such a vast array of skills and understanding that to encapsulate that variety in a word or phrase is difficult if not impossible. From those many visits - some recounted in *The Plumb Line* - there will be many varied memories which add new perspectives to the man.

But if I am forced to attach one personal descriptor to Henry it would be that of the *man with the common touch*. Rarely can you find someone who is at ease with the smallest UK farmer and equally at home in the City with leading financiers or in Downing Street with the Prime Minister. As he has moved onwards from his role as President of the NFU, his meetings have continued to increase his knowledge of people further, from subsistence farmers in poor African countries to royalty around the world. The tale goes on. In his role as a senior member of the House of Lords he has assumed an ever more public important role, but unlike many before him - and after - he has lost none of that *common touch*. He has never been duped by fancy words. He has always been able to break a position down into logical segments that, once explained, bring breathtaking clarity to a situation and, in so doing, create obvious solutions to problems that seemed to the lesser person insoluble.

His time as the President of the European Parliament was a particular testament to such analytical and diplomatic skills, coping with Yasser Arafat or indeed the Pope on their visits to Strasbourg. In both cases he found ways round the intricate problems of diplomacy which permitted important steps forward with minimal distress and anger to those opposed to such visits. His logic has always been that dialogue is a better route than combat. It is so obvious, but regrettably it is ducked by many world leaders as it requires a vastly greater amount of work to ensure that the outcome does not unintentionally inflame or incite matters (albeit in a totally unintended way) resulting in a worse position than was started with.

With Henry, the phrase *'nothing ventured, nothing gained'* springs immediately to mind. Henry was not one to shrink back from *'venturing'* as his calling of the first World Food Summit in Rome in 1996 showed. Many at the time poo-pooed it as a charade; but that there is to be a 'Five Years On' meeting in 2001 proves that opinion wrong. It may not have solved all the problems, but it has focussed attention on them in a way that nothing else has, and Henry continues to do so in addressing the issues of how we will feed the world within the constraints of sustainable farming systems.

So what of the book itself? It acts as a marvellous refresher, a reminder, that in our current desire to move forward using science as our benchmark, we would be all the poorer if we ignore the history of our country, and for farmers the history of our industry. That is particularly true of the last five decades or so since the second World War. Reading this book, as you have done, with the comfort of a full stomach – thanks predominantly to British food - it is very easy to forget the origins of post-war farming. In 50 years we have seen the demise of the carthorse and its replacement with the tractor. Even that is too simple a statement for the *little grey Ferguson* of the fifties bears little resemblance to the tractors of today. With no cab and a heating system comprising army surplus greatcoats and an upright exhaust to insert heat inside, these old tractors have been replaced with sophisticated machines in which the seats alone cost more today than the old grey 'fergie' in its entirety. What in their time were revolutionary Ferguson hydraulics, which moved us from trailed implements for the first time, are now controlled by sophisticated computer systems which permit an almost limitless set of variations in how we can set up our equipment. And today's technology goes even further with the use of equipment which, in real time, can sense the intensity of crop cover. In the time it takes to drive over a patch of ground it can decide how much nitrogen fertiliser needs to be applied and in what way to meet the needs of the crop. This application is then recorded on to a contour map using Global Positioning Systems and finally compared with the yield map from the on-board computer on the combine harvester.

In this period a good yield for a crop of cereals has risen from an average of 1.25 or 1.5 tonnes per acre to over 3 tonnes and at best well over 4 tonnes. The biblical two seeds where one grew before has been exceeded by a considerable margin, and the benefit, in the main, passed on to the consumer - and forgotten. Recent outrage in the UK press that the good old British loaf of bread was to rise by 6 pence because of the 'poor harvest' illustrates just this lack of knowledge and understanding. That the total value of our wheat in the final loaf in no way approaches 6 pence proves the point; the wheat price may have risen from lows of last year of around £60 to £80 per tonne, but as little as four years ago wheat was trading at £120 per tonne. Henry Plumb quotes Socrates: 'No man is a statesman who is ignorant of wheat.'

In the same period we have seen improvements in the genetics of our dairy cattle coupled with significant improvements in dairy nutrition. This has led to consistent year-on-year improvements in dairy yields per cow in the national herd by about 2 per cent per annum over a sustained period, with dramatic improvements in the technology in the dairy parlour reducing the need for labour and at the same time improving the standard and longevity of our milk, which is second to none in Europe – and in the world. Imagine the frustration, then, for farmers to witness their high value product being regularly sold for less than the price of a bottle of water. Small wonder that farmers the length and breadth of the country feel despondent. For them, basic values have been turned on their head.

Such values could not have been more clearly illustrated than at my eldest son's recent wedding. Having offered to buy the wine, I found the wine list offered predominantly French wines. These were not an option, so having consulted a friend, who is a wine master, I acquired wholesale some very good wines some of which had travelled half way around the world. I reflected on the grower's time and effort that had gone into producing them: the breeding of the best vines; the initial planting; the training; the annual pruning; the protection from disease by regular spraying; the picking, mostly still by hand; the production of the wine itself; the maturation of the wine and storage; the bottling; the transport; and the promotion and marketing of it. And I thought of the work of the hotel: storing the wine for a few days; opening the bottles and pouring them; and washing up the glasses afterwards; oh and yes, to be fair, the hire of the glasses as well. How many peoples' livelihoods depended on each of these two parts, the growing and the serving? And what was the relative cost? The former cost was only half of the latter. I was told that I had secured a good deal from the hotel who couldn't have been more helpful, and that the disparity could have been much worse, undervaluing the producer's contribution even more.

All this leads me to the conclusion that in today's society we have come to value food too lightly, and that this is a real danger, for undervaluing anything leads to a tendency to be wasteful. But of course you could then say that, from *The Plumb Line* perspective, I am ignoring the needs of the Third world countries to whom Henry has also devoted so much attention. But the reality is that, in the crazy world in which we live, they pay a far greater share of their income and work longer hours for their staple diet than we do. Valued in hours of work to produce the food on which to live for a week changes the issue to a different perspective. The recently agreed *'Everything but Arms'* treaty is meant to yield real benefits for the world's poorest countries, but it will not do so if we collapse their internal prices as has happened in previous attempts. Rather the opposite, for by valuing their food higher we will give them more disposable income from the surplus that they can sell from their farms.

And it is at this point that history as described in *The Plumb Line* brings us almost full circle. The problems of British farming in Henry's term as President of the NFU revolved around some of the very same problems that we grapple with at world level today. British farmers over the years have valued fiercely their independence within their businesses. They have consistently believed that their farming businesses (which on acreage alone are the biggest by far in Europe) were big enough for them to be meaningful players in the market place. It was not the case in the 1970s, and it surely is not the case now. Since then we have had the endless consolidation not only of our retailers (in the UK the big three supermarkets account for around 60 per cent of the food market), but also elsewhere in the chain. The phenomenon of concentration in the U.S. has led to a situation where we even have major companies controlling more than one sector of the same food chain. The catering sector is not immune form this internationalisation either. As it assumes an ever-greater share of the market place for food, you can now find the same French company providing the catering in the Sydney Royal Opera House, the Chicago International Conference Centre and our own Royal Show!

Is such globalisation likely to go away? The clear answer is 'No'. Indeed the chances are that, with another round of world trade talks looming this autumn under the WTO, there will be further liberalisation. Against this background, the need for better structures both pre and post farmgate is critically needed today in a much more urgent way if our farming and horticultural industry is to thrive and prosper. My recent visits to Germany and France, amongst other countries, highlighted this need. After stripping out the currency effects, German farmers still benefit from milk prices around 2 to 3 pence per litre higher than ours, depending upon outlet, and cereal farmers £5 to £7 per tonne more for their wheat. Why? Because they have an understanding of the crucial need to work together to develop the economies of scale that even our biggest farmers cannot emulate, and to create a balancing force in the market place to balance the size of those other companies with whom farmers have to deal. For the inputs we only have to look at the different effects on fertiliser price in the last twelve months between France and ourselves. France, the only other major country to use ammonium nitrate as we do, has been insulated from the extent of price rises that we were experiencing because their product is held in bulk in a controlled number of stores operated by a handful of farmers' co-operatives. The response of farmers to the economic power of other actors in the food market must be to co-operate.

Never has the message and work detailed in *The Plumb Line* been more in need than it is today. Never has the need to learn the basic fundamentals of business - to sell retail and buy wholesale - been so desperately needed. We must learn from our historical failings and not repeat them. *The Plumb Line* could not have been more timely in reminding us of this.

INDEX OF ORGANISATIONS

ACCA   Agricultural Central Co-operative Association

ACMS   Agricultural Co-operation and Marketing Services

ACP   African, Caribbean and Pacific Countries

ACP-EU   African, Caribbean & Pacific Countries and European Union

ACT   Agricultural Central Trading

ADAS   Agricultural Development and Advisory Service

AMDEC   Agricultural Market Development Executive Committee

BAMDO   British Agricultural Marketing Development Organisation

BCL   Bougainville Copper Ltd

BIF   Bougainville Interim Government

BIG   Bougainville Interim Government

BRA   Bougainville Revolutionary Army

BSE   Bovine Spongiform Encephalopathy

BTG   Bougainvillle Transitional Government

CAP   Common Agricultural Policy

CBI   Confederation of British Industry

CD   Christian Democrats

CDJ   Creutzfeldt-Jakob disease

CDU	Christian Democratic Union
COGECA	Comité Général des Co-opératives Agricoles de la CEE, (Committee of EEC Farmers' Co-operatives)
COPA	Comité des Organisations Professionelles Agricoles de la CEE, (Committee of EEC Farmers' Unions)
COREPER	Council's technocratic preparatory body at Permanent Representation level)
DEFRA	Department of Environment, Food and Rural Affairs
DUP	Democratic Unionist Party
EC	European Commission
ECHO	European Union's Humanitarian Office
EDG	European Democratic Group
EEC	European Economic Community
EMS	European Monetary System
EMU	Economic and Monetary Union
EP	European Parliament
EPLF	Eritrea Peoples Liberation Front
EPP	European People's Party
EU	European Union
FAR	Forces Armées Rwandaises
FCB	Farmer Controlled Businesses
FCO	Foreign and Commonwealth Office
FMC	Fatstock Marketing Corporation

FNSE   A Fédération Nationale des Syndicates d'Exploitants Agricoles

GATT   General Agreement on Tariffs and Trade

GDP   Gross Domestic Product

GDPS   Guarantee and Deficiency Payment Scheme

GMO   Genetically Modified Organisms

IFAP   International Federation of Agricultural Producers

IMF   International Monetary Fund

ITMG   International Truce Monitoring Group (Bougainville)

LEAF   Linking Environment and Farming

MAFF   Ministry of Agriculture, Fisheries and Food

MCA   Monetary Compensatory Amount

MEP   Member of the European Parliament

MP   Member of Parliament

NAAFI   National Association of Agriculture, Farming and
            Industry

NEDDY   National Economic Development Council

NFU   National Farmers Union

NGO   Non-Governmental Organisations

OPEC   Organisation of Petroleum Exporting Countries

PASOK   Panellinio Socialistiko Kinima (Greek Socialist Party)

PIDA   Pig Industry Development Authority

PNG   Papua New Guinea

PNGDF	Papua New Guinea Defence Force
RASE	Royal Agricultural Society of England
RDE	Rassemblement des Democrates Européens (EP Group of French Gaullists and Irish Fianna Fail)
RDS	Rural Development Service
SEA	Single European Act
SPLA	Sudanese People's Liberation Army
SPLM	Sudanese People's Liberation Movement
TMG	Truce Monitoring Group
TUC	Trades Union Council
USDA	United States Development Agency
WTO	World Trade Organisation
YFC	Young Farmers Club

INDEX OF NAMES

Butler, Sir Richard NFU President, 1979-1985, Dep. President, 1971-79, Vice-President, 1970-71

Callaghan, James Lord, Labour politician, Home Secretary 1967-70, Prime Minister 1976-79

Cassidy, Brian MEP, Conservative politician

Castle, Barbara Baroness, Labour politician, Cabinet Minster in 1960s and 1970s, Leader of Labour group in EP, 1979-89.

Catherwood, Sir Fred, Chairman of NEDDY, MEP, Conservative politician

Catlin, Charles President of the National Federation of Meat Traders' Association, early 1970s

Cattell, George NFU Director-General, 1970-78

Cerreti, Cassanmagnago ACP-EU Co-President

Chalker, Lynda Baroness, Minister for Overseas Development

Chambrier-Rahandi ACP-EU Co-president, Gabon

Chan, Julius Prime Minister of Papua New Guinea

Charles, Eugenia Prime Minister of Dominica

Chichester, Giles MEP, Conservative politician

Chick, Simon Dorset farmer

Chirac, Jacques French MEP, Prime Minister, later President of France

Churchill, Sir Winston, Conservative politician, Prime Minster 1940-45, 1951-55

Clarke, Kenneth Cabinet Minister 1985-97, Conservative politician, longest continuously serving Minster since Lord Palmerston in the early 19th century.

Cockfield, Francis Arthur Lord, British Conservative Vice-President of the EC Commission

Corrie, John UK Conservative MEP politician, Co-President ACP-EU Joint Assembly

Cossins, John NFU Vice-President 1974-76

Cowen, Tom NFU Vice-President 1966-69

Craxi, Bettino Prime Minister of Italy, Socialist politician

Crespo, Enrique Baron Spanish MEP, Socialist politician

Cresson, Edith French Socialist politician, Minister of Agriculture, Prime Minister, European Commissioner

Cripps, Anthony Member of the Northumberland Inquiry, 1968-69

Cripps, Sir Stafford Labour politician, expelled from his party 1939-45 for supporting a 'Popular Front' against Chamberlain, Chancellor of the Exchequer 1947-50

Crotty, Kieran Irish citizen, challenged the ratification of the SEA

Curry, David Conservative MEP politician, now MP

Daksager, Paol Danish Commissioner for Agriculture

Dankert, Piet Dutch MEP, Socialist politician, President of the EP, 1982-84

Darbishire, David NFU Vice-President 1971-73, NFU Council Delegate, Warwickshire, Chairman FMC

Davies, Ieun Young Farmers' public speaking competition

Davies, John NFU Council Delegate, Pembrokeshire

Day, Sir Robin television and radio journalist

Day, Wallace NFU Council Delegate, Devon

Debatisse, Michel MEP Chairman National Farmers' Union France

Delors, Jacques French Socialist politician, President European Commission

Dentash, Rauf Turkish Cypriot nationalist politician

Donelly, Brendan Conservative MEP politician

Douglas, George Lincolnshire farmer, friend of Sir Emrys Jones

Duke of Northumberland Chairman Committee of Inquiry, Foot-and- Mouth 1968-69

Eastwood, John Largest UK producer of broiler chickens

Elles, Diana Baroness, Vice-President EP, Conservative MEP

Elles, James Conservative MEP politician

El-Turabi,Hassan Alsdalla Secretary-General, National Islamic Front, Sudan

Engholm, Basil Permanent Secretary of MAFF

Esmieu, Jean-Claude EC Delegate in Khartoum, Sudan

Eyadema, Etinienne Gnassingbé President of Togo

Fáil, Fianna Irish politician

Falk, Sir Roger Chairman Central Council for Agricultural and Horticultural Development (1967-75)

Farqueson, Ronnie Chairman of the NFU Cereals Committee, 1960

Ferranti, Boz Conservative MEP politician

Figures, Ernesto Argentinean politician, Minister of Agriculture

Fischler, Franz Austrian European Commissioner for Agriculture

Forth, Eric Candidate in European Elections1979, later MP and Minister of State

Fraga, Manuel Founder of the Spanish Alianza Popular

Francis, Ona Leader of BIG

Franco, Itama Brazilian politician

Garang, John Guerrilla leader, Sudan

Gatling, Tony and Mary Warwickshire farming friends

Gaulle, Charles de French General and President, 1958-1969

Genscher, Hans-Dietrich German Liberal politician and Foreign Minister

Giansilly, Jean-Aubine French MEP, Gaullist

Gill, Ben NFU President, 1999 -

Gillis, Alan President of Irish Farmers' Association

Godber, Joe Minister of Agriculture under Ted Heath

González, Felipe Leader Spanish Socialist Party

Gorbarchev, Mikhail Leader of the Soviet Union

Gromyko, Andrei President USSR

Gundelach, Finn Olav Danish European Commissioner for Agriculture

Habsburg, Baron Otto von German politician MEP

Hague, William Leader of the Opposition 1997-2001, Conservative Politician

Hannay, Sir David UK Permanent Representative in Brussels

Hassan, Sir Joshua Chief Minister of Gibraltar

Heart, Jon Chief-Executive RASE

Heath, Sir Edward Prime Minister, 1970-74

Herlitzka, André Secretary General, COPA

Herzog, Chaim President of Israel, born in Belfast

Hoosen, John NFU Council Member

Howe, Geoffrey Lord, Conservative politician, Home Secretary and Deputy Prime Minister, Chancellor of the Exchequer under Margaret Thatcher

Hughes, Cledwyn Minister of Agriculture, 1970

Hurd, Douglas Lord, Conservative politician, Home Secretary, Secretary of State for Northern Ireland, Foreign Secretary

Hussein ibn Talal King of Jordan

Jackson, Caroline MEP Conservative politician

Jackson. Christopher MEP Conservative politician, now Liberal

Jepsen, Marie MEP Danish politician

John Paul II Polish priest, Pope from 1978

Johnston, Stanley MEP Conservative politician, known for his action against the practice of culling seals in Canada

Jones Parry, Emyr Deputy Director of EP President's Cabinet, Counsellor UK Permanent Representation in Brussels

Jones, Sir Emrys Director General of ADAS and Principal Royal Agricultural College Cirencester

Juan Carlos King of Spain

Junker, Karin German Socialist politician MEP

Kabui, Joseph Vice President of BIG

Kaputin, Sir John ACP-EU Co-president, 1995-97 PNG, Chief negotiator PNG Government, now Foreign Minister

Kaunda, Kenneth President of Zambia

Kauona, Sam Commander of BRA

Kellet-Bowman Conservative politician MEP

Kingsland, Baron Life Peer

Kinnock, Glenys MEP ACP-EU Vice-President , Socialist politician

Kirk, Kent MEP Danish Conservative politician

Kitchener, Horatio British General and administrator

Klepsch, Egon President of the EP 1992-94, German Christian Democrat politician, Chairman EPP

Knapp, Joseph Administrator of the Farmer Co-operative Service of the US Department of Agriculture

Knotnerus, Carl Dutch Agriculturalist, President of COPA 1974

Knowles, Ken NFU General Secretary and Administrator

Koffigoh, Joseph Prime Minister of Togo

Kohl, Helmut German Conservative politician, Chancellor, Leader of the CDU

Kouchner, Bernard French MEP, Chairman Committee of Development and Co-operation, Minister of Health, France

Nicholson, Sir David MEP Conservative politician

Nickerson, Sir Joseph Chairman Nickerson Seeds

Nixon, Richard President USA

Normanton, Sir Tom MEP Conservative politician

Ormesson, Jean Olivier d' French MEP, Member of the French National Front, Owner of Chateau Ormesson

Özal, Turgut Turkish Islamic right-wing politician, Prime Minister

Paisley, Ian Northern Ireland politician, cleric, leader of the DUP, MEP

Pangaloss, Theodorous Greek MEP, Minister (PASOK)

Pannella, Marco Italian MEP, Leader of the Italian Transnational Radical Party

Paul, Staes Belgian MEP

Pauwels, Hans Richmond Europe Imports

Peart, Fred Minister of Agriculture

Perinat, Marquess of Spanish MEP, Vice-President EP, Negotiator for Alianza Popular

Perry, Roy MEP Conservative politician

Pflimlin, Pierre President EP, 1984-87, former Prime Minister of France

Pinheiro, Joao de Deus European Commissioner for Development and Co-operation

Pires, Lucas Member of the Portugese 'Partido do Centro Democrático Social'

Pisani, Edgard Minister of Agriculture, France, and Commissioner for Development and Co-operation

Plunkett, Horace Founder of the Plunkett Foundation

Prior, Jim Lord, Minister of Agriculture

Prodi, Romano President of the Commission

Prout, Chistopher Conservative politician MEP

Provan, James MEP Conservative politician, now Vice-President EP

Punset, Eduardo Spanish MEP, Centro Democrático y Social

Putten, Maartje van Dutch MEP, Socialist politician

Quinn, Joyce MEP, MP, Minister of State for Food & Agriculture

Rabin, Yitzhak Labour Party Leader Israel, Prime Minister

Ramsay, Robert Director EP President's Cabinet, EDG Secretary General

Rank, Arthur Lord, Chairman Animal Health Trust

Rattle, Simon Conductor of the Birmingham Symphony Orchestra

Reagan, Ronald President USA

Ridley, Nick Member of Parliament, Conservative politician

Roberts, Dame Shelagh MEP Conservative politician

Robinson, Heather Member of Parliament, Jamaica

Rogalla, Dieter German MEP, Socialist politician

Rose, Bryan Senior Administrator EP, now Director General for Research

Royle Lord, Member Assembly Council of Europe an WEU

Sakharov, Andrei Soviet physicist, human rights campaigner

Veil, Simone First President of the
EP 1979-82, French Minister of
Health

Vinci, Enrico Secretary General of
the European Parliament

Voss, August Eduardovich
President of Supreme Soviet, USSR

Warner, Sir Fred Ambassador to
Japan, MEP, Conservative Politician

Watt, Percy President NFU
Scotland

Weipers, Sir William Professor,
Head of the Veterinary Faculty at
Glasgow University

Weldegiorgis, Audebrhan ACP
Vice-President, Eritrea

William Wilberforce Nineteenth
century politician, leader of the
antislavery movement

Williams, Sir Gwilym President
NFU

Williams, Tom Minister of
Agriculture

Wilson, Eric President of COGECA

Wilson, Harold Prime Minister,
1964-70; 1974-76

Wilson, Colonel Jock NFU
Treasurer, Chairman Pigs
Committee

Winegarten, Asher NFU Chief
Economist

Woolley, Harold Lord, President
NFU

Yamani, Ahmad Zaki Saudi
Arabian politician, Oil Minister

Zenawi, Meles President of
Ethiopia